Democracy in Contemporary Japan

Democracy in Contemporary Japan

Edited by
Gavan McCormack &
Yoshio Sugimoto

M. E. SHARPE, INC.
ARMONK, NEW YORK
LONDON, ENGLAND

First published in the United States in 1986 by M. E. Sharpe, Inc.,
80 Business Park Drive, Armonk, New York 10504.

First published in Australia in 1986 by Hale & Iremonger Pty Limited,
80–90 Chapel Street, Marrickville, NSW.

Available in the United Kingdom and Europe from M. E. Sharpe,
Publishers, 3 Henrietta Street, London WC2E 8LU.

Library of Congress Cataloging-in-Publication Data

Democracy in contemporary Japan.

    Bibliography: p.
    Includes index.
    1. Civil rights—Japan—History. 2. Democracy—History.
I. McCormack, Gavan. II. Sugimoto, Yoshio, 1939–
JC599.J3D46   1986   321.8′0952   86-17744
ISBN 0-87332-397-1
ISBN 0-87332-398-X (pbk.)

Printed in the United States of America

MA   10 9 8 7 6 5 4 3 2

Contents

5

Japanese Names

The Japanese convention that family name precedes personal name is
generally followed in this book. However, those Japanese who either
live in the West or have chosen to adopt the opposite (Western) convention of personal name followed by family name in their writings in
English are identified accordingly. In the table of contents, for example, Sugimoto and Sibatani are listed in Western order, but all
other Japanese names are in Japanese order, surname first. Un-
certainty may be resolved by reference to the index where all persons
named in the text are listed in alphabetical order according to their
family names.

Contributors

Buckley, Sandra. Assistant Professor, Department of East Asian Languages and Literature, McGill University.

Hidaka, Rokurō. Professor, Kyoto Seika University, Japan: author of numerous books in Japanese, including *Contemporary Ideology, Selected Essays by Hidaka Rokuro on Education, 19 May 1960, Flight from Freedom, Reflections on Contemporary Thought*, and in English, *The Price of Affluence*, Tokyo and New York, 1984, Melbourne, 1985.

Igarashi, Futaba. Lawyer, Tokyo. Co-author of *The Substitute Detention System and Civil Liberties*, Tokyo, 1981 (in Japanese).

Kawanishi, Hirosuke. Professor, Chiba University. Author of *The Reality of Enterprise Unionism, On the Minority Labour Union Movement* (both in Japanese).

McCormack, Gavan. Senior Lecturer in History, La Trobe University. Author of *Japanese Imperialism Today* (with Jon Halliday), London and New York, 1973; *Chang Tso-lin in Northeast China 1911-1928*, Stanford, 1977; *Cold War Hot War*, Sydney, 1983.

McEachern, Doug. Lecturer in Politics, University of Adelaide. Author of *A Class against Itself: Power and the Nationalization of the British Steel Industry*, New York, 1980; co-author of *Colonialism and Capitalist Production*, London, 1982.

Mackie, Vera. Lecturer in Japanese, University of Adelaide.

Morris-Suzuki, Tessa. Lecturer in Economic History, University of New England. Author of *Showa: An Inside History of Hirohito's Japan*, Sydney, 1984.

Mutō, Ichiyō. Director of the Pacific-Asia Resource Center (Tokyo); member of Editorial Board of *Ampo: Japan-Asia Quarterly Review*; Lecturer in Department of Sociology, State University of New York at Binghamton.

Sibatani, Atuhiro. Professor, Kansai Medical University. Formerly chief research scientist, Division of Molecular Biology, CSIRO, Sydney, Professor of Biochemistry and Biophysics at the Research Institute for Nuclear Medicine and Biology, Hiroshima University. Has authored 14 books, mostly on moral and social issues in science and technology, including *Essay on Antiscience, Critique of Biotechnology, What is Science to Me?* (all in Japanese).

Smith, Beverley. Honorary Research Fellow, Centre for Asian Studies, University of Adelaide.

Sugimoto, Yoshio. Reader in Sociology, La Trobe University. Author of *Popular Disturbance in Postwar Japan*, Hong Kong, 1981; *The Ultra-controlled Japanese Archipelago*, Tokyo, 1983 (in Japanese); and co-author of *Japanese Society: Reappraisals and New Directions*, Adelaide, 1981; *Images of Japanese Society*, London, 1986; and *Japanology Reconsidered* (in Japanese), Tokyo, 1982.

Yamazumi, Masami. Professor of Education, Tokyo Metropolitan University. Author of *Textbooks, School Textbooks, Imperial Rescript on Education* (all in Japanese).

Introduction:
Democracy and Japan

Gavan McCormack
and
Yoshio Sugimoto

The 'modern' transformation of the Western world was accomplished by what has sometimes been described as the dual revolution: capitalism and democracy. In the non-European world, no nation has made greater strides than Japan to achieve the transformation of its productive economy by the adoption of the institutions of capitalism, albeit of a distinctive hue, and the attention of the world has focused on it in countless studies. But *democracy? Japanese democracy?* Not a single monograph has been published on the subject in English.

Throughout the world, 'democracy' is a prized value. It is part of the boast of both the world's major systems, East and West, that they represent it in their own distinct forms — liberal and people's — while much of the Third World aspires to attain it. This fact alone indicates that the word is not always thought of in the same way. The basic sense of the triumph of the *demos,* the common man, in a society in which his interests are paramount, is one which no government would wish to deny, but it embraces a profound ambiguity, for what are the interests of the common man? How are they to be interpreted and implemented? How are contradictions between the interests of different groups of 'common people' to be mediated?

In very general terms, we would suggest that there are certain political and economic preconditions for democracy: majority rule, minority rights, division of powers prominent among the former, and socio-economic equality among the latter. Just as the former set of conditions (but rarely the latter) is present (with some qualifications and to differing degrees) in advanced capitalism, so the opposite tends to be true of the countries commonly described as 'socialist'. However, both of the current world systems are deficient in one important dimension: in neither are human creative and cooperative capacities given due expression and in neither is the scope for grassroots control

9

over areas of life and work maximised. There are fundamental obstacles to this: the deep structure of market, continuing scarcity and
the association of value with price in Western capitalism on the one
hand, and the bureaucratic and irresponsible structures of 'actually existing socialism' on the other.

Democracy, in short, is not merely a set of institutional arrangements expressive of formal popular sovereignty; it is also an aspiration
or orientation of a society towards maximum free expression of its
citizens, maximum devolution of power from centralised governments
and their bureaucracies to citizens and their freely cooperating organisations. We are broadly in agreement with the list of definitive requirements of the democratic order as set out by Joshua Cohen and
Joel Rogers in their recent study of democracy in the United States:

> civil rights and civil liberties, public subsidy for organized competitive po-
> litical groups, egalitarian distributional measures, public control of invest-
> ment, workplace democracy, equal opportunity, and a foreign policy
> informed by the principles of democratic legitimacy that underlie the
> domestic system.[1]

In this regard, the Japanese constitution is perhaps most democratic at
least in its spirit and letters, if not in its practice and application. It
covers almost all the prerequisites of democracy: 'entertainment of
fundamental human rights', 'respect for individuals', 'equality under
law', 'freedom of assembly, association, speech, publication and all
other forms of expression', and 'right to enjoy the minimum of healthy
and cultural life'. It also incorporates a unique renunciation of
militarism and commitment to the values of peace. But, the fact that
movements to maintain, defend, or even to realise the values apparently entrenched in the constitution are seen in the contemporary
Japanese context as reformist suggests that mere formal analysis of the
country's constitutional and legal structure is not enough.

Through the course of Japan's modernisation and industrialisation
from the Meiji restoration onwards, the common people were
dragooned, manipulated, mobilised, and exploited in the relentless
pursuit of the elusive goal of equality with the West. There was little
room for spontaneous, cooperative popular movements in this Japan.
Its spirit was summed up in the slogan of the 1930s: *messhi bōkō* (extinguish the self in service to the state). Japanese etatisme was demanding and total.

In the early decades of this century the very word for democracy,
minshushugi or 'people-rule-ism', was anathema in Japan because of its
implicit *lèse majesté*, since only the emperor could rule. Despite the
overtly repressive nature of prewar Japan, the conceptual equivalents
of the Western notion of democracy emerged in a variety of forms. In
the period immediately after the Meiji Restoration the conservative
'national right' elite was pitted against various democratic 'people's

right' groups, whose notion of *minken* (people's right) was rooted in traditions of popular struggle from the feudal period and became the catchphrase of grassroots social movements for decades in the late nineteenth century.

At the climax of the period of Taisho democracy which followed the end of World War One, Yoshino Sakuzō (1878-1933) formulated the distinctive Japanese concept of *minpon shugi* (people-first-ism). While falling short of challenging the framework of emperor sovereignty, he stressed that the objective of politics should be the welfare of the people and the decision-making process should be based upon their will. A somewhat different notion of democracy was that for which the prewar anarchist Ishikawa Sanshirō (1876-1956) coined the phrase *domin shugi* (people-of-the-soil-ism). This stemmed from the agriculturalist tradition and stressed the defence of agriculture, nature and ecology against industry, civilisation and environmental disruption. Ethnographic studies and research on mass culture reveal that many kinds of 'democratic', egalitarian and flexible practices existed in those rural hamlets and urban communities which were relatively free of the penetration of legal-bureaucratic forces of industrial capitalism. The renowned ethnographer, Yanagita Kunio (1875-1962), devised the term *jōmin* to convey the image of the ordinary nameless and voiceless men and women who contributed to history from below, and an even more inclusive notion, similar to that of 'common man', was captured by the word *shomin*.

In the postwar period, for the first time, some of the key institutional structures of popular sovereignty were established. The emperor was displaced from his central location in the state and declared a 'symbol', and one of the main extra-parliamentary centres of power in pre-war Japan, the military, was liquidated. Other extra-parliamentary centres, however, were bypassed by the reform, notably the concentrations of private corporate power (the *zaibatsu*), although there was a short-lived and half-hearted move to break up the largest of them. There were similar indecisive moves against the bureaucracy, although that section of it most directly identified with repression and thought control, the Home Ministry, was broken up and police and education powers drastically decentralised. In short, Japan did not experience a radical reconstruction of its state system such as occurred in Germany, but a partial reform. The defining character of the US impact during the 1945-52 period may be seen in retrospect to have been the purging of elements of the Japanese state which were inimical to the US. The implanting of democracy was limited by the fact that it was instrumental to this main purpose, much as some members of the occupation thought of their mission as a crusade for democracy.

Since the end of the US occupation of Japan, it is clear that the political infrastructure of democracy is in place: universal suffrage, regular elections, responsible cabinets. Equally clearly, it is a capitalist democracy; industry is privately owned and controlled in a market-regulated economy. True, some large caveats have to be entered: a significant number of people do not bother to vote — four million or about 33 per cent of the eligible electorate in December 1983, for example — but that is far better than the United States where almost half the electorate does not bother to vote even in a presidential election; there is a considerable gerrymander, such that a rural vote may be worth as much as four urban votes, an imbalance that the High Court has ruled unconstituional, and the ruling Liberal-Democratic Party would not have enjoyed a majority in several elections it 'won' had votes all been of equal worth; money and the machine are at least as important as policy in determining political fortunes; and, alone among major capitalist countries, Japan has seen no change of government for 30 years and faces little prospect of it.

Except for a short-lived socialist-led government in 1947-8, conservative rule at the national level has in fact been virtually unbroken since the promulgation of the Meiji Constitution in 1889, and the absence of a serious opposition threat has allowed the coalition of bureaucratic, business, and conservative political power to become thoroughly entrenched. The so-called 'democratic forces' of the political opposition, deprived of any realistic prospect of power, have become less able to project an alternative vision: rightwing and leftwing socialists split in the 1950s; the Communist Party and the New Left engaged in bitter confrontation in the 1960s; and the factions of the New Left have fought each other fiercely since then. Rather than presenting a challenge to the lack of democracy elsewhere in Japanese life, the 'democratic' movements of the left have themselves frequently been plagued with their own 'internal emperor system'.

Pluralism and populism constitute the central tenet for some sections of citizens' movements, which are analysed in the chapter by Smith. The countless struggles in postwar Japan in the name of the people *(jinmin)*, the autonomous citizenship *(shimin)*, and local resident communities *(jūmin)*, express a force of great energy and variety. The democracy of these movements is something that allows for and draws inspiration from amorphous, inarticulate and ambiguous ideas of the masses, and which stands in opposition to the clear-cut, articulate and unambiguous concepts which elites impose from above. Yet Smith's picture is somewhat bleak, showing a divided and dispirited movement, lacking any coordinated strategy and less capable in the 1980s than at any time in the postwar period of mounting serious challenge to the corporate and bureaucratic versions of a 'restructured' Japan.

Much of the history of postwar Japan has been one of gradual erosion of local autonomy and reestablishment or enhancement of central, bureaucratic authority, a process particularly evident in matters of police and education. Most of the chapters of this book interpret this process of bureaucratisation and centralisation — the enhancement of state power — as inimical to popular democracy. We are interested in particular in the degree to which a democratic spirit informs the Japanese body politic as a whole, the extent to which responsibility, initiative and, above all, power have been devolved to the grass roots level of the Japanese *demos,* the people. An astonishingly high proportion of the Japanese people, 90 per cent, pronounces itself content with the status quo, but that is scarcely decisive, given the degree to which the universalisation of mass production and mass consumption has been extended in Japan from conventional commodities through the area of 'culture'. Abundance of consumer goods is a measure of capitalist development, but not necessarily of democracy.

Doug McEachern's paper analyses in broad terms the dilemmas of the major capitalist states of the postwar period, focusing on the tension between political representation ('formal democracy') and economic growth (successful capitalism). His thesis immediately raises the broad question of the state and the various projects for its reorganisation on the part of the leading capitalist democracies in the early 1980s: monetarism, 'Reagonomics', Thatcherism, 'small state-ism', and, in Japan, 'administrative reform'. He sees the process in terms of the quest for a formula of renewed economic growth through a reduction in the power of organised labour and a reduction in public subsidies for welfare, unemployment, and health, which involves a historic swing away from the tendencies of the 1960s and 1970s towards incorporation of labour, with government and business, as part of the tripod of state. What is striking about McEachern's broad-canvas picture of trends in the capitalist democratic state is the distinctiveness of Japan. Where the process of incorporation of labour as a partner in the Western state was effected through policies affecting the central representative institutions of labour, such institutions exist only at a very underdeveloped level in Japan, where only a small part of the work force is organised at all and most of that in enterprise unions (on which see the chapters by Mutō and Kawanishi). So, although Japan is a central part of the world capitalist system, facing similar problems to those confronting other capitalist countries, Japan is, at least in some respects, structured differently and therefore likely to respond differently.

McEachern describes the present juncture as analogous to the interwar years in the sense that there is no longer any consensus on an appropriate method for integrating representative political institutions and economic growth. He does not labour the analogy with the 1930s, but it is clear he is outlining a contemporary crisis of no mean dimension.

His paper is the only one in the volume by someone who is not a 'Japan specialist'. It was commissioned because we believe that Japan is too important to be left to specialists alone, and are convinced that Japan specialists (and the general reader) have much to learn from the reflections of a political scientist expert in the recent history of Western capitalist democracy, even though his paper necessarily raises more questions than it answers.

McCormack's paper pursues the strictly Japanese dimensions of the crisis. He argues that the central postwar Japanese consensus, around economic growth, has gradually lost force as that objective has been achieved. He analyses a confluence of external and internal pressures pushing the country in the direction of a major military commitment and active partnership with the US in a North Pacific NATO-type alliance on the one hand, and a sharp increase in state controls and in the statist-orientation of crucial institutions on the other. He sees Japan as facing a qualitative break with the 40-year postwar period of 'economism' as a result.

Sugimoto focuses on some aspects of the warp and weft of the Japanese social fabric, whether derived from the militaristic, authoritarian past or more recently conceived, which predispose the society towards an even finer mesh of constraint and control. Morris-Suzuki's paper concentrates on the social implications of the new technology, exploring the illusory character of the technocratic utopia and the reality of deepening alienation in the 'information society'.

On the whole, overt political repression would seem to be relatively rare, and manipulation and control by subtle, covert, or ideological means much more common. Nevertheless, the practices of overt repression which Igarashi vividly describes in the law enforcement area suggest that minimum human rights are less than secure.

Yamazumi looks at the crucial area of education, Mutō and Kawanishi at the labour movement, Buckley and Mackie at the particular implications for women, paying close attention to the implications of recent legislation in the area of women's rights, while Sibatani concentrates on the management of science and questions of scientific ethics. All are fundamentally concerned with questions of freedom and control.

The overall picture is of Japan as a materially abundant and dynamic society, but a society which, however well articulated, is total and inclusive in structure and ethos and coordinated from a series of highly placed power centres utilising techniques of manipulation and control.

Yet, however total and inclusive the structure, there are those who refuse or prove unable to occupy their allotted place within it, as well as those who, for one reason or another, are denied a place. Their lot has to be weighed in any assessment of the quality of the structure; the perspective of those who are simultaneously insiders and outsiders of Japanese society differs fundamentally from that of those who are comfortably ensconced within. Two examples of these categories, both deserving of treatment in full, are the mentally ill and the Korean minority.

Japan has 330,000 people in mental institutions, of whom about 80 per cent have been compulsorily committed (compared with 44,870 confined in prisons). The immensity of the Japanese figure may be understood when it is compared with the figure of 120,000 in the United States, despite the fact that the population of the latter is nearly double Japan's, and while the US figure has steadily fallen since the mid-1950s, Japan's continues to grow. 80 per cent of those in Japan's mental institutions are held behind bars, and various forms of ill-treatment, including physical assault, solitary confinement, deprivation of food, and indiscriminate drug dosage, have been widely reported in recent years, including cases of patients being beaten to death. Various international bodies, including the International League for Human Rights and the International Commission of Jurists, have protested to the Japanese government on behalf of this huge yet generally invisible minority.[2]

Japan also has approximately 700,000 resident Koreans, many the descendants of the slave labour force imported into Japan during the war, most of them effectively exiled from their homeland by reason of war, division, and continuing political instability. Though 2,000 Koreans graduate annually from Japanese universities, as 'non-nationals' they are ineligible for employment in the public service, whether as diplomat or dustman, and are equally excluded from employment in the major Japanese corporations by the operation of elaborate discriminatory screening procedures. Most therefore, have no alternative to work in small and middle scale enterprises or in Korean owned companies. Their experience suggests that the cohesiveness of Japanese society is achieved through selective *exclusion*.

At the Yasukuni shrine to Japan's war dead the spirits of some 20,000 Koreans who died while serving in Japan's imperial army are enshrined. After their death, however, Korea ceased to be Japanese, and although those who had died remained 'Japanese', their families became 'Korean'. Calls by their Korean families to have these names deleted from the list of enshrined 'heroes' have been rejected, since they died as 'Japanese'; yet their families, as 'non-Japanese', have no 'Japanese' pension settlement.[3]

The weakness in Japan of a sense of universal human values (on which see also Sibatani's essay in this volume), and the deep-rootedness of the prewar notion of inviolable Japanese polity (*kokutai*), is evident in this confusion of citizenship with blood membership in a family state lineage. One of the most trenchant critics of modern Japan, the emigre Korean philosopher Chung Kyungmo, believes that the notion of popular sovereignty, established in Europe with the execution of the monarchs of Britain and France, and in America with the revolution and the Declaration of the Rights of Man, remains foreign to Japan. He suggests that the secret of Japanese economic success may be found more in the *inadequacy* of the Japanese personality — the continuing capacity for total and unquestioning performance of roles prescribed by those in authority — rather than its maturity and fullness. [4]

'Internationalisation' has so far had little impact on the core areas of Japanese identity. Multiculturalism, Australian-style, stands at the opposite pole of social formations from Japan's highly integrated and articulated model.

Looking at contemporary Japan from the depth of his experience of prewar and wartime society, Hidaka sees an unmistakable trend away from democracy and in the direction of what he calls a 'control society'. The mechanism of 'distribution of the profits', which he describes, ensures the consent of the masses of the people to the system, which therefore is able to retain the formal structures of parliamentary democracy.

Yet some of the most astute and intelligent foreign scholars of Japan single out the strong Japanese bureaucratic tradition, whose current flowering Hidaka finds so disturbing, not only as the key to Japan's material achievements and social harmony, but also as positive attainments worthy of emulation. Thus Ronald Dore speaks of the Japanese as 'born bureaucrats', a 'people that accepts bureaucratic control easily', and finds in the Japanese people's skill in creating and running bureaucracies precisely the quality which will enable Japan to contribute to 'the building of a new international society'. [5] And Chalmers Johnson praises the achievement of the Japanese bureaucracy which has restricted the legislative and judicial branches of government to 'safety valve' functions. [6]

Our perspective is that prosperity and order are not in themselves goals necessarily related to democracy. The formula by which Japan manages to combine industrial growth and social harmony could as well be described as corporatist, though labour plays much less a role than elsewhere in advanced capitalism since it is incorporated at the level of the enterprise rather than through any central representative organisation. Preoccupation with systemic efficiency at the expense of voluntaristic choices cannot but diminish the quality of life of the Japanese. [7]

Over 50 years ago one Japanese scholar used the phrase 'cool fascism' to describe the kind of control state he perceived being born in 1930s Japan. [8] Others have used formulas like 'friendly fascism' (to describe tendencies in the United States)[9] or, more recently, 'democratic fascism' of Japan in the 1970s.[10] What they mean is a society in which the masses of the people are mobilised to serve state purposes 'through means which are heavily bureaucratic, within structures that are superficially democratic, and according to processes which ensure the consent of many of the people . . . '.[11] From this perspective, democracy cannot be reduced to a static institutional arrangement in which voting rights are ensured. The actual operation of democracy cannot be assessed without considering the degree to which the population participate in the political process where their interests are affected. To the extent that law represents and protects the interests of limited, often privileged, groups of society, even civil disobedience which breaks law may be regarded as an act of participatory democracy. The fundamental question which we canvass in this volume is the extent to which democracy as a participatory process is operative in contemporary Japan.

The fact that some outstanding scholars can see elements of a model for emulation in Japan's development of the 'control society', while others describe it as a form of fascism underlines the importance of focusing the most careful attention on studying what is going on. We hope that this book will serve that purpose.

Combining democracy with growth: the search for a formula

Doug McEachern

Japan is often described as 'unique', and undoubtedly much about it is unique, in the sense of being highly specific to that country. This is not to say, however, that the Japanese people have a peculiar or unique morality, for the values of Japanese society are in essence the shared values of humanity, or even that the Japanese economic system is unique, for that system is clearly capitalist. What is unique is the political system. Though categorised loosely as 'democratic' and formally structured in representative and responsible political institutions, there is much that is unique about the way that Japan has adopted the institutions of representative democracy. This stands out starkly when the process of adapting those institutions to maximise economic growth in the postwar Western world is examined.

To illustrate the uniqueness of the Japanese political system, we have adopted the unusual practice of inviting an expert in Euro-American politics and political theory who is not a Japan 'specialist' to delineate what he sees as the general lines of development of the Western state in the postwar period. Dr McEachern's article draws attention to the fact that the Japanese formula for growth rests upon a strikingly different balance of social forces.

The Editors

Western debates over Japanese political development are frequently characterised by attempts to use familiar definitions to measure the reality of Japanese experience. This has been true for the debate about the Japanese past: 'was it feudal?'; the interwar period, 'was it fascist?'; and for the present, when the character of the political system is examined, 'is it a liberal democracy?' On this last question, notions of democracy are derived from idealised versions of the Western system, frequently without considering the historical development of that system and without reflection on the ends served by 'liberal democracy' as a 'system of power'. In this paper I have sought to go beyond the popular description of the workings of a supposedly liberal democratic system and to concentrate on the extent to which the changing forms and patterns of political representation, through partly competition and

18

the electoral process and through direct negotiations between class organisations and the state, are linked to the pursuit of economic growth.
My purpose is not to suggest that Japan's economic success has been
based on a pattern of political representation but rather that, when
considering Japan's economic growth, attention needs to be paid to the
way in which the Japanese political system and its particular style of
political representation has resolved the tensions between rule and accumulation that underlay the development of the formal and informal
levels of political representation in other industrialised capitalist countries in the postwar period.

Introduction

Prolonged worldwide economic recession of the early 1980s focuses attention on the importance of the relations between forms of political
representation and conditions of high and secure economic growth. It
is not just the fact of formal electoral participation that is significant,
though that provides the basis for the democratic claims of the system.
What matters is the complex, changing, formal and informal ways in
which social classes are organised and brought into the political
process, for it is on this pattern that the size and scope of state action
depends and, through that, prospects of economic growth are secured.
These forms of representation include institutions for economic and
social planning that are based on consultation between representative
class organisations, or even direct negotiations between government
and those class organisations, or policies (such as prices and incomes
policies) that depend on acceptance by these class organisations and
over which, as a result, they have a veto.

Political responses to the recession reveal tension between two
aspects of state action, one concerned with maintaining social stability
to ensure the maintenance of class relations upon which the economic
system is based, the other with promoting capital accumulation.[1] It is
such forms of representation, linking political and economic
processes, that seek to combine these two tasks in mutually reinforcing
ways. It cannot be assumed that it is always possible to find arrangements that will successfully balance these two tasks, or that solutions
once found will be durable. Such arrangements are not static. They
contain implications for future economic, political and social development and, as economic growth weakens and declines (for whatever
reasons), these arrangements need to be reworked in an attemp to discover or rediscover a social basis for a new period of sustained economic expansion. The argument here is not that these various forms of
representation either 'cause' or 'explain' economic growth but, instead,
that they form an essential social base upon which can be constructed
economic policies that may, in particular circumstances, generate expansion and affluence.

The political system is based on formal equality, symbolised by the equal right to vote. Formally it dominates all areas of society, including the economic. The economic sphere on the other hand, is marked by great and small forms of inequality over the distribution of wealth and income, and over access to, and control of, the production process. How is it that representative and political equality have not been used to transform the economic system, at the very least to reduce the size and significance of wealth and income inequality, and to end the class privileges of private ownership of the major means of social and economic production? This question underlies some of the early debates over the extension of the franchise.

How could political equality be granted without undermining the economic inequality so essential to capitalist production? One possibility was suggested by J. S. Mill, who recognised a need to extend the right to vote to the propertyless males and to women, if only because there were no effective arguments to deny such an extension after granting a limited widening of the franchise to include traders and manufacturers.[2] Mill shows a characteristic sensitivity and advocates greater access to education as the solution. Through education the propertyless would come to understand the system and would not act in ways to undermine its essential features, since these guaranteed their freedoms.

Miliband, in his recent *Capitalist Democracy in Britain,* extends such an argument to the whole campaign for reform that both widened the franchise and subsequently modernised the political, economic and social system.[3] For Miliband, the political system acts as an engine of containment, limiting and transforming the challenges of the working class, so that their actions are not able to damage capitalism's long term viability. He makes this claim in two ways: firstly, by treating voting, formal political equality, and the electoral and parliamentary processes as the key institutions that blunt social challenge, in that the act of granting the various reforms lessens the growth of potentially dangerous campaigns. In this he cites many examples of class- and system-conscious politicians who argue the need to make concessions in just this way. Secondly, he examines the attitudes and political perspectives of the major class organisations of the British working class, the trade unions and the Labour Party, and reveals the extent to which these are easily confined within acceptable limits.

I argue a different case from Mill and Miliband. It was not just education or the fact of political equality that rendered the system safe. The role of the working class has been more substantial than they implied. Indeed, the challenge from the class organisations of labour has been an important part of the very process by which the system was adjusted to the task of running a capitalist economy, once the era of liberal market society was destroyed by the profound interwar depression. It was because of this challenge that the role of the state was expanded and the trade union movement brought, gradually, closer to the centre of the political stage, setting the scene for the major political conflict that has characterised the management of this recession, the dispute over the size and the role of the state.

Postwar political and economic reconstruction
Although not all societies that industrialised and did so within a capitalist framework had a liberal past, the era of a society largely co-ordinated through market institutions passed away with the variety of solutions to the depressions of the 1920s and 1930s.[4] In all cases, it was the extension of the state into areas of the economy and society from which it had been previously excluded and the increased range of state actions that paved the way for recovery and world war: the giving up of the gold standard and free trade in Britain; the rise of the Nazi Party in Germany; the Popular Front in France (its weakness paralleling the weakness of the recovery in France); and the tightening of authoritarian rule in Japan. All expressed a similar kind of distancing from the preeminence of the market solutions.

Some countries, such as Germany and Japan, had less far to travel, since the state had played a very important part in promoting both capitalism and industrial development. The solutions to the depression may have ended the liberal era, a tendency reinforced by the rise of larger and larger capitalist enterprises in the form of monopolies and cartels, but they did not solve the problems of how state actions would be co-ordinated with a still predominantly privately owned economy. This problem was initially and pragmatically solved for the fighting of the war, but the new arrangements linking the political and economic sphere were only consolidated during the political and economic reconstruction after World War Two.

Using Britain as an example, it is possible to see what this process involved. On the basis of an elected Labour government, the state expanded its role, largely through the nationalisation of a number of basic industries, most of which had become problems for their private owners but which could, with the adequate provision of state investment funds, be extremely useful for promoting the more profitable operation of privately owned manufacturing industry.[5] There were two exceptions, the profitable steel industry, nationalised in 1949 and the only industry denationalised after the election of 1951, and the Bank of England, which was given public status as a central banking institution but still retained its important role as a link between government and the private banking sector. It was only through nationalisation and the rules for the conduct of the nationalised industries that the British state sought to intervene in the operations of the productive economy; planning was eschewed. A degree of Keynesian fiscal manipulation was adopted, but there was no full scale Keynesian revolution. The trade unions were the basis upon which this process of expanded state action was constructed. It was their depression grievances that identified the targets for nationalisation and it was their presence in the political system that formed the basis for this consolidated state role.[6] The promise of full employment, the construction of a greater system of state provision of welfare, and the nationalisation programme were the indicators of the significant presence of the working class within the political process. Even though this construction of a mixed economy did not end or transform capitalism, instead merely acting to modernise its structures and to provide the basis for a new period of expansion, it would not have happened at the time that it did nor in the way that it did without the influence of the trade unions and their social democratic political party. It is significant that the Labour government did not seek to create planning institutions to guide the development of the private sector, and that it did not set up durable institutions to involve the organised trade unions in on-going debates about national economic decisions. Instead, these were avenues, logical concomitants of what had been done, that could be explored when the era of growth started to weaken and new initiatives were required to discover other sources of expansion.

Other industrialised capitalist countries did not follow the same path as Britain. The United States, for example, simply consolidated the position of the state inherited from the New Deal reforms while adding a limited degree of government fiscal policy to its existing means for supporting private capital.[7] Its major assistance to the private sector derived from its role in the international arena, through defence procurement contracts, through schemes to make the world safe for the free operation of US corporations, as seen in the international trade and finance arrangements negotiated as part of the peace settlement with its wartime allies.[8]

In the defeated countries of Germany and Japan, the United States also played an important part in shaping postwar economic growth and its social basis. In Germany, for example, the United States was the dominant force in reconstruction and, by its actions, promoted a reformed trade union structure (conceived and implemented by the British delegation), further weakening a trade union movement already weakened by Nazi rule. This continued weakening was reflected in the trade unions' acquiescence in the moves *not* to nationalise those sections of German business most compromised in the ascension and rule of the Nazi Party. Instead the emphasis was on setting up institutions of co-determination in the heavy metal industries with vague commitments to extend this reform to other sections of industry at some later date. Co-determination was a continuation of the Weimar

experiment in works councils and was a vehicle for worker participation in company management in a way that neither strengthened
the position of trade unions nor weakened the strength of German
business and management.[9] It was a form of political representation
with the scope for tying workers and managers closer together in the
pursuit of growth and was, in many ways, part of the social basis for
the wage restraint upon which the rapid postwar recovery was
constructed.

With the return to power in Germany of conservative Christian
Democratic elements, and the regime's obvious attachment to neo-
classical and quasi-free market ideology personified by Ludwig
Ehrhard and the social-market doctrine,[10] there would seem to be few
parallels between the situation in Germany and that in Britain or most
other industrialised capitalist countries.[11] But this is to mistake the
rhetoric for the reality of the shape of the German economy and its
mode of operation. The ideology stresses a minimal and marginal role
for the state, largely confined to setting broad rules for economic conduct and protecting, to a certain extent, the needs of those who can not
survive in the market society. In practice, the moves to reprivatise the
economy and to reduce the scope and significance of state action were
not as impressive as the ideology suggests. The state still owned or was
dominant in significant areas of the national economy, largely in infrastructure it is true, but with some presence in the fields of finance
and manufacturing.[12] The federal structure of the German state and
the concern not to discriminate between different firms in the
economy did mean that co-ordinated use of the state sector to promote
growth and to remove obstacles to growth was not possible. In terms of
the broad relationship between the state and the economy, what the
moves to reduce the size of the state achieved was simply to bring Germany in line with the situation created by the expansion of the state in
its European rivals.

The events in France lie somewhere between those of Britain and
Germany. The size of the state sector was rapidly expanded with the
nationalisation of the property of some sections of business strongly
implicated in the period of Vichy collaboration.[13] In this way the
French state came to own a major car firm, much of the basic infrastructure and a significant part of the financial system. Unlike in
Britain, the French state left these units more or less free to conduct
themselves as if they were still in the private sector. The instrument
chosen to promote growth and the modernisation of the basic infrastructure was the system of indicative planning which used very loose
guidelines and persuasion to promote and co-ordinate investment so
as to boost growth.[14] Though the actual contribution of planning to
the rapid (and unprecedented) postwar growth in France has been dis-
puted,[15] it is clear that in the years before state action and planning the

French economy stagnated and in the years since it has prospered. The planning process, at its peak and basic levels, was meant to work on the basis of tripartite discussions between labour, capital, and the state. In practice the trade unions have either chosen not to participate or have been neglected, and the planning process, for much of its time, has been a collaboration between big business and the state in promoting their common goals, modernisation and expansion.[16] Again, this incomplete pattern of trade union association with state and business goals through formal consultation procedures formed a basis for future experiments, if and when the tendency for high growth slackened.

As in Germany, postwar occupation created the basic pattern of class-state relations that were the social basis of Japan's re-emergence as a significant capitalist power. During the 1930s, the state had gained a significant presence within and wide powers over the private economy. The reform of the state, which reduced its military capacity, did not alter the fundamental relations between the state and major businesses. Indeed the efforts to reform the structure of industry and the role of the *zaibatsu* may have served to reinforce the role of the state.[17] It was at this time that the structure of enterprise unionism was created as an outgrowth of employee organisation in the wartime economy.[18] The significance of enterprise unionism in postwar Japan has been widely analysed and the contrast with European developments noted.[19] If the social integration of workers through forms of representation is important, the consequences of this Japanese solution will be substantial. Integration is achieved at the level of the work place. Such enterprise unionism places barriers in the way of, and may indeed render irrelevant, the articulation of working-class concerns through a social democratic political party in the electoral sphere.

The challenge of affluence

The new forms of class representation embodied in this postwar reorganisation provided the social base for economic growth, social development, and increasing standards of living in all the major industrialised capitalist countries. Although economic fluctuation remained, serious downturns were avoided and many countries reported growth rates far higher than their historical averages. Such was the case in Britain, France, and Germany. New technologies were introduced into the production process, synthetics became commonplace parts of everyday life, and consumer goods came into the hands of more and more families. The Japanese economy shared in and exemplified the growth of the long boom. It was during this time that Japan became a force in the international relations of the Asian and Pacific region and was poised to become a major force in the American and European markets.[20] The experience of affluence also promoted the development of political movements to challenge the characteristic social consequences of that economic success. The apparent identification of the trade unions with the goals of business and the state was the starting point for the development of radical student politics and the growth of citizens' movements concerned with the results of the unbridled pursuit of growth on the environment and the health and welfare of local communities.[21] These groups seem to be more deeply entrenched in Japan, perhaps because the option of reintegration with the trade union movement was not as possible in the absence of a viable social democratic political force.

What I want to discuss here is not that flowering of material life, nor the fact that many commentators felt that this proved that capitalism as a system of class exploitation no longer existed.[22] Instead, I wish to examine the extent to which prolonged growth and affluence, and the apparent ability of government to control economic developments in such a way as to avoid severe recessions, affected the balance between accumulation and social control. One of the attractions of these new arrangements was that they could satisfy both demands without undermining one or the other; the need for social peace could be fulfilled without weakening the basis for continued accumulation; there would be sufficient economic surplus generated to raise the standards of living of the bulk of the population, to fuel greater investment and to leave the state free to provide both infrastructure for business and social support for the working population. Under the particular circumstances of the postwar long boom, the experience of affluence created challenges to the social order of quite a distinct kind; these challenges were neither anticipated nor resolvable within the context of continued affluence.

The longer growth continued the more people came to assume that affluence was an assured condition that was changing the framework of debate about the social alternatives. This can be seen in books written by authors of sharply contrasting political persuasions. J.-J. Servan-Schreiber's *The American Challenge,* written before both the weakening of the long boom and the dramatic events of 1968, captures the spirit well.[23] Economic growth is assured, the new issues concern the participation of all sections of society in the debates about how the surplus is to be spent, a making real of the potential of the planning mechanism. He also indicates a new concern with the impact of growth on the environment and the character and consequences of new technology. J. K. Galbraith, in *The Affluent Society,* argues from the position of assured growth for a re-orientation of economic and social priorities away from pure economic expansion towards greater social development.[24] Baran and Sweezy in *Monopoly Capitalism* make the case that too great a surplus and not scarcity was the major problem threatening the continued expansion of the system.[25] True to their marxist heritage they, of course, anticipated a future downturn without being precise in their arguments. They also saw a shift in the area of social debate and demands. Herbert Marcuse, in his most misunderstood book, *One Dimensional Man,* accepts the permanence of consumer satisfaction and raises large questions about the consequences of continued development and introduction of newer forms of automated technologies and machines that could think.[26] None of these authors anticipated the dramatic ways in which the question of continued accumulation would be posed in the late 1960s, ironically, just at the time when the growth of the long boom was faltering.

The student movement in the 1960s, especially when, as in France, linked to working-class struggles, challenged the rationale of the system, the logic of its continued economic and social priorities. The main areas of concern for these movements were democratic participation (based on a critique of the increasingly bureaucratised character of life in industrialised capitalism) and the character and desirability of new technologies (based on a critique of the way in which technologies could shape the human character of social development). It is the question of democratic participation that is most relevant here. Whether it was the Students for Democratic Society in the United States, the Trotskyist 'groupuscles' in France, or the 'Joint Struggle Committees' in Japan, the critique of formal political equality and representative democracy was similar.[27] Formal political representation was not relevant to the lives most people lived most of the time. It was significant every few years, at the time of elections and referenda, but the institutions in which most people worked and lived were not democratic in even that limited, representational form. Bureaucracy was the most common form of social organisation from the office, factory, and hospital to the school, and, in a bureaucracy, the decisions were made at the top; there was a downward hierarchy of control and the role of most people was to do what they were told. The challenge of these social movements was to ask, how can a society claim to be democratic when all its major institutions are as dictatorial in form as the Central Committee of the Communist Party of the Soviet Union? The proposed forms of direct associational democracy were significant because they embodied the critique in, more or less, practical form. These movements challenged the rights of managers to manage and demand far greater participation of, for example, workers in their work places and students in their schools and universities. The authority of experts and technocrats was challenged. Without such authority and deference, it would be extremely difficult (though not impossible) to run a class-based system of social production with an unequal pattern of economic and social rewards. It was certainly perceived as a threat by the relevant powerful sections of these industrialised capitalist societies.

Accompanying this critique of the legitimacy of the most common forms of social control went a critique of the means and ends of technology. This can be seen in the developing hostility to the uncritical acceptance of science and its products, and growing suspicion about new technology, which was seen as an increasingly effective form of social control. Indeed, doubts were expressed about the appropriateness of growth as a social objective at all. The rejection of growth, in the name of ecological protection or on broader social grounds, and the hostility to technological innovation, constituted significant challenges to the normal responses of capitalist industry to problems of accumulation and profitability. The campaigns against pollution, which stressed the social costs of private advantage, would have significantly added to business costs should business have had to bear the cost of any improvements in pollution controls, and would have placed further barriers in the way of private, profitable investment, except in industries manufacturing and installing pollution control devices. It seems fair to observe that if these movements had continued and if the social and economic circumstances that enabled them to flourish had persisted, then the health of capitalist enterprises would have been impaired. As it happened, the first thing to go was the certainty of growth, and though remnants of these movements still provide critiques of the logic of industrial development, they are less effective now than they were.[28]

The failure of these movements need not detain us here. It was the fact of this opposition and the character of its criticism that makes this interlude important. It highlights a weakness in the original postwar strategy to combine high rates of economic growth and a degree of increased affluence with a stable social order. The fact of growth and affluence was thought to give the system immunity from the kinds of social problems and the potential threats of the interwar depression years. What the events of the late 1960s reveal is that affluence, by itself, contains no long term guarantees that the population will remain socially passive. Indeed, removing scarcity from the agenda and seeming to be able to control economic development so as to remove the threat of unemployment had the effect of activating a new kind of criticism that was just as unsettling as that of depression times. Potentially, the situation was even more difficult since full employment served to strengthen the position of the trade unions and, although it is true that this gave them a stake in the existing social order that they were reluctant to lose, to give them a more secure base from which to challenge the prevailing priorities of the capitalist production process.

Between the boom and recession

In the aftermath of the weakening of the long, postwar period of growth and before the onset of the major recession of the 1970s and 1980s, there was a period in which governments experimented in attempts to recapture the chances of growth. It is instructive that in many cases governments extended the schemes for the more direct representation of class organisations in national policy making that had been implicit but incomplete in the postwar reconstruction period. This can be seen most clearly in the efforts to extend planning procedures and to operate forms of prices and incomes policies, both of which were undertaken as important initiatives in the attempt to recapture growth. Such an effort underlay the events in Britain, where the growth of the long boom slackened early and the attempt to find sources of growth was more prolonged than elsewhere. The first initiative came from a Conservative Party government with an attempt to imitate French planning and to set up the National Economic Development Organisation with a tripartite structure, embracing organised business, state representatives, and trade union people.[29] There were also various regional and sectoral versions of the same all seeking to pool information about the barriers to increased output, efficiency, and viability, but also seeking to harmonise relations between the 'social partners' in the pursuit of growth. In the context of this paper, the setting up of these institutions appears as an attempt to generalise the social basis of postwar growth and to implant it deeply in all parts of the British industrial economy. The fact that it did not produce some effective form of nationally co-ordinated industrial effort[30] does not detract from the significance of the initiative, the persistence of the arrangements, nor the implications of the social perspective embodied in them.

Along with the attempt to co-ordinate investment and effort in the industrial economy went state-sponsored forms of prices and incomes policies, once again based on attempts to link together business, labour, and the state in some coherent framework.[31] The problem of growth was behind this effort since it was assumed that lessening the rate of wage increases would boost the level of profits and, hence, investment, thereby preparing the way for future economic expansion, with more secure employment as the incentive for trade union complicity. All the efforts at securing prices and incomes policies failed, because the trade unions were in a position to protect themselves against moves that would have weakened their bargaining ability without guaranteeing higher growth and secure employment.[32] When the government shifted its attention from constructing these agreements to reforming trade unions to make them more amenable to such policies, then the growing strength of the trade unions was revealed. This image of increasing trade union presence culminated in the dramatic

1973-4 miners' strike, which provided the occasion for the Conservative Prime Minister, Ted Heath, to gamble away his Party's electoral majority.

It is revealing to note that in other major European countries similar moves occurred. In France, both before and after 1968, there were attempts to extend the planning process to include incomes, first in the public sector and then in the wider economy, on the basis of a concern with the whole growth context.[33] Although growth was much more secure in France, the incomes measures were not noticeably successful. On the planning front, there were moves to encourage trade unions back into 'participation' and to give these initiatives a more secure and broader social base. In the Federal Republic of Germany, the onset of temporary recession, and the change towards a Social Democratic Party-dominated government, saw experimentation with economic policy and with a form of consensus-building 'concerted action' programme.[34] Once again, the impetus was the need to produce conditions that would re-establish growth. The institutions of concerted action were made up of representatives of business, labour, and the state, along with a group of designated 'economic experts'.[35] The role of these meetings was to discuss the 'objective orientation data' provided and to agree, more or less, on a framework for wage settlement that would be consistent with rapid economic recovery. Although the trade unions had welcomed the opportunity to take part in what they saw as the making of national economic policy, their attempts to make concerted action into something other than a forum for agreeing on wage restraint were unsuccessful. Wage restraint was agreed, below the rate of recovery, and the rapid return to profitability of German firms resulted. The renewal of wage restraint in conditions of strong recovery led to illegal, unofficial strikes largely in the metal industries. These strikes gained very substantial nominal wage increases, often returning the situation to what it had been before concerted action was introduced. Such success may also stand as a symbol for increased trade union strength in the full employment economy and a sign that the extensive weakening of the years of Nazi rule and postwar reconstruction had finally been overcome.

In terms of the relationship of forms of political representation to the pursuit of economic growth, the interlude between the end of the long boom and the onset of the recession was most revealing. In their own distinct ways, most of these initiatives to promote a return to conditions of economic growth were based on promoting more or less direct forms of political participation by representative class organisations. The demands of the 'end-of-affluence' radicals were a response to the real problems confronting the organisation of capitalist production at that time. Nevertheless, as so often is the case, such demands were taken up, transformed, and implemented in ways that were far less socially challenging than their original proponents intended. Regardless of the extent to which it was a deliberate policy, these consultation and participation schemes all addressed the contrast between formal political participation in elections and the actual irrelevance of democratic forms to the making of the major decisions of national policy and the conduct of affairs within the work place. It may be that these schemes were introduced with the hope that they would pacify the working-class organisations that took part; the assumption being that the leaders would be so flattered, or so compromised, by participation that they would be either unable or unwilling to campaign against the sacrifices demanded. Such pacification was not the automatic consequence of coopting trade unions into these schemes. The very fact of creating these new institutional forums for direct and formal consultation with trade unions was seen as a sign of trade union strength (if it had been otherwise, neither business nor government would have been interested in such gestures) and the persistence of full employment only reinforced that strength. Given the circumstances, trade unions were in a position to use the new institutions to demand further changes in the way in which capitalist societies would be managed.[36]

As for Japan, the uniqueness of its balance of institutional and class forces was already evident at this time. The challenge mounted by the student movement at the end of the 1960s against the system of alienating, bureaucratic education in the universities, continuing military links with the United States, and the prospect of corporate servitude beyond graduation, was quickly contained. In the process of pacification in the early 1970s, the precise proportions of responsibility that should be attached to internal (factional) disintegration on the part of the student organisations, suppression by forces of the state (on which see the McCormack introduction in this volume to Igarashi's chapter), and co-option (on which see Hidaka's analysis of the 'distribution of the profits'), remain to be elucidated; but the transformation was unquestionable. The universities, administratively reorganised, began the transformation into bastions of conservatism. In the world of labour, co-option in the confines of enterprise unions (described by Mutō and Kawanishi in this volume) made unnecessary the corporatist strategies of other capitalist countries. Trade unions did not need to be incorporated at the national level; they were already incorporated at the level of the enterprise. The freedom of bureaucratic and corporate manoeuvre in Japan on the eve of the oil shocks was unprecedented in advanced capitalism.

The recession, phase one
When the industrialised capitalist countries plunged into the recession after the Middle East war of 1973 and the dramatic increase in oil

prices, the first response of most governments was to continue exploiting the avenues of participation already opened up by the postwar settlement and the initiatives after the end of the long boom. Even though the recession was characterised by the combination of unemployment, inflation, and declining output that confounded Keynesian (and many other) assumptions, it did not, at least in the initial stages, discourage attempts to use state policy to offset the severity of the recession. In Britain, under a Labour government, there was a sharp increase in the size of the state through nationalisation, state assistance to threatened firms, and the increased funds needed to support those unemployed by the downturn in the manufacturing sector.[37] Within the framework of the Social Contract, the initiatives taken by the state also increased. Those largely took the form of attempts to make effective the assumptions behind the wage restraint component of the Social Contract. The National Enterprise Board and the Planning Agreements were both created to make it more likely that the benefits of wage restraint would be translated into higher investment and growth. Underlying the Social Contract negotiations was the assumption that the private sector had been failing in Britain and that, if left to its own commercial judgements, it would not substantially increase its investment, regardless of the levels of profitability.[38] This period of state expansion was predicated on the increased presence of trade unions in the deliberations over national economic policy, which is precisely what the Social Contract represented.

In France, the first response was a similar intensification of state efforts reflected in the increased reliance on 'contractual' arrangements to smooth the campaign against inflation while maintaining France's record of high growth.[39] Given continuity of the conservative government, and given that the trade unions did not suddenly find themselves projected into the centre of the political sphere, the expansion of the state in this period cannot have been simply the result of the increased political presence of the trade unions. Perhaps the lack of such social base for these new moves explains their relatively limited character and their early replacement by new forms of small state and partly monetarist policies in 1976, with the appointment of Raymond Barre as Prime Minister.[40]

In Germany, the pattern was similarly muted. Nonetheless, the position of a Social Democratic government did see some moves to increase the presence of trade unions in both the national decision making process and at the factory level, through the attempts to extend the scope of co-determination.[41] And though the United States does not have a particularly 'interventionist' state (although the political actions of the state have been important for the well-being of private American capital operating as a coherent system),[42] under the Carter

Presidency, the scope of state action increased as did its regulation of business activities, especially on environmental and social matters.[43]

This first period of response to the recession saw a series of moves to create, recreate or intensify the social basis for a new period of economic expansion. The key objective of such policies was to involve trade unions in national policy making in ways that would contain the strength gained by these organisations as a result of the hang-overs from full employment, and to provide a breathing space for the reassertion of social stability in the face of the onset of sudden and prolonged recession. The extent to which new institutions were created to achieve this by 'incorporating' trade unions in the processes of government encouraged many social commentators to regard these developments as threatening the status of parliamentary representation. Such a concern was misplaced, exaggerating as it does the previous significance of parliament which had really been displaced by cabinet and executive government when the franchise was extended, and parliament was no longer the exclusive preserve of the dominant class. This period of representational initiative encouraged a resurgence of literature on the character of corporatism and its significance in the present period and its relationship to the essential characteristics of industrialised capitalism.[44] Some saw it as a threat to the existing system of electorally-based political representation; some saw it as the creation of a totally new social system, neither capitalist nor socialist; some praised these developments as offering the only hope of social stability in troubled times; some saw it as the rise of a system that would extinguish individual liberty and destroy free enterprise; others stressed the potential of such direct forms for the representation of class organisations to generate social containment of a developing labour-based movement of opposition.[45] In almost all cases, the extent and significance of the changes was misinterpreted. The extremely limited sense in which the trade unions did more than formally participate in decision making was not appreciated, and the alleged veto powers of the unions were slight and undermined by the uneven continuation of recession.

The recession, phase two
The response to the second phase of the recession that followed the sharp rise in oil prices in 1978-9 was a second kind of strategy that only makes sense when its actions are measured against the pattern of changes in class representation since the end of the long boom.[46] In Britain, France and the United States, governments came into office that were formally committed to strategies based on monetarism and reducing the size of the state. The new strategy used the monetarist analysis to support the campaign to withdraw the state from the economy rather than as a real doctrine to shape policy responses to the

continued recession. It is true that monetarism and the revival of the
ideas associated with Hayek symbolised the rejection of Keynesian
politics and the consensus that had underlain the period of postwar expansion.[47] Nonetheless, its own imprecisions made it a dangerous
guide to action and, although monetary policy was given greater emphasis in this period, monetary policy alone was not considered
enough to change the political and social framework within which
state economic policy was being formed. The emphasis was twofold:
reduce the size of the state *and* reduce the political presence of the trade
unions, where this had been the basis for the expansion of the state's
role. Where the trade unions had been most significant, there the neo-
liberal response was most determined. Where the expansion of the
state had come with only a limited increase in the presence of the trade
unions, here the policies were more muted and pragmatic. Britain ex-
emplifies the first position; France and Germany, the second. Japan
once again followed a quite distinctive path.

The Thatcher Government introduced new trade union laws to re-
strict union organisational abilities and their recourse to strike action.
The negotiations between government and trade unions which had
been such a characteristic feature of the preceding period came to an
end, partly because the government rejected the legitimacy of such
trade union participation and partly because the trade union movement was reluctant to deal with the new and obviously hostile government.[48] Negotiations over general levels of pay settlement were no
longer relevant. The government was also committed to a direct
reduction in the state's share of the economy and in its broader economic role. For this reason it encouraged limited sales of state assets.
The most significant was of shares in North Sea oil. The basic shape of
the state sector has not been changed and the state still plays a substantial infrastructural role and is still, through British Leyland, at the
centre of manufacturing industry. Although some attempts were made
to reduce the scope of welfare provision, the severity of the recession
has meant that the size of the welfare component of the budget has
steadily increased. Of more significance than these moves to take the
state out of the productive economy has been the impact that the broad
contractionist policies have had on manufacturing industry. Since the
advent of the Thatcher Government and its distinctive style of policy
this has shrunk rapidly.[49]

Other countries have not pursued their policy packages with as
much enthusiasm or indifference to the impact of unemployment.[50]
The record of these policies have been fairly consistent. In the initial
phase, they increased inflation, output slumped dramatically, and unemployment increased steadily. The longer the policy was applied the
more the economy contracted and there has been a recent fall in the
rate of inflation. The greatest achievement has been to make this

recession more like its predecessors, with low output, low investment and high unemployment, while inflation becomes of diminishing significance. The control of the money supply does not appear to be directly related to the reduction of the rate of inflation, and the size of the state, relative to the Gross Domestic Product, does not seem to have been substantially reduced.

The one enduring achievement of the combination of these policies and the severity of the recession has been to pacify the trade union movement and to reduce its political presence. Perhaps this period was necessary to make that expansion of the state in the initial period of the recession less significant for private capital, without directly increasing the prospects of renewed capital accumulation, growth and affluence.

Japan's experience after the ending of the long boom is rather different from the other major industrialised capitalist countries. Again it was the different social basis of growth that conditioned the character of that response. Enterprise unionism and the absence of an effective political voice for the trade unions made the 'corporatist' experiments of other places irrelevant.[51] This relative exclusion meant that the challenge of prolonged international recession could be met by closer co-ordination of the state and the dominant private firms without too much regard for the concerns or complaints of the working population.[52] Japan's role as an export economy also reduced the significance of these objections. Despite the great trade successes of the Japanese in this present recession, it is not clear that these successes will be enduring, partly because of the talk in Washington in the early spring of 1985 about 'trade war' and 'retaliation' and partly because of the unpredictable effects in Japan of the pressures (described in the chapter by McCormack) for Japan to shoulder military commitments in Northeast Asia comparable to its economic scale.

The Japanese working class is not only marginalised in industrial terms because of the split between general and enterprise unions and the character of the enterprise unions themselves, drastically limiting their impact on both the conduct of business and state, but it is marginalised in electoral terms too, since no matter how radical the parties of opposition they are handicapped by the long entrenched electoral gerrymander. But, if labour is politically marginalised, business is not. Not only is the Liberal-Democratic Party very much open to business in the sense that money is the key to electoral funding and to the relative strength of factions, so too is the state itself. It is not that the bureaucracy directly articulates business's wishes; the role of MITI as the centre of a quasi-planning system, especially in its response to the problems of international recession and contraction of trade, shows that this is not the case. Nevertheless the framework of state action serves to promote and secure capital accumulation and to manage the interaction between the Japanese and world economy.

Conclusion

This paper has presented an account of postwar developments in terms of the association between economic growth and changing forms of class representation. As governments have sought to respond to the challenge of protecting and promoting economic growth, the pattern has been one of increasing experimentation with increasingly formal arrangements to get the organisations of labour to negotiate with business and the state over economic development and the levels of wage settlement. Some of these institutions have been tripartite in character, but just as often they have promoted direct negotiations between trade unions and the state. Even when not part of a corporatist project, the attraction of these new institutions included the possibility of harmonising the interests of capital and labour in the mutually beneficial process, within industrialised capitalism, of the pursuit of growth. These institutions have rarely worked in that way since both business and labour have good grounds for suspecting that their interests are not always as compatible as these schemes presuppose. Labour organisations have grown more and more suspicious of the attempts to persuade them to limit their wage increases for some increasingly remote improvements in investment, economic growth, and employment. Business clearly became suspicious of the increased legitimacy of trade unions in the 1970s and this was linked to their enduring suspicion about expanding the role of the state. But both groups may have learnt from their experience of the small state alternatives that there are worse alternatives than encouraging institutionalised and structured negotiations between the 'social partners'.

The events of the late 1970s and early 1980s suggest that something quite significant happened in the first phase of the recession. The sudden development of business and political hostility to the role of the state cannot just be explained by the persistence of the recession, since the major changes occurred before it was obvious that the recession would last. It is true that business organisations have often expressed hostility to the expansion of the state, especially when some political party is proposing a new campaign of nationalisation. Nonetheless, during the years of the boom and immediately after its end, business organisations seemed to have become accustomed to an active and expanding state, at times encouraging moves towards more state initiatives. The transformation of conservative politics is no less surprising. Traditional conservatives, especially in the years of growth, endorsed the positive role of the state and had no trouble in managing the kind of mixed economies generated by the postwar settlement. Towards the end of the 1960s something was stirring within the political imagination of the leading figures of these parties. The initial attitude of Britain's Ted Heath to competition and the role of the state suggests as much. His reversion to a more active role for the state was seen as a sign of political realism. Somewhere in the 1970s the criteria of realism shifted, and the conservative orientation of these parties moved towards neo-liberalism, with the emphasis on reducing the size and significance of the state. Conflict over the role of the state returned to the political stage.

This was the culmination of that whole line of developments outlined in this paper: the gradual, relentless expansion of the options for direct class representation in the debates over national economic policy. That these options were increased for business was less relevant than the fact that they conferred new status on the trade unions and gave them more formal influence than they had previously had. If the trade unions had simply participated without seeming to have become more influential, the matter would probably have been of limited interest. The significant aspect of the initial period of the recession was that, in some countries, the importance of trade union influence could be measured in the expanded and changed parameters of state action. This was true of welfare and social concerns, but also of the greater interest in the operations of the private economy and the attempt to impose social objectives on normal business decisions. Pollution control, environmental awareness, the social consequences of investment decisions, and the need for greater investment, economic expansion, and more secure employment were all examples. The role of the state expanded, as it had done before, to offset the consequences of the economic downturn, but this time the expansion of the state was seen as a threat to the long-term viability of the private economy. Partly this may have been an ideological assessment, responding just to the increased size of the state. Partly, it may have been a response to moves by the state against the private prerogatives of management, especially over investment. Partly, it may have been a result of state moves into the manufacturing heart of the industrialised capitalist economy. The expansion of the state may have been sufficient to activate the concerns of business and conservative politicians. When this was linked to an increased trade union presence in the political process then such concern was heightened. Exploring the logic of the connection between postwar economic growth and various forms of class representation had brought the process to a very difficult and ambiguous stage. If not challenged, did this development have the potential to harm the private component of capital accumulation? The appearance of governments dedicated to monetarism and small state strategies has certainly removed the ambiguity while reducing the political presence of the trade unions and presiding over increases in unemployment that further weakened their bargaining positions.

Industrialised capitalism, in some countries, is coming to the end of one phase in its political development. As yet no government has found a strategy that can assure the social dominance of private capital, social stability *and* a return to conditions of profitable economic expansion. The consequence of the institutional presence of the trade unions may have been solved, at least while unemployment is increasing. The problem of the increased significance of the state has not yet been tackled. The limited attempts to reduce its size have all been unsuccessful, and still the private sector, even with extensive government support, has not been able to find the investments that will lead to secure growth. In this way the present period resembles that of the interwar years when the old liberal order had passed away and the new pattern for integrating state initiative and private enterprise had not yet been found. A similar problem, the new social basis for capital accumulation in the context of expanded state actions, has been posed, only this time the private sector has less of the manufacturing area in which to operate.

In Japan, as elsewhere, the size of the state, the range of its actions, its attention to the provision of welfare, are all shaped by the balance between the forces of business and labour. But that balance is uniquely weighted in favour of business.

The Japanese formula for making the system safe for private accumulation and pacifying the workforce is not to be found in the area of representational politics or in schemes of 'corporatist' political representation at a national level. The roots of the successful Japanese formula probably extend back into the years of authoritarian rule prior to 1945 which shaped the trade unions and made them less socially significant than, say, their British or Australian counterparts. Incorporation of labour at the level of the enterprise also made it less necessary to create political structures to incorporate trade union ambitions at the national level. But within this pattern of effect and consequence much remains unclear. While the gradual expansion of the home market and increasing levels of consumption have obviously played a part in marginalising the political claims of the unions, and the cultural and ideological apparatus has also played a role of some significance in pacifying the population, some would see postwar Japan as the success story of social stability through growth, in which the Japanese people are integrated through the success of the economy so that broader strategies of incorporation will not be needed so long as the economy does not falter.

The emphasis within Japan placed on the need for radical state restructuring ('administrative reform') suggests that confidence in the continuing durability of the Japanese solution is anyway waning rapidly. All the same, it is the distinctly Japanese combination of high technology in production coupled with a passive trade union movement that has been the inspiration for other capitalist states in their efforts to manage the recession and to prepare the way for success in any future expanding world economy. While Japan in the mid-1980s is the butt of much criticism in Washington, London, and Paris, it remains the object of envy and emulation.

Beyond economism:
Japan in a state of transition

Gavan McCormack

Introduction

There is a sense in which Japan's modern history, since the opening of the country by Commodore Perry's 'Black Ships' in 1854, has proceeded in alternating waves of openness, liberalism, and rationality on the one hand, and contraction, repression, and atavism on the other. The first phase lasted from 1854 until approximately 1882-83, ending with the crushing of the 'Liberty and People's Rights' movement and the establishment of an imperialist and expansionist orientation towards the Asian continent, particularly Korea. A second, but weaker, wave of democratic movement rose to challenge the structures of absolutism and imperialism during the years following World War One. It receded in the early 1930s, however, and the collapse of August 1945, imposed by forces from outside, was necessary to dissolve the structures of the Meiji state.

Nearly forty years have passed since then, and to the contemporary historian there are abundant signs that the postwar state, put together as a kind of joint venture by General MacArthur and Yoshida Shigeru, has developed cracks and fissures of a kind which suggest another major shift in character may be imminent. This chapter attempts some generalisations about the character of the postwar state, looks at the pressures for change from within and without that have been generated by it, and considers some possible scenarios for change.

There have been two main characteristics of the postwar Japanese state. The first is its economistic orientation. Governments have been primarily business-oriented. They have been cautious, bureaucratic, diplomatically low profile, relatively tolerant of social diversity, and pursuing limited military goals. Ideology has been very low key, particularly since the 'high growth' and income doubling policies adopted in the early 1960s. The economistic postwar political tradition established by Yoshida and continued especially through the cabinets of Ikeda (Hayato), Satō (Eisaku), Tanaka (Kakuei), Miki (Takeo), Ōhira (Masayoshi) and Suzuki (Zenkō) has only briefly wavered in the direction of a higher *political* and Cold War activist profile, notably under Mr Kishi (Shunsuke) in the late 1950s, but now is subject to greater strains than ever before. Is Yoshida's economism still viable? Does such a concept still define the basic orientation of the governments of Mr Nakasone Yasuhiro, who became Prime Minister on 26 November 1982?

The second distinguishing feature of the postwar Japanese state has been the relative weakness and subordination of Japanese nationalism. The prewar Japanese state found the period of alliance with the Western powers most fruitful for growth and strength, and that of isolation and extreme nationalism from the beginning of the 1930s brought the country eventually to disaster. The postwar leadership embraced more or less enthusiastically alliance with the world number one power — the United States. Independence in 1952 came on the condition of the stationing of a substantial force of US troops in a chain of strategically located bases up and down the country. The bilateral security treaty with the US meant a permanent (if also voluntary) curtailment of Japanese sovereignty. But it was acceptable because it was profitable, and it has continued to be accepted so long as economism, the priority of growth and profit, has constituted the underlying consensus. Furthermore the priority to growth and profit has contained within it one expression of sublimated nationalism — the aspiration to equality of status with the advanced countries of the West, and the sense of progressive approximation to that goal made tolerable the absence of the normal trappings of nationalism — an independent foreign policy and a military force commensurate with its economic status.

The prewar Japanese state was integrated around an ideological mix of *tennōsei* (imperial absolutist nationalism) and economic growth or modernisation, with the balance of the mix fluctuating. In the postwar state, nationalism, in the very attenuated form of catch-up with the West, has now been clearly accomplished — indeed over-accomplished since there is nothing that most Western countries would now like more than to catch-up with Japan — but Japan remains constrained within the Security Treaty alliance with the United States so that the other trappings of nationalism are still unfulfilled, and even the indignity of occupation by US troops continues. The closer the goal of economic parity with the West has become, the more the quest for substitute goals has preoccupied political leaders. Tanaka's 'Remodelling the Japanese Archipelago', Miki's 'Clean Politics', Suzuki's 'Harmony' and 'Administrative Reform' all represent more or less feeble efforts to find a substitute symbol of sufficient attractive, mobilising force to serve as an integrating pole for the emerging economic super-power. The problem is whether the truncated, semi-dependent and military mini-power bequeathed by Yoshida has not itself reached the end of its viability. Some Japanese scholars have already begun to recognise the transition point that has been reached by referring to the postwar state as a 'moratorium' state,[1] implying that the normal accoutrements have been missing but that the peculiar circumstances under which this occurred are to be of limited duration. If such thinking is correct, and if the economistic and semi-dependent Yoshida state has reached very near the end of its viability, then what are the directions in which it might be recognised?

The range of options appears limited. Japan may on the one hand opt to become a neutral, non-aligned, peaceful and peace-oriented country, committing itself to realisation of the values expressed in its constitution while applying its considerable resources, both human and technical, to the task of furthering human dignity and equality by closing the North-South gap.[2] This step would call for radical changes: the gradual closure and dismantling of the existing US base structure from Japan and withdrawal from all military aspects of the existing Japan-US relationship being undoubtedly the most substantial. This would not be inconsistent with the transformation of the existing defence forces into a citizen defence force designed to defer any conventional military assault, although the multi-faceted economic diplomacy, which would be inherent in it, and the detachment from super-power alliances and nuclear systems would make any such assault unlikely.

On the other hand, Japan could move towards the attainment of military super-power status, thus complementing its existing economic might and becoming a 'great power' in the full sense of that very loaded word. Once such a commitment was entered upon, the extension from 'conventional' to nuclear weapons is one which would be likely to follow quickly. According to one estimate, Japan could produce nuclear weapons within two months if it so determined.[3] Whether a military super-power Japan would continue to embrace the alliance with the United States, albeit on an equal basis, indefinitely, or would prefer to pursue an independent road, perhaps forging alternative alliances with China, ASEAN, even the Soviet Union, is of course impossible to predict, but entry upon this path would soon reveal whether Japan's prewar traditions of militarism had been completely broken or not.

That the pressures for abandonment of the status quo are very strong is clear. These pressures are of two main kinds, external and internal, and it is well to remember that the major shifts in the structure of Japanese state and society in the past have commonly resulted from precisely such a convergence.

Pressures for change

(a) Foreign Pressures

External pressures directed at radical change in the existing Japanese state stem especially from the United States. These pressures are based on both military/strategic and economic grounds.

The economic grounds are plain. The problem is that of the sorcerer's apprentice. Japan has turned its supposedly dependent or subordinate status within the Security Treaty alliance system to its own benefit to such an extent that in one after another economic sector it has outstripped the United States. Japan, with 0.3 per cent of the world's land area and 3 per cent of its population, now accounts for over 10 per cent of its GNP. Japan is already the world's second largest economy, after the US, and in 1984 on a per capita basis its GNP should actually surpass that of the US. Its goods have progressively displaced those of the US in world markets and this process is seen as a contributory factor in the US recession and the collapse of several central sectors of US manufacturing industry and consequently in the social problem of mass unemployment. Although it is a figure to be used with caution because of the internationalisation of production, the balance of the bilateral trade has grown to be massively and apparently chronically in Japan's favour. The Japanese surplus, in *billions* of dollars, between 1978 and 1983 was as follows:

1978	11.6	1981	15.8
1979	8.7	1982	16.8
1980	9.9	1983	18.0

and in 1984 reached a staggering 34 billion dollars.

The solutions that have been canvassed in the US to this problem range from the more or less economic — either Japanese self-restraint in exports or outright US protection — through the military-economic — that Japan fill the trade gap by large-scale purchase of US military hardware or else pay a fee, perhaps something like 2 per cent of its GNP,[4] to the US as a defence tax — to the comprehensively sociopolitical demand that 'Japan must change its cultural tradition' so that its people would buy more foreign goods.[5]

The common American belief that Japanese economic growth has been achieved at least in part because Japan has 'enjoyed' the benefit of US defence, thus being able to divert resources which would normally be required for defensive and military purposes into industry, is a major factor in the US thinking. Now that Japan has achieved economic super-power status, it should defend itself and play a more active role in the defence of the Northeast Asian region, or pay a realistic sum to the US for doing it for them. Whichever option Japan adopted would have not only military but also large economic consequences: militarily, the US could reduce its force levels in Northeast Asia and thus strengthen its position in the Middle East; economically, Japan's adoption of a much expanded military role in the region would lead to a substantial increase in military hardware purchases from the US, thus helping to bridge the trade gap.

More speculatively, it may be that there is an inverse ratio linking militarisation of the economy and growth, in which case Japan's burgeoning GNP and trade surpluses could be expected to be weakened as a direct result (and even in a closely related proportion) as military expenditure increased. According to figures drawn up by Harvard's John Kenneth Galbraith comparing the performance of leading industrial countries over the period 1960 to 1978, while Japan's proportion of military expenditure to GNP remained below 1 per cent, its real economic growth rate averaged 8 per cent per annum. In the case of Italy, Sweden, West Germany, and France, whose military expenditure ranged between 3 and 4 per cent, productivity increased at the rate of approximately 6 per cent. For Britain, the figures were military 5 per cent, productivity 3 per cent. For the United States, the figures were military 7 per cent, productivity 2 per cent.[6] Whether or not the relationship is as mathematically neat as such figures suggest is, in a sense, beside the point. By compelling Japan to turn a significant proportion of its resources and energy into the military field, Washington might reasonably expect both to blunt Japan's drive for world economic dominance and to strengthen strategic pressures on the Soviet Union in Northeast Asia.

Despite such an expectation, however, it is sobering to reflect that these pressures might achieve the precise opposite of what is intended: enhanced Japanese weight in the world economy leading to further destabilisation of trading relations between the leading capitalist powers as Japan lifts its current restraints and launches upon a major drive to develop a weapons export capacity for its rockets and tanks comparable to its automobiles and industrial robots, and tensions in Northeast Asia further escalated as Japan commits itself to a forthright anti-Soviet posture.

American (and other) pressures on Japan rest upon an unproven and unlikely assumption (though that does not lessen its force). It is assumed that Japan has been and is being defended from some enemy or enemies by the US forces stationed in the country.

But what threat does Japan face? One of Japan's leading defence experts, Inoki Masamichi, formerly president of the Defense Academy and now head of a private research institute on security matters, has stated that the Soviet Union is 'not a military adversary to Japan' in the

sense it is to the United States, and that military confrontation between Japan and the Soviet Union was only likely to occur in the event
of war between the United States and the Soviet Union elsewhere in
the world spreading to the region.[7] Another senior Japanese defence
expert, Maeda Hisao, who was until 1980 chief of the first research
office (security policy) of the National Defense College, in a book published in 1980 expressed the view that

> The mutual expansion of the global military strength of the US and the
> Soviet Union is merely a strategy game between the two countries . . .
> Geographically, Japan is the safest country in the world because it has no
> area of military conflict with any of its neighbours. With a certain amount
> of self-defense capacity, Japan need not fear a military conflict in nearby
> countries affecting us. It is untrue that US naval forces secure our sea lanes
> because there is no reason why Japan should become subject to a naval
> blockade. The security treaty was something 'imposed' on Japan. All that
> has been said in defense of the fact, e.g., Japan's postwar peace has been
> secured by it; Japan is a member of the Western regime; Japan has been
> protected by the US nuclear umbrella, etc., has been hogwash.[8]

Maeda pointed out that, even if the Soviet Union should harbour
dreams of conquering Japan, such a conquest would be of no value.

> Japan is famous for having no natural resources of its own. Without being
> able to keep the population fed, how could the Soviet Union maintain the
> 'revolutionary government' it established in Japan?
>   Will it suppress with naked force a discontented population of 120
> million, which is more than the total of the six Eastern European countries?
> An army of 100,000 or 200,000 will not do. Will Moscow throw half a mil-
> lion or even 1 million troops into Japan? But where would they be brought
> from?

Since 1978, there has been a succession of defence studies, emergency
studies, joint tactical studies, Far Eastern emergency studies, sealane
joint studies, and the like within the 'Guidelines' for US-Japan Defense
Cooperation that were then established; all have been based on the assumption that Japan would become involved as a result of world-wide
American-Soviet confrontation expanding to engulf it. Even a former
commander of US forces in Japan is on record as agreeing that a
limited Soviet attack on Japan could only occur in the context of such a
showdown.[9]

   The location of American strategic bases on Japanese soil is precisely what renders it vulnerable in any exchange between the super-
powers, neither of which has any particular reason to love Japan and
both of whom might be expected to welcome the opportunity to con-
fine their exchanges to locations like Japan well removed from their
own shores.

   In other words, the possibility has to be faced that the US bases in
Japan have existed to serve American rather than Japanese goals: to

retain a powerful lever of influence over Japan on the one hand, and to facilitate US involvement in military and political operations of a counter-Soviet and, not necessarily related, counter-revolutionary character through the region on the other.

Japan's provision of base facilities then appears as one aspect of the price it has paid in the postwar years for its economic growth: from the late 1940s it is clear from the US policy planning documents that the Japanese role was seen as part of an integrated US military/economic strategy for the containment of communism and revolution in the region. The Japanese role in the division of labour drawn up by the planners of that period was actively economic, passively military, but as that economic role, in sustaining anti-communist regimes throughout the region, became more substantial, balancing and reinforcing the US military role in Asia in particular by its economic involvement in South Korea, Taiwan and Indonesia, the US came to insist that *mere* economic collaboration with it was not enough. Japan should play an overtly military role too. Thus, from the time of the Miki cabinet in 1975, consultations on increased military cooperation commenced, and increasingly since then the Japanese have been asked to step up their fiscal outlay on defence and to assume major responsibility for the anti-Soviet defence of their segment of the Northeast Asian arc. The Americans have at times put specific figures on the kind of budgetary allocation they would find satisfactory — anything from about 1.4 per cent of GNP to 3 or 4 per cent of GNP — and are impatient with the objection that constitutional or legal constraints make this impossible. As US Defense Secretary Brown put it late in 1980, the Japanese choice was a simple one of 'Guns or Caviar'.[10]

This pressure, at core essentially American, has become increasingly international. Early in 1984, the top-level US-Europe-Japan think-tank, the Trilateral Commission, added its voice to the call for Japan to 'use its growing economic power to take over part of the global defence burden now assumed by the US'.[11]

Such pressures, when translated into the concrete Japanese political context, imply the revision or drastic undermining of the 1946 constitution, the abandonment of the Japanese self-restraining ordinances of the 1970s against arms exports, an increase in defence spending well above the current self-imposed figure of 1 per cent of GNP,[12] and a transformation in character of the Japanese role within the US-Japan Security Treaty from exclusive focus on defence of Japan's own shores to active participation in the 'free world' defence system throughout the region. They also imply a gradual shift of military/strategic questions from the periphery to the core of Japanese political life and in due course a much enhanced role for the military in the determination of state policy.

And what, it may be said, could be objected to that? What could be wrong with Japan falling into line with other advanced Western countries and contributing in proportion to its economic weight to the defence of the Western alliance? The peculiar conditions which applied when Japan's constitution was drafted in the wake of war no longer apply. Like other parliamentary democratic regimes, Japan in the 1980s should be able to cope with the existence of an army without succumbing to militarism or fascism of the 1930s or 1940s variety again.

This kind of thinking is extremely common among Western commentators and in the Western media which generally supports Washington in its efforts to secure major changes from the Japanese on these matters. The doubts are more commonly expressed by Japan's near neighbours. The following, from an article by a prominent South Korean political scientist,[13] expresses them succinctly:

> Once a bona fide military build-up programme gets started it will create its own dynamics, and those who advocate such a course as a means of appeasing the Americans are likely to be overtaken by those who would like to build an autonomous defence capability and to move away from what is considered a subordinate relationship to the US . . .

He adds:

> A stepped-up Japanese military build-up would almost certainly bring about a Soviet reaction that would accelerate the arms race and increase tension in the area.

That tension in the area is already at critical levels was demonstrated during the Korean Air Lines affair of 1983; if Professor Han's analysis is correct, these tensions will be heightened to the extent that the US has its way in shifting Japan onto the course of full-scale military buildup.

The base line of the early 1980s, from which Washington would like to see a quantum increase in military spending, already warrants Japan the position of world's No. 8 military spender, after the United States and Soviet Union, the other three nuclear states, China, Britain and France, the oil power Saudi Arabia, and the NATO core country, West Germany.[14] The existing ceiling of 1 per cent GNP, an important limitation although it has allowed considerable increases over the past decade because of the constantly rising GNP, is almost certain to be breached in the coming financial year, and Japanese Finance Ministry sources estimate that a 2 per cent of GNP expenditure would put Japan into No. 5 position in world military rankings, above Britain and France, while 3 per cent would make it No. 4 after the super-powers and China.[15] It is surely significant that even the supposed political leader of the forces opposed to Japan's remilitarisation, Mr Ishibashi Masashi, chairman of the Japan Socialist Party, should remark in 1984 that Japan's defence spending was 'bound to exceed that limit (1 per cent) and climb to the level of 3 or 4 per cent, equalling that of North Atlantic Teaty Organization members'.[16] If Ishibashi is right and such a programme is now underway, the point of the existing self-denying ordinances on the non-possession, non-manufacture, and non-admission to the country of nuclear weapons will also be drastically weakened.

Furthermore, the potential for neo-nationalist resurgence in Japan, fed by pressures of trade wars and intervention by other Western powers attempting to divert Japan's policies along lines which suit their own interests, should not be forgotten. Mr Nakasone himself, for all his protestations of commitment to the US alliance, clearly harbours the aspiration to independence from the Americans. In his English *apologia* he writes:

> I believe that true independence is impossible as long as a nation chooses to depend in large measure on the military power of another country for its territorial security.[17]

He went on to express the view that a constitution that left any room for doubt on the legitimacy of so doing should be revised.

The Japanese dilemma arising from the intensity of these pressures from its most important ally, the United States, deepened markedly from the end of the 1970s as those pressures were reinforced from a different quarter: China. The change in Japan's relations with China from non-recognition to normalisation (1973) to alliance (1978) was a shift of historic proportions. In part the Japanese government was following the American lead set by Nixon and Kissinger, but the relationship quickly gathered its own momentum, driven by a deep well of pro-China sentiment on the Japanese side, fed by war guilt, cultural rapport and economic ambition, and on the Chinese side by the pragmatic 'Four Modernisations' commitment of Deng Xiaoping and his associates.

The China which Japan moved to embrace in the late 1970s was also choosing the American side in the antagonism between the great powers. Ominously, one of the first fruits of the shifting pattern of relationships in East Asia was China's 'punitive' expedition against Vietnam early in 1979. China came to assume a central role in the anti-Soviet strategy of revived 'Cold War' that dominated Washington thinking with the advent of the Reagan administration.

By reason of its close alliance with the United States (though the relationship was only officially recognised as such in 1981) and its new treaty of 'peace and friendship' (1978) with China, Japan's pretence to an omnidirectional diplomacy of benevolence became more difficult to maintain. The balance of power in the Western Pacific and Northeast Asian region appears to have shifted heavily against the Soviet Union as a result of the closeness of Washington and Tokyo, Seoul, and Beijing. This new balance of alliances has been the context for the Soviet militarisation of its Kurile Island territories (claimed by Japan) and its greatly stepped up military, especially naval, presence in the Soviet Far East and Western Pacific waters.

Unlike the Cold War of the 1940s and 1950s, in which Japan was able to play a low-key role, though providing important military facilities to the Americans, in the 1980s Japan stands exposed and vulnerable. Its embroilment in US nuclear strategy in particular can no longer be described as protection under a 'nuclear umbrella'; rather does it place the islands at the forefront of any 'limited' superpower nuclear exchange and thereby threaten Japan with extinction. The layers of fantasy in which the relationship was long shrouded have been left in tatters by the rapidly escalating tensions of the region. Though Japan may be in the process of settling its historic account with China, its overall geopolitical security has been diminished rather than enhanced as a result of the circumstances within which that rapprochement has occurred.

Japan's increased 'contribution' to international society is not to be exclusively military, however. Indeed, it was characteristic of the division of labour between the United States and Japan in Asia from especially the mid-1960s that while the military burden was borne primarily by the United States Japan concentrated on economic 'aid' to sustain favoured regimes. While Japan is now called upon to assume a more equal role in military matters, it is *also* under enormous pressure to step up its 'aid'. These are two items of government expenditure exempted from budgetary cuts and actually steadily increasing.

The Trilateral Commission meeting of March 1984, already mentioned above, recommended not only a substantial increase in Japan's defence spending, but also made a specific call for Japan to undertake to make up the entire $US3 billion shortfall in World Bank aid programmes for Third World countries.[18] The recommendations of this informal, but highly prestigious foreign policy forum, which is made up of 200 top business, political, and academic figures from the US, Japan and Europe, carry considerable weight.

The political character of Japanese 'aid' is clear enough. That the three main recipients of such 'aid' for the period 1960 to 1981 should be Indonesia, South Korea and the Philippines, three countries strategically crucial to the US and 'Free World' system which all face recurrent problems of acute political dissent, should speak for itself.

What the Trilateral Commission seemed to be saying was that the character of this 'aid' should be expanded from a regional to a world scale, commensurate with the general expansion of Japan's economy from regional force in the 1960s to world power in the 1980s. As a world economic power, and especially a trading power, Japan has a great deal at stake in preventing any breakdown of the US-centred world economic order.

Naturally it is right to prefer that Japan concentrate on economic rather than military expansion, but there are problems with the notion none the less.[19] First is the extremely low proportion of official development assistance relative to economic assistance, a mere .2 per cent in 1981 or thirteenth of the 17 member countries of DAC and far below the internationally agreed figure of .7 per cent. Second is that a much higher proportion of Japanese 'aid' is in terms of tied loans and grants, that is, tied to the purchase of specific Japanese goods or services, than is the case with other advanced countries, and frequently the projects targeted for such 'aid' are those earmarked as important for Japan's long-term strategic resources security. The underlying consideration is the furthering of Japan's 'comprehensive security'. Third is the tendency for large infrastructural developmental 'aid' to be channelled into recipient countries in ways which feed corrupt bureaucratic and business networks in both Japan and the recipient country. If Lockheed and Grumman-type scandals occur even in the bilateral relationship between Japan and the United States, many Japanese are convinced they occur on an even larger scale in relations between Japan and South Korea or Indonesia.

A glance at the official government rationale for increased 'aid' to ASEAN illustrates some of the problems. In a February 1981 report on 'Economic Cooperation', the Ministry of Foreign Affairs gave three main reasons for stepping up its ASEAN-directed 'aid'.[20] They were that the strategic importance of the area had increased since the end of the Vietnam War and Japan 'as a pacifist country' should contribute to strengthening it; that 'aid' could help to reduce frictions aising from the 'overpresence' of private Japanese capital in the area; and that the Malacca straits were strategically vital to Japan and Japan's aid to the area generally could help to offset its 'external economic vulnerability'. In short, Japan's national interest was the predominant consideration. A different report, prepared in 1980 by an influential business grouping, added a gloss to the effect that Japan should assume primary 'caretaker' responsibility for the ASEAN region in the same way as the US for Latin America and the European Community (EC) for Africa.[21]

External pressures on Japan to step up its profile as an 'aid' power are likely to be accommodated within the framework of such thinking, with its primary emphasis on Japan's national interest and its dominance of the Asian region. It is significant that both the Japanese government and the major powers bringing pressure to bear on Japan should think of Japan becoming simultaneously a military great power and an 'aid' great power. While a massive increase in the proportion of untied Official Development Assistance funding in Japan's 'aid' would represent a significant step, it is doubtful whether the rest of Japan's 'aid' programme will do any more for Asia than would a Japanese military buildup.

(b) Domestic Pressures

It is, however, the peculiar conjuncture of external and internal factors for change which makes the time of the Nakasone government so important. There are, it should first be understood, far more elements of continuity in Japan's postwar 'democratic' state with its prewar 'fascist' state than are commonly recognised, and certainly far more than in the case of, say, Germany or Italy. The preservation of the emperor and the bureaucracy served to cushion against radical change; the corporate structure and the political leadership too maintained significant elements of continuity, and some scholars have argued that the collectivist mind-cast of prewar *tennōsei* (emperor system) itself survived the defeat and postwar reconstruction in transmuted form. Thus Kogawa argues:

> Since *Tennō-sei* was a total system of politics, legislation, society, family, custom and communication, the society that it had once permeated retained a homogeneous network through which cultural capital and information could circulate. In the post-World War II period, this very convenient circuit was fully utilized to produce an American consumption-oriented society.[22]

At the level of national politics, there are two particularly striking facts about Japan in the postwar period. One is simply that there has been no real change from conservative power throughout the entire period and the possibility of change occurring in the near future seems slight. The second is that, from the brief glimpses of the inner workings of the Japanese system afforded by the revelations of the Lockheed and Grumman scandals of the 1970s, corruption, and the operation of power brokers with strong roots in prewar fascism, continue to play an important role. There is general agreement in Japan in the early 1980s as to who are the most powerful political figures in the country: Kishi Shunsuke and Tanaka Kakuei. Kishi's record includes designing Japan's wartime economic and manpower planning blueprints and being one of the signatories to the declaration of war against the US in 1941. After the war he was imprisoned for three years as a major 'war criminal'. He rose to become Prime Minister (1957-60), and has been at least as powerful since then as power-broker and king maker. His links with nationalist and ultra-nationalist bodies of prewar lineage are undisputed. Tanaka was Prime Minister in the early 1970s till forced to resign as a result of massive corruption charges for which he was convicted in 1983. Despite that, he continues to control the largest faction in the Japanese Diet. Some political commentators in Japan see the 1983 cabinet of Mr Nakasone as a marriage of the old rightist forces from the camp of Mr Kishi with the plutocratic elements around Mr Tanaka. Western commentators have, on the whole, been so overwhelmed with the apparent economic rationality and efficiency of Japanese business as to have directed little attention, so far, to the evidence of fissures in the political superstructure.

The electoral strengthening of the conservative camp, particularly since the 1980 election, is itself testimony to the general rightwards shift of society.[23] The left has been demoralised and confused by the problems of Japanese affluence, and by the transformation of China and the adoption, *even in China,* of a frankly 'learn from Japan' line, and while the left has contracted, the so-called 'centre' parties have moved right and the ruling Liberal-Democratic Party (LDP) even further right. The Komeito, a party which for long was identified with peace, neutralism, and defence of the constitution, has softened its tone on all of these and has entered an apparently unconditional embrace with the Chon Du Hwan regime in neighbouring South Korea,[24] while the Democratic Socialist Party (DSP) has expressed 'complete agreement' with the US on the 'Soviet threat' and on the need for US warships to maintain a nuclear presence in Japan.[25]

In 1980, Shimizu Ikutarō, a prominent intellectual who had been at the heart of the democratic, anti-US treaty renewal movement in the late 1950s, declared his support for massive military strengthening and the acquisition of an independent nuclear force.[26] It is possible that he was merely acting as a maverick, somewhat like the novelist Mishima Yukio a decade earlier, but it is more plausible to see his action as heavily symbolic, reminiscent of the switch by prominent prewar leftists to endorse the then imperial state and prefiguring the general rightwards shift of his generation.

Those positions, which ten years ago were advocated only by peripheral groups to the far right of the LDP such as the 'young Turk' organisation known as *Seirankai,* have now become respectable and adopted by the centre of the party. These include constitutional reform (i.e. deletion of the constitutional statements of commitment to a pacifist, non-military position), a strong moral and patriotic content to education, stricter textbook censorship (to weed out pacifist, anti-war, anti-nuclear expressions, or historical allusions to the excesses and atrocities committed by imperial Japan in the 1930s and 1940s), emasculation of the radical public-sector based trade unions, revision of the legal and especially the penal code, the restoration of Yasukuni, the shrine to the nation's war dead, to the centre of a national cult. It is a comprehensive and interlocking programme.

Administrative reform

During the 1970s the Japanese bureaucratic and business elite came gradually to view the Japanese state as constructed in the 1940s and 1950s by Mr Yoshida as anachronistic, and the programme that goes under the innocuous-sounding title of 'administrative reform' (*gyōsei kaikaku* or *gyōkaku*), heavily promoted since the late 1970s, embodies nothing less than a fundamental and thorough-going restructuring of that state.[27] Japan's experience of the decade beginning in approximately 1971 helped feed a sense of crisis in the country which was little appreciated outside it because of the overriding impression of Japan's economic success and apparent invulnerability. But invulnerability is something felt by very few Japanese. Instead, their profound impression, based on Nixon shocks, oil shocks, resources scares, trade disputes, demands for a higher Japanese military share in the 'Western alliance', ever swelling budget deficits, rapidly aging population, and flattening curve of economic growth, is of a Japanese ship of state being tossed about rudderless in all directions, and extremely vulnerable in a highly unstable world.

It was during the Suzuki (Zenkō) cabinet, late in 1980, that Mr Nakasone, then Minister in charge of the Administrative Management Agency, launched the task of 'administrative reform'. Most attention in Western reporting of the process he thereby launched has concentrated on one aspect: the fiscal problem of reducing Japan's huge public sector deficit.[28] Considered in this light, Japanese 'administrative reform' resembles the 'Reagonomics' and 'Thatcherism' of the United States and Britain. The attempt to reduce the public-sector deficit by paring the welfare budget, reducing public service personnel spending, or selling off deficit-ridden public corporations to the private sector in the pursuit of a goal of 'small state', while insisting on the sacrosanct quality of expenditure on defence expenditure, is common to all. However, the Japanese programme is no mere fiscal reform; it is the design for a radically different Japan.

Two keynotes are 'increased contribution to international society' and 'realisation of a dynamic welfare society'.[29] Both are somewhat vague, but the profile of recent budgets make clear that one major planned 'contribution' to international society is to be in the military area. While all other areas of expenditure are either cut or held to zero growth, the military and foreign 'aid' segments alone continue to climb.

The notion of a 'dynamic welfare society' or a 'Japanese-style welfare society' is one which rests heavily on the spirit of self help, and which would move much of the burden of welfare from the state (European-style welfare) to families or private corporations. The resolution of the

39th General Assembly of the Liberal-Democratic Party in 1981 included the following sentence:

> The time when politics could pander to or stir up excessive demands among the people is past. Now what is demanded both of politics and of people alike is the spirit of self-help grounded in understanding of a stormy new age. While striving to foster such a spirit, we call upon the various strata of the people to put an end of softness and indolence and wake up to their responsibility and role in this new age.[30]

To avoid 'advanced country disease', which seems to mean a process of 'enervation' and 'stagnation' of society resulting from 'softness, dependence, and acquisitiveness', the will to work has to be revived.[31] However healthy that will may seem to outside observers, the Japanese perspective is different. This goal is sometimes described as the cultivation of a 'lean and hungry attitude' (*hangurii seishin*),[32] which is pretty much what foreign adherents of the 'Japanese way' think is the very stuff of Japan.

If welfare needs are no longer to be met, or at least not to be met in full, by the state, it will also be necessary for Japan to engage in some heavy promotion of the 'group mentality' that constitutes another part of the popular Western image of Japan. Thus the report of the Special Commission on Administrative Reform:

> From now on, it will be necessary to further develop the special character of our country's society. We will have to plan to implement a welfare (system) in which an appropriate share is met by a highly efficient government, but which is based on the solidarity of home, neighbourhood, enterprise, and local society, which is in turn founded on the spirit of self-help and independence of the individual.[33]

In plain terms, this means the government is going to pay less but try to revive the institutions of a supposed traditional Japanese 'special character' to meet the difference. Whatever this putative Japanese 'special character' may once have been, it has been drastically eroded by urbanisation, industrialisation, and prosperity, as even the language of the Commission implicitly accepts. To restore it will call for an active interventionist role by the Japanese state authorities.

What Japanese business and bureaucratic think-tanks have come up with as their prescription for the twenty-first century is a revival of the work ethic and village-type social relations. A dose of 'Japanese-ness' is as much seen as a remedy for 'advanced country disease' in Japan as in the United States, Europe and Australia where 'learn from Japan' has become a watchword.

Nothing could speak more eloquently of the power of the myth of 'Japan Incorporated' which is thus invoked as the solution to Japan's own problems. The vision that drives the architects of the blueprints for the new Japan is compounded of classic early capitalism and the

spirit of the decade which was most crucial in their formation: the
1940s. For half of that decade, submergence of the self in total commitment to the collective enterprise (which happened to be war) was the
unifying axis, while in the other half real hunger was the scourge.
Throughout, the virtues of hard work and comradeship were palpable,
and the experience of that decade was crucial to the generation that
leads Japan today.

It is at this level that 'administrative reform' crosses from fiscal
policy into the territory of education, propaganda, and myth-making,
or that it moves, in the words of the chairman of one of the first sections
of the Commission, from concern with 'things and money' to 'reform of
the mind of the Japanese people'.[34] The people must be conditioned to
adopt a 'lean and hungry attitude'. Mr Nakasone himself is one of the
most eloquent advocates of this task of spiritual renewal:

> We need a thorough-going educational reform that will fundamentally
> change the existing system of education. The administrative reform, so to
> speak, should be a a spiritual preliminary to the educational reform we
> need.[35]

Indeed, for Mr Nakasone, 'reform' is much too modest a word to
describe the process. In July 1981, waxing enthusiastic about the goals
of the *gyōkaku* programme, he used the word *ishin,* which can be loosely
translated as meaning a transforming and renewing upheaval, and
proclaimed:

> the Meiji Restoration (1868) was the first *ishin* and Japan's defeat in World
> War II the second. The current administrative reform ought to be the third
> *ishin* for Japan.

He added:

'Past *ishin* have normally been carried out through coups or civil
war'.[36] This is not the language of the conservative politicians who
have been more or less faithfully following the 'Yoshida Line' in post-
1945 Japan. It is precisely the stress on spiritual renewal, mobilisation,
and nationalism which lead one to seek parallels in the history of fascism rather than elsewhere in conservative politics.

In 1978, before he became Prime Minister, Mr Nakasone gave the
following statement of his political beliefs:

> I believe that faced with this crisis the responsible politician must make
> plain to the people his 'philosophy' and his 'passion'. The reason is that
> democracy is in crisis as the Japanese islands are besieged by political and
> economic tidal waves from north, south, east and west, the authority of the
> state is damaged and the people are swayed by unease and anxiety. Further-
> more, this sense of crisis is aggravated by the excess of information that is
> characteristic of an excessively free pluralistic society. Various miscel-
> laneous value systems are rampant. It is regrettable that there are no com-
> mon rails upon which to restore order. It is the responsibility of the

politician to *smash through the status quo* (sic) *(genjō o daha)*, create a popular consensus and open up for Japan a wide world oriented towards the future age.[37]

From this, the radical vision that inspires Nakasone can hardly be doubted. It became evident during the term of his first ministry, however, that it could be tempered in practice by pragmatic political judgement and a readiness to compromise and 'tack' in adverse winds. After a decline in the fortunes of his party in local elections in the spring of 1983, and a strong indication of public alarm over the radical rhetoric of militant anti-Soviet sentiments during his visit to Washington, he showed that he was aware of the dangers of advancing too far beyond the political consensus and tacked back into familiar consensual territory. However, despite the assurance of a prominent academic member of the 'Administrative Reform Commission', on the basis of personal acquaintance with Nakasone and careful study of his speeches, that Japan under Nakasone can be expected to maintain course in the pursuit of 'peace and mutual prosperity',[38] it would seem legitimate, and prudent, not to discount too heavily his expressed commitments, and to watch what moves may be taken towards increased ideological and educational conditioning or political mobilisation in the direction of the consensus he desires.

The linkage between military-strategic, economic, and ideological-educational aspects gives the project its comprehensive character. Thus, while in official circles administrative reform is tied to the notion of a comprehensive security system *(sōgō ampo taisei)* or to that of a crisis management system *(yūji taisei* or *kiki kanri taisei)*[39] critics sometimes use the expression 'general mobilisation system' *(sōdōin taisei)* after the wartime totalitarian system adopted in 1938. But by whatever sobriquet it may be known the immensity of the programme may not be doubted. It involves no less than the shift from a form of social integration around the goals of growth, productivity, and catchup with the West espoused by Yoshida and his heirs, to one of social integration around the notions of 'security', 'patriotism', and the nation, in short the transition from a business orientation to a state orientation. Whether the apparently hedonistic and consumer-oriented Japanese people of the 1980s are capable of being diverted onto such a track may be doubted, although shifts of comparable moment have occurred in popular thinking before.

The economic imperative for change derives not only from the desire to revive and promote a 'hungry' work ethic but also from deep structural changes. The Japanese economy is being rapidly transformed from one based on steel, chemicals, automobiles and electrical goods to one centred on information processing, new (ceramic) materials, biotechnology, nuclear power and aerospace. In the 1990s these 'new' industries are expected to account for as much of Japan's

GNP as the 'old' manufacturing sector of the high-growth 1960s and 1970s.[40] But the scale of research and investment required in the 'new' sectors may be beyond the range of existing individual or even inter-linked corporate capacity, i.e., be such to require organisation on the scale of *national* projects, with national budgetary and staffing pro-visions, thus rendering necessary revision of the existing systems of research and development, corporate finance, and, last but not least, labour.[41]

One may, of course, doubt the appropriateness of the Special Ad-ministrative Reform Commission's view of what steps should be taken to bring Japan forward to the twenty-first century while yet believing that far-reaching reform is desirable. Indeed, the Commission's prescriptions fly in the face of the most widely accepted consensus among Japanese people on what needs to be done. In a *Yomiuri* newspaper opinion survey of 2 November 1981, when asked where they felt cuts in public spending should be made in order to meet the fiscal crisis, 52.5 per cent replied 'defence', 22 per cent 'economic cooperation' and 18.4 per cent 'the public corporations', while the reply to the question as to which areas should be preserved free from cuts gave first priority to social welfare (53.7 per cent), second to education (39.1 per cent), and third to public enterprises (10.6 per cent).[42]

Since the Commission, in corporatist rather than parliamentary democratic style, was made up of members of the business, bureaucratic and political elites, rather than elected representatives of the people, it is perhaps not surprising that it should have called for in-creased spending on defence and reduced welfare and education, while promoting the most 'successful' unit of Japanese society, the pri-vate business corporation, as the model for the transformation of the entire society,[43] but there is a popular consensus which stands against its programme, and Nakasone and his associates will indeed have to fight to 'smash through' this consensus in order to implement their vision.

The constitution

The comprehensiveness of the 'reform' project does not need stressing. It has important implications for labour, the citizens' movement, women, and education. The constitution, however, is central, and the question of its revision has subtle ramifications in all other areas.

The existing Japanese constitution, adopted in 1946, was designed to prevent Japan ever again following the militarist path which had brought it into such devastating conflict with the other countries throughout the region. It included, therefore, one clause that was un-precedented in the consitutions of the world, Article 9:

> Aspiring sincerely to an international peace based on justice and order, the Japanese people forever renounce war as a sovereign right of the nation and the threat or use of force as a means of settling international disputes. In order to accomplish the aim of the preceding paragraph, land, sea, and air forces, as well as other war potential, will never be maintained and the right of belligerency of the state will not be recognized.

Despite the apparently unequivocal renunciation of 'land, sea, and air forces', Japan has come to maintain quite considerable armed forces. They are known, however, not as 'Army, Navy, and Air Force', but as 'Land, Sea, and Air Self Defence Forces'. The constitutional prohibition has been evaded on the somewhat casuistical ground that the constitution could not have been intended to deny the inherent right of the state to self-defence. The problem is not easily conjured away, however, and there are increasing doubts as to the constitutional propriety of participation in multinational military manoeuvres or belonging to an alliance (with the United States) which is not directed exclusively at the defence of the Japanese islands. The 1980 *Defence White Paper* made it clear that Japan

> going beyond the defence of its territories, will make major contributions to the maintenance of peace and security in Asia.[44]

In short, this means that Japan's military preparations are an integral part of Western military bloc confrontation with the Soviet Union.

There are other problems with the constitution too, all of which may be subsumed under the general question of the appropriateness of *this* constitution, which in effect was foisted on Japan, a defeated aggressor, in the peculiar circumstances of the immediate aftermath of war, for Japan, the contemporary sovereign nation and economic super-power.

So the question cannot be escaped. But revision requires a two-thirds majority of both houses of the Diet, followed by a national referendum (according to Article 96). So, although the goal of revision has been urged at the highest level on both sides, American and Japanese, almost from the time the ink on the document dried, and has been part of the programme of the Liberal Democratic Party since its establishment in 1955, Article 96 has so far presented an impossible barrier.[45]

Revision or no revision, the problem remains. If revision is adopted in the interests of 'autonomy' the way is thereby opened to a stronger nationalism and a more open militarism; if revision is *not* carried out, the constitution will simply continue to be further subverted and the same reorganisation of the state will be pursued, but compounded by deepening cynicism over the irrelevance of the nation's basic charter. The direction of the emerging consensus is in favour of revision. LDP and mainstream conservative national politics is divided over the strategic desirability or the timing of the step, *not* over the principle itself.

It is only in relatively recent years that the prospect of marshalling sufficient support to satisfy the requirements of Article 96 has begun to appear a possibility. Mr Kishi's Assembly for the Establishment of a Sovereign Constitution was set up in 1970 and functions as a liaison front to galvanise mass support on the issue. The forces expressly committed to revision are now composed of a Dietmen's League for the Establishment of a Sovereign Constitution *(jishu kenpō kisei giin dōmei)* and a similar Citizen's League *(kokumin kaigi)*, while an alternative rightist grouping, known as the Citizens' Association for the Defence of Japan *(Nihon o mamoru kokumin kaigi)*, is committed to the promotion of Japan's defence strengthening *regardless of* the success or otherwise of constitutional revision.[46]

The spectrum of organisations mobilised under Mr Kishi's banner is a representative array of the contemporary Japanese reactionary right-wing. It embraces organisations of youth and veterans, the association of families of bereaved veterans, the central organisations of Shinto and Buddhist shrines and temples *(jinja honchō* and *busshō gōnenkai)*, the World Anti-Communist League and the Political League of the *Seichō no ie* religious organisation. The World Anti-Communist League is the political organisation of the Korean-based Unification Church of the infamous Reverend Sun Myung Moon. The *Seichō no ie* (literally: 'house of growth') is a Japanese new religion of a very fundamentalist and nationalist character. Set up in 1930, it flourished in the period of prewar militarism and fascism, the period when many religions were crushed.[47] With approximately one million members today, its political wing is especially active. Among other things, it stands for the 'national spirit', constitutional revision, anti-communism, the nationalisation of the Yasukuni shrine to the spirits of the war dead, and opposition to abortion. It is reported to have links with Jerry Falwell's 'Moral Majority' movement in the United States and within Japan it has established a strong influence on the LDP from within. Both former Prime Minister Fukuda and current Prime Minister Nakasone are advisers to the organisation, and many other prominent LDP politicians are closely connected with it.[48] Indeed 230 Diet members attended a meeting under its auspices held in March 1982. Former Premier Fukuda (Takeo) remarked on that occasion:

> Religion and politics are like the two wheels of a cart; only when religion and politics are fused together will a perfect society be created on earth for the first time.[49]

Since 1976, this same broad alliance of forces has been campaigning strongly in the form of an 'Association to respond to the spirits of the heroes' to restore state Shinto and to have the emperor, Prime Minister and military leaders worship regularly and publicly at the centre of the state cult. In 1980 Mr Kishi took his constitutional revision campaign to local and prefectural assemblies across the country, organising resolutions and mobilising signatures on petitions. One of the slogans adopted, calling for 'complete renewal of the age' *(jidai o isshin)*, well sums up the radical and comprehensive restructuring ambitions which are encapsulated within the call for constitutional revision.[50]

The other broad front, neo-conservative in character, links such elements as senior politicians, businessmen, military officers, certain union groups, intellectuals, doctors, and its foundation and orientation was very much influenced by the Shimizu manifesto.[51]

The above groups committed to change, either via revision of the constitution or despite its non-revision, also share a considerable area of agreement on basic objectives with a wide range of other organisations on the right — the patriotic, ultra-nationalist, occasionally fanatical anti-communist groups whose members are often uniformed and organised in quasi-military fashion and whose links with the criminal underworld are strong.

The present juncture

After the fall of the Tanaka cabinet in the early 1970s, Japanese politics entered a period of short-lived, unstable cabinets as two factions jostled for power in what was known in Japan as the 'Tanaka-Fukuda War' *(Kaku-Fuku sensō)*. The rise of Mr Nakasone and his cabinet in November 1982 would seem to mark at least a temporary resolution of these differences in a fusion of the economistic/plutocratic camp of Mr Tanaka and the nationalist/patriotic camp of Mr Fukuda (a close political associate of Mr Kishi).[52]

A second feature of the political scene in the early 1980s is that the dominance of the ex-bureaucrats of the Finance and International Trade Ministries which was pronounced throughout the major post-war cabinets has shifted to former members of the Home Ministry, officials with a background in police or education or in defence and military fields.[53] Gotooda Masaharu, himself a former police chief and in 1984 head of the Administrative Management Agency, stresses the difference between other bureaucrats who pursue their own sectoral interests first and the old Home Ministry men who put nation first.[54] One pointer to the shift in the bureaucratic balance that is now underway is that up until the late 1970s graduates of the University of Tokyo entering the public service had a first preference for Finance or MITI postings; from the early 1980s their top choice has been the Police Department.[55] The emerging elite would appear to have detected a pendulum swing away from fiscal and economic matters to a revived emphasis on the traditional Home Ministry tasks of social control and manipulation.

Despite the links which exist with prewar and postwar rightist and nationalist groups, Mr Nakasone placed great stress on the improvement of relations with the US; in this crucial sense, therefore, his is still a muted nationalism.

The political record of the Nakasone government is instructive. One of Mr Nakasone's first acts in office was to visit South Korea where he lavished high praise on the Chon Du Hwan regime, spoke of the 'common ideals of liberty and democracy' the two countries shared, and announced a Japanese aid commitment of $4 billion, larger than Japan has entered into with any other country and as much as the total of Japanese economic involvement in South Korea during the entire period of the postwar relationship from 1965 to 1981.[56] The Chon with whom Mr Nakasone professed identity of views on peace and democracy came to power via a series of coups d'etat and a veritable blood-bath at Kwangju in May 1980 and his regime depends still on the continued denial of many basic democratic rights.

From Seoul, Mr Nakasone's next visit was to Washington, where he made a series of commitments: to defence of the sea-lanes up to a distance of 1000 nautical miles from Japan, closure of the straits leading southward from the Pacific seaboard of the Soviet Union, and to the transformation of Japan into an 'unsinkable aircraft carrier' (fuchin kūbō) which could block the Soviet Union's backfire bombers.[57]

There are, as a matter of fact, only three straits by which Soviet shipping passes into international waters, of which only one, the Tsugaru Strait between Japan's Hokkaido and Honshu islands, is exclusively within Japanese territory. One of the other two, Sōya Strait, lies between Hokkaido and Sakhalin, while the other, Tsushima Strait, lies between Japanese and South Korean territory. The South Korean government was not consulted about this Japanese pledge, and Seoul was obviously alarmed. As the *Korea Herald* (27 January 1983) noted:

> This strategy also leaves open chances for Korea to be embroiled in a conflict against its intention . . . Japan's defense plan is aimed almost totally at its potential adversary, the Soviet Union, which hardly comes into play in our defense preparations.[58]

The same editorial also called attention to the US Fiscal 1984-88 Defense Guidelines which envisage US counter-offensives against North Korea, Vietnam, and Soviet coastal areas in the event of any Soviet attempt to seize Gulf oil reserves in the Middle East. In other words, both South Korea and Japan are rapidly losing their autonomy and being sucked into dependent and vulnerable positions in the superpower rivalry.

In expressing himself in such militantly anti-Soviet terms in Washington, Mr Nakasone won an enthusiastic reception from his hosts, but by courting US favour and volunteering his country as an integral part of the American Far East strategy, Mr Nakasone may also have been clenching his teeth as he suppressed his nationalist instincts. He was indeed echoing South Korea's Chon Du Hwan who, in 1981, declared *his* country 'a fortress for the defence of the United States and Japan in the Pacific'. Nakasone's pledges of enormous funds to support Chon's regime also smoothed the way to his welcome in Washington, where the shoring-up of that regime against the pressures of the Korean democratic movement and the forging of close trilateral links between Washington-Seoul-Tokyo as part of a general strengthening of its Northeast Asian anti-Soviet position have been given high policy priority. The reinforcement of economic and political links between the three countries is gradually being matched in the military field too.

While the Japanese government denies that Washington, Seoul, and Tokyo are linked by any trilateral military alliance, and that denial is correct in a literal sense, there undoubtedly is a high and increasing degree of defence cooperation and coordination between Washington and Seoul on the one hand, and between Washington and Tokyo on the other. The third side of the triangle, Tokyo-Seoul, is still represented only by a thin line of consultations and occasional officer exchanges. But, since the existing control and coordination of all three forces by Washington is well developed, it may be that two bilateral treaty relationships, both heavily dependent on Washington, are actually preferred by the Americans to a full trilateral relationship which would contain at least the potential for a combination of the two Asian partners against the United States and an assertion of their local and regional interests against the global, super-power obsessions of the Americans.

It is true that on his subsequent ASEAN tour in May 1983 Mr Nakasone did his best to damp the fears that had been rising in Southeast Asia (and in Japan)[59] about the direction his government was taking, insisting that Japan's military would remain strictly limited and of a purely defensive character, that Japan would never become a nuclear power, never possess 'offensive weapons', and that it would strictly adhere to the three non-nuclear principles.[60] The same message was also repeated to visiting Australian Prime Minister Bob Hawke in February 1984. The profession of commitment to such peaceful objectives was welcome, but since it is an open secret that Japan has turned a blind eye to the breach of its non-nuclear principles for decades, and continues to do so, it is difficult to avoid scepticism. *This* Nakasone, surely, was the one who has been described in Japan as 'the weathervane'.

Conclusion

The central thesis of this chapter is simple, and may be restated in a series of points.

(i) Japanese political life — the Japanese state — is facing a fundamental reorganisation. The economistic orientation established by Mr Yoshida in the immediate aftermath of defeat in the war and persisted in throughout the postwar era is approaching its end. As Japan achieves preeminence in the world economy, merely 'catching-up' or attaining equality with the West ceases to be a meaningful goal. A new integrative principle is sought.

(ii) Mr Nakasone stems from and has directly associated himself with the anti-mainstream, nationalist, political-rather-than-economistic priority element in the LDP. He stands for a high military profile, revision of the constitution, export of arms, comprehensive administrative reform in which the internal powers of the state would be greatly increased and patriotic, nationalistic values officially propounded. He is firmly anti-communist and anti-Soviet, and his nationalism is tied uneasily to the profession of unequivocal commitment to the US line, especially in Northeast Asia.

(iii) The Nakasone cabinet fused formerly contending plutocratic and rightist camps. Nakasone's success occurs in an atmosphere of conspicuous rightwards shift in Japanese politics, in a situation where the left is fractionalised and demoralised. Conservative political hegemony in the society has been reinforced by the deep-rooted consumerist orientation towards private satisfaction on the one hand and insecurity stemming from the oil shocks, intensifying cold war and severe economic pressures from the US and the EC on the other.

(iv) The central contradiction of the rightist camp during the whole postwar period has been on the issue of nationalism, since Japan's identity has been predicated upon its formally dependent status within the security alliance with the US. Whether Nakasone can effectively appeal to the symbols of nationalism — national greatness, a strong army, the national shrine cult, etc. — without also challenging the basic structures of dependence remains to be seen. Continued American and European pressures on Japan run the risk of provoking the frustrated nationalist spirit that Nakasone and his colleagues so carefully nurture. The old Home Ministry officials who are at the forefront of the Nakasone government have a clear public record of antipathy to US influence on Japan.

(v) Japan's defence orientation has shifted from one concerned with the capacity to resist attack on its own shores to one of collaboration in a world-wide anti-Soviet crusade. Japan's vulnerability is unquestionably increased as a result.

(vi) Japan's right is moving at both the central and local level away from a conservative, management of the state and economy role, to a radical-romantic and visionary restructuring of state role. In place of the postwar democratic spirit — for all its flaws — Nakasone offers his appeal to the spirit of patriotism, nationalism and a reinforced military. Nakasone's ideological lineage can be traced back to prewar radical rightists like Kita Ikki as much as to the postwar bureaucratic pragmatism of Yoshida Shigeru. There are no obvious parallels among contemporary Western statesmen.

(vii) Conservative Western governments, journalists and scholars, who urge upon Japan a rapid and substantial expansion of the country's armed forces and a much larger contribution to Western defence, pay too little attention to the overall nexus within which Japan is moving to meet such demands. They make neither economic nor military sense. Economically, the US-Japan trade imbalance might be mollified in the short term by increased Japanese purchases of US military hardware, but in the longer run competition will simply be expanded as rivalry spreads to the arms trade too; militarily, Japanese rearmament heightens tensions in Northeast Asia and renders Japan itself hopelessly vulnerable as a target in any nuclear superpower exchange.

(viii) There is every indication of the consolidation of a Northeast Asian alliance, political, economic and military, linking the US, Japan, and South Korea. Yet such an alliance can be no stronger than its weakest link, and the Chon Du Hwan regime, installed by a bloody coup in 1980, is far from stable and experiences rising anti-Americanism. All its massive military weight will not prevent its becoming a send Iran or Nicaragua or perhaps Philippines unless the demand of its people for democracy is met. Unlike these cases, however, an explosion in South Korea will not easily be contained since the Korean peninsula is embedded, like Germany, right at the centre of the Cold War, and since the US has made clear its intention to use nuclear weapons in any renewed outbreak of war in Korea. (Not only is Korea itself a storehouse for US nuclear weapons but the Edwin Reischauer and Daniel Ellsberg revelations of 1981 made clear that the US regularly brings such weapons to Japan too.) There will be no stability in Northeast Asia, and therefore no enduring stability for Japan, without a solution to the Korean problem. US appreciation of the highly militarised and anti-communist Korean state reinforces pressures on Japan. Is Chon Du Hwan's Fifth Republic, resembling as it does the national defence state of 1930s Japan, to be the model for the 1980s?

(ix) The failure of Japan to generate any alternative to the line of full, militarised dependent integration in the US Cold War strategy can only make it harder for those elsewhere who are trying to develop such a strategy for their own countries.

(x) Japan's defence cannot be advanced by being tied to superpower nuclear rivalry, but only through the promotion of peace and the diminution of tensions, through de-nuclearisation and closer economic, social and political lines across bloc frontiers.

If, however, Japan were to undertake a new 'export drive', putting its resources and energies to the task of exporting to the world the peace principles enshrined in its constitution, it might find there a task requiring a more single-minded and intense effort than any the country has so far undertaken, but one which would earn the support of the world's peoples and also provide a worthy vision 'beyond economism' to inspire the Japanese people themselves.

The manipulative bases of 'consensus' in Japan

Yoshio Sugimoto

Pitfalls of the 'learn-from-Japan' thesis

The Japanese are beginning to show a certain high-handedness in their dealings with foreign countries: many businessmen are confident that the Japanese economy has outperformed the economies of other industrialised nations, and some high-ranking officials do not hide their feeling that Japan can now learn very little from overseas. Public opinion polls show a consistent rise in the proportion of persons who feel that Japan is the best place in the world to live. The nation's mood is one of confidence, assurance, even impudence. Japanese tourists increasingly assess their host countries on the basis of the availability or not of the goods and amenities they enjoy in Japan.

The chorus of praise for Japan presented by some American and European scholars abets this scornful attitude.[1] The common theoretical assumption behind the praise is that the degree of a society's success can be gauged primarily through such economic indicators as national income, productivity, and technological development. Viewed in terms of these indicators, Japan's phenomenal economic growth in the recent decades is clearly outstanding. Hearing the chants of praise from abroad, Japanese have understandably become self-confident and have developed feelings of superiority.

The increasing popularity of the Japan model has opened up a new horizon in scholarly debate on patterns of social development. Until recently, historians and social scientists have been divided into the convergence and divergence schools of thought. Supporters of the convergence theory argue that, as nations industrialise, they become increasingly similar in their social structure and value orientation. By

An earlier version of this chapter was published in *The Age Monthly Review*, vol. 3, no. 11 (March 1984), pp. 14-15.

contrast, the divergence school claims that the culture and traditions of each society are so entrenched that, even after industrialisation, they remain intact and distinct.[2]

In both convergence and divergence theory, the central frame of reference has always been Western Europe and the United States. The emergence of Japan offers the possibility of an alternative axis, the Japanese model. Even the idea of reverse convergence has emerged; according to this, industrialised nations are now developing patterns of social relations of Japanese, rather than Euro-American type.[3] The current upsurge of the 'learn-from-Japan' campaign has healthy implications in comparative sociology, where Western countries have long been regarded as the unchallenged leaders of development in the international context. On the other hand, the 'learn-from-Japan' thesis appears to be based on numerous biases.

In work situations, for instance, the level of worker satisfaction in Japan is not as high as the 'learn-from-Japan' advocates tend to assert. According to a large-scale three-nation study of 6,000 white-collar employees of Japan, USA, and Britain carried out by Sengoku Tamotsu and his associates at the Japan Youth Studies Centre, a significantly higher proportion of Japanese employees said that the following statements accurately reflected their feelings:

    (a) My future career is at the discretion of my superiors.
    (b) Since my colleagues are my rivals as well, they would not defend me if I made mistakes in my job.
    (c) If I offer to resign from my company, the management would not make an attempt to dissuade me.
    (d) The job most suitable to me is not my current one.
    (e) If I could restart my job at the age of fifteen, I would not choose my present job.[4]

According to a cross-national survey of youth from 18 to 24 years of age in 11 countries conducted by the Office of the Prime Minister of Japan, Japanese youth is highly egoistic, self-centred, and oriented to personal interests; levels of frustration against family and school are highest among the nations surveyed. Compared with other nations, youngsters in Japan tend to show a distinctly low level of concern and sympathy with others. For example, in response to the question, 'What would you do if you found someone lost in the street?', only 29 per cent of Japanese respondents replied, 'I would offer assistance', recording the lowest figure among the nations under inquiry.[5]

To understand consensus we must understand conflict. To understand conformity we must understand deviance. If conformity and consensus bring benefits to individuals and groups, at what costs are these benefits secured? The 'learn-from-Japan' advocates fail to see a correlation between the success and failure of Japanese modernisation. While their books and articles mention such darker aspects as environmental pollution, sexual discrimination, the disparity between big and small business, poor housing, and the pathological effects of frantic competition for entrance into prestigious schools, negative phenomena are nevertheless treated as though they were isolated from the more positive aspects. The Japan-model advocates lack what C. Wright Mills described as 'sociological imagination', the capacity to shift from one perspective to another.[6] They fail to see consensus from a variety of perspectives — that is, they fail to examine it in the contexts of political, economic, and social structures which constrain the behaviour and consciousness of individuals and groups.

In any society, all component parts are interdependent and interrelated. Economic growth occurs at the cost of environmental disruption. Concentration of business activity in large cities forces workers to endure long rides on packed commuter trains. Any serious discussion of Japan's development should evaluate the cause-and-effect relationship between favourable and unfavourable factors. A balanced assessment of Japan's modernisation is particularly important when the Japanese experience is being considered as a developmental model for other nations to emulate. If failure and success are two sides of the same coin, any country attempting to fashion itself after Japan must be ready to accept both the strengths and weaknesses of the model.

The current 'learn-from-Japan' argument has an in-built bias toward elitism. *Japan as Number One*, by Harvard Japanologist Ezra Vogel, is the classic statement of 'learn from Japan', yet the samples upon which Vogel bases his assessment of Japanese society are drawn heavily from the elite sector, namely government and big business and employees in these organisations.[7]

Advocates of the 'learn-from-Japan' thesis give credit for Japan's success to a concentration of men of high calibre in the central government and large corporations. They have a point, but their argument assumes that those working in small and medium industry and local government agencies are inferior in intellect and ability. These ardent sympathisers with the Japan model project this centralisation of intellect as the core requirement for economic development. They see it is an ideal pattern for distribution of human resources. Naturally, the elite employees in the central government and leading corporations find this meritocracy concept appealing. However, few studies have examined how it impinges upon the life conditions of the subordinate groups of Japanese society.

As the 'learn-from-Japan' literature has dominated the publication market both inside and outside Japan, it appears that numerous researchers on Japanese society have lost sight of two fundamental questions: who defines the contents of consensus; in whose interests is consensus formed? The focus of analysis from this perspective must centre upon the degree to which groupism itself is an explicit ideology

directly communicated by dominant to subordinate groups in an attempt to routinise the obedience of individuals to the so-called needs
of the company, school, or state. To the extent that the prevailing consciousness is internalised by the broad masses, a routinised psychic
structure for compliance is created. Why do so many companies
gather their employees together at the start of the day's work, exhort-
ing them with pep talks and the singing of the company song? Why are
the streets lined with so many posters and billboards urging drivers
and pedestrians to observe this rule and that? One must examine the
possibility that these phenomena are not cases of Japanese group
orientation but testimony to the pervasive pressures of social control in
Japanese society.

If workers usually do conform to company norms which values in
Japanese society persuade them that they *ought* to conform? What
sanctions are applied to what kinds of behavioural and attitudinal in-
subordination on the part of employers? Furthermore, how do workers
themselves feel about their conformity? Here we are referring to what
Richard Sennett and Johnathan Cobb call the 'hidden injuries of class'.
They write:

> In the adult . . . there is a split between conscious belief and inner convic-
> tion — in secret he feels ashamed for who he is. Class is his personal respon-
> sibility, despite the fact he never had a chance.[8]

If we are to have any genuine sociological understanding of the existential situation of workers in Japanese society, we must address our-
selves to the complexity of worker consciousness in terms of the inner
contradictions (which may never be resolved) that emanate from the
external social, economic, and political contradictions of the society.
As Sennett and Cobb note: 'workers can be both angry and ambivalent
about their right to be angry'.[9]

Conflict is not something rare and pathological but rather a reflection of the competing interests in society. Many Japan specialists and
industrial relations experts tend to perceive worker-employer consensus as a positive value, without seriously acknowledging that the
systematic engineering of worker satisfaction is one of many forms of
legitimation of worker exploitation and alienation.

One must not overlook the possibility that Japan's so-called unique
groupism is, in fact, part of an authoritarian political system. Systematic control by management and officialdom is a characteristic of
Japanese society. Most of the theories of the Japan watchers tend to
confuse the results of authoritarian control with voluntary consensus.
What many scholars describe as groupism is the phenomenon of standardisation of thought and action. This may in fact be the product of
psychic repression induced by ideological domination. It may be that
in the name of groupism some sections of Japanese society have per-

fected the production of Herbert Marcuse's 'one-dimensional man', or C. Wright Mills' 'cheerful robot'.

As illustrated in Figure 1, Japanese groupism tends to be founded on control from above. In this sense, it is qualitatively different from more spontaneous group action from below (cell D) and is similar to what Hidaka Rokurō calls Japanese 'me-ism' which is subject to manipulation by authorities.

FIGURE 1   RELATIONSHIP BETWEEN INDIVIDUALISM/GROUPISM AND AUTHORITY

Unit of Action / Orientation to Authority	Individual	Collectively
Subject to authority (control from above)	(A) Japanese 'me-ism'	(C) Japanese groupism
Resistant to authority (spontaneous from below)	(B)	(D)

Japanese technology of social control

In order to investigate the possibility that the so-called Japanese group orientation may be a euphemism for the Japanese method of efficient manipulation, we examine some specific forms of social control in Japanese society.

As the institutional backbone of state supervision of individuals, the twin system of family registration *(koseki)* and resident registration *(jūmin tōroku)* deserves special attention. In the *koseki* system, the government possesses files on the birth, marriage, death, and crime records of members of each household unit throughout the nation. In the resident registration system, each household unit must report to municipal authorities whenever there is a change in the composition of the household or a change in its residential address. Copies of documents from these two systems are required for school entrance, job application, and other crucial occasions. Checks are then made to see whether a 'stain' exists on the applicant's record. In some instances, divorce, residence in minority communities, and even parental divorce are treated with suspicion. These twin institutions serve as powerful deterrents to non-compliance and have been used to discredit minorities, dropouts, and deviants. Foreign residents in Japan are subject to similar constraints, being required to carry a finger-printed certificate of alien registration. Those refusing to comply risk being arrested.

In the field of law enforcement a similar arrangement exists. More than half a million households, or about one in fifty, are organised as 'households for crime prevention' and are closely associated with police stations.[10] The *kōban* (police box) system, which Singapore and Los Angeles are determined to emulate, is essentially a community-level information-gathering network to siphon data about apparently 'undesirable' elements and suspects. For the system to work, the notion of the policeman as a benevolent community figure must be continually propagated. At each *kōban,* as much information as possible is filed about each household in the area under its supervision. A high degree of penetration into every nook and corner of society characterises the Japanese police system. In this situation ideological control — in Gramsci's term 'hegemony' — is in full swing.[11] The agencies of social control promote a worldview supportive of the established order in every area of life until it becomes part of the 'world taken-for-granted'. With the successful implementation of this process, self-policing becomes a daily reality.

The Japanese education system is rife with problems. The 'examination hell' is intensifying, and school violence has increased sharply in recent years. In this context, the school recommendation *(naishinsho)* system operative in most prefectures has become a powerful means by which middle-school teachers manipulate their students. In assessing applications for admission to high school, about one quarter of a student's marks come from a confidential assessment of the student made by the classroom teacher in the final year of middle school. Since the teacher provides both academic and character references, student scores may be manipulated on the basis of teacher preference. In a widely reported court case,[12] one student was not admitted to the high school of his choice because his middle school teacher commented negatively in the confidential report on his record of political activity. Students thus have to calculate what a particular teacher may write on their *naishinsho* before they act. From an early age, attempts are made to remove spontaneity from their behaviour. The control mechanism here is not shame, but rather the threat that the door to upward mobility will be closed. This is a case of what Sennett and Cobb call the 'ideology of self-blame': students are made to feel 'personally responsible for the labels of ability' they bear.[13] As a passive judge, the teacher

> 'gets away with' restricting freedom of someone in his charge by replacing the problem of limited freedom with the problem of an inferior person, asserting his dignity — the superior will not control, he will impassively judge.[14]

This 'game of disguised power' is played out in full in what is known as the 'examination hell'. Behind it is an obvious assumption that the more prestigious the university from which one graduates, the higher economic and status rewards one can expect. While the empirical validity of this premise itself has been a subject of controversy,[15] the important point is that it is effectively propagated by the examination industry, including preparatory schools *(yobikō)*, after-school coaching schools *(juku),* and publishers specialising in the production of sham examinations and magazines for students preparing for entrance examinations. Japan is perhaps the only country in the advanced capitalist world in which tens of thousands of high school students tune into a one-hour coaching programme designed to prepare them for university entrance examinations. This programme is broadcast every night through a commerical network throughout the nation.

A more subtle form of control from the vantage point of the children is the supervision of textbooks. The Ministry of Education has reassumed certain of its earlier censorship functions and now has the right to approve all textbooks. Its insistence on petty changes which hinder the publication of textbooks written by leading historians and social scientists is well known.[16] So too are its more blatant attempts in recent years to change the account of Japan's aggression in Asia during the 1930s and 1940s.

The flow of foreign ideas into Japan is subject to similar control. Although the Diet finally passed legislation in August 1982 to enable national and other public universities to appoint foreigners as tenured professors, the new law still provides that such appointments may be made only with the approval of the Ministry of Education and that a foreign staff member may not be head of a department.[17] Moreover, the Ministry of Education quickly sent a circular to public school administrators of secondary schools asking that they not hire foreign staff.[18] Given the fact that the number of prefectures doing so has increased rapidly over the past few years and that approximately 30 foreigners have been so employed, some interpreted this move as an attempt to reverse the trend toward providing students with a more internationalised education and to keep out a Korean minority for whom teaching is an avenue for upward social mobility.

Many schools have strict dress codes which specify hair length and uniforms. Although universities tend to be more relaxed in this regard, junior colleges for women place special attention on the private lives of their 'young ladies'. Some student dormitories continue to require that 20-year-olds be back by 10.00 p.m. every evening. The girls are forbidden to drink alcohol either in the dormitory or outside.

Numerous other practices are used to regiment children. There is a good deal of emphasis on military order. Attention is given to *kiritsu* (standing), *rei* (bowing), and *chakuseki* (sitting down). Outside the classroom, students are often told *'ki o tsuke'* (Attention!) or *'mae ni narae'* (Get your lines straight!). Prizes are given for perfect attendance, a prestige denied to children with weaker physical constitutions who are prone to illness. Until recently many high schools refused to accept physically-handicapped children on the grounds that they would be unable to pass the physical education courses necessary for graduation.

Although corporal punishment is not now officially condoned, teachers are able to cause their students considerable physical discomfort. One survey by the Education Office of the Tokyo Metropolitan Government revealed that teacher violence greatly exceeded student violence. Moreover, nearly all of the students who had been classified as problem children had at one time or another experienced a beating at the hands of their teacher.[19]

Work is an area where multifaceted social control is most skilfully perfected. The sharp sex-based division of the labor market in Japan is well documented.[20] Entry requirements, application procedures, and selection criteria in the recruitment process of major companies are differentiated along gender lines at all levels, particularly that of university graduates. Furthermore, large corporations recruit graduates for career-line appointments in a specified month each year from a handful of prestigious universities which the companies designate.[21] This so-called university designation system is a key reason for intensive competition for entry into high-ranking universities. Pre-employment social control includes a background investigation of prospective employees. Most major companies spend considerable sums to hire private detective agencies to investigate short-listed applicants.

Once employed, individuals are placed in a work situation conducive to group pressures and 'group policing'. White collar employees do not receive private rooms or partitioned work space. Rather, under the ōbeya (large stable) system, they must work under the watchful eyes of their workmates. According to Michael White and Malcolm Trevor, Japanese practices have been successfully applied to British firms include management-worker mingling, as in common staff canteens, and managers' willingness to muck in and get their hands dirty if necessary.[22] It is possible to interpret this as a mode of legitimation of the myth of status equality, company solidarity, and shared interests. As Frank Parkin and others have shown,[23] those who are brought into immediate face-to-face contact with management personnel are faced not with the abstract concept of class differences but with the 'operationalised' and tangible representations of power relations. As workers experience the illusion of equality in one sphere and the reality of inequality in another, they cannot avoid feeling ambivalent toward management. This contradictory dual position makes it difficult for workers to articulate their class position and cultivates worker compliance to management ideology and company norms.

Company regulations range from the necessity to obtain permission to leave the premises at lunch time to requiring employees to obtain affidavits from train companies if they are late to work because of a train delay. In applying for vacation leave, employees are often asked to indicate their reasons and/or destinations if travelling. Some regulations require that employees use only the employees' elevators and toilets, others forbid socialising with customers or the bringing of personal articles to work without special permission. Employees also receive admonitions on how to wear the company pin, how to bow, the phrases to use with customers, and how to position one's feet when standing. They are instructed about how to sing the company song and how to behave while attending morning ceremonies or eating in the cafeteria, and so on.

The Total Quality Control (TQC) movement which has spread across Japanese firms over the last several years perhaps best epitomises the Japanese technique of manipulation and regulation. The initial version of quality control in the United States was Statistical Quality Control (SQC) in which the purpose of the exercise was to check each commodity thoroughly so as to decrease the number of defective goods shipped out of the firm. After the importation of this method from the United States, Japanese management expanded its application to the workers themselves.

The basic unit of the QC movement in Japanese firms is a group of 10 to 15 members in the same section or division. Each group is expected to present as many proposals as possible to improve both the quality of products and the conditions of the work arrangements in order to maximise the level of productivity and the efficiency of marketing. Within this framework, QC groups are supposed to compete with each other in producing proposals for adoption by management. Since the number of proposals per group is the crucial index of competition, each group member is under constant pressure to think of ways and means to 'improve' his or her company. In this process, each employee inevitably conceptualises his work setting not from the worker's but from the manager's point of view. While this movement does not involve physical coercion, its primary function is the production of employees totally devoted to the company. In some firms, the TQC movement is labelled as the JK (*jishu kanri*) activity, meaning literally voluntary control. The phrase epitomises both the purpose and function of the activity: it is a mechanism of controlling employees under the guise of voluntary commitment. According to a Japanese QC circle manual:

> The ultimate purpose of the QC circle activity is to alter the attitude of each employee to his life in general and his job in particular. Each member of the circle must have a missionary dedication in engaging with this movement. The primary purpose of the QC circle must be the combination of this

missionary dedication with the determination to change the employee's mind for the maximisation of company profits.[24]

QC circle activities are often accompanied by collective singing where employees are required to sing company songs together. Characterised by official and moralising phrases, these songs are designed not only to inculcate company norms but to hammer company identity into employees in an emotional fashion. Gramsci might have described this as a method to 'undermine creative and critical thinking and break down the impulse to resist exploitation'.[25] C. Wright Mills would regard this as a case of 'rationality without reason'.[26]

Such legitimation appears to be quite conspicuous even among labour unionists. According to a national survey on the consciousness of members of *Sōhyō* (the largest national federation of unions), those who are oriented to social change constitute only about 5 per cent, as compared with 25 per cent in a similar survey conducted 15 years earlier.[27] Gramsci would see in contemporary Japan numerous situations where corporate managers grab every opportunity 'for increasing productivity by regulating the complete moral-psychological being of the worker'.[28] As he put it, 'the new type of worker will be a repetition, in different form, of peasants in the villages'.[29]

In his work on class inequality and political order, Parkin distinguishes three major meaning-systems: (a) the *dominant* value system, the source of which is the major institutional order; (b) the *subordinate* value system, the generating milieu of which is the local working-class community; and (c) the *radical* value system, the source of which is the mass political party based on the working class. In the context of the present discussion, the subordinate value system which, according to Parkin, promotes *accommodative* responses to the facts of inequality and low status, is of particular interest. This system is accommodative, as it is generated by the tension between two levels of normative reference. On the one hand, it is a system of meaning which cannot oppose the *abstract* moral order of the dominant class. On the other hand, it comes into conflict with this moral order in the *situational context* involving concrete choice and action; there is no inconsistency between two apparently contradictory survey results showing that a majority of workers who agree with the *general* proposition that hard work is a virtue also respond affirmatively when posed a *concrete* question of whether they want more holidays or not.[30]

The Japanese technique of social control therefore appears to be based upon the rooting out of elements of potential political opposition from the subordinate value system by ensuring that the dominant moral order is reproduced at the level of specific face-to-face existential situations. With police boxes and households for crime prevention established in every community, the law enforcement power of the state cannot remain an abstract concept. It is brought into the day-to-day experiences of the masses. The confidential report system in educational institutions makes teacher authority concretely visible in the daily life of students. With the expansion of QC circles in firms and plants, the specific work environment of the subordinate class is increasingly dominated by the normative order of the superordinate class.

What the 'learn-from-Japan' advocates are praising is the Japanese technology of translating dominant moral order into specific daily contexts, thereby reducing the total experiences of the masses under domination. As Mills put it:

> The society in which this man, this cherished robot, flourishes is the antithesis of the free society — or in the literal and plain meaning of the word, of a democratic society.[31]

The attitude and behaviour patterns of the Japanese in various social groups must be analysed in terms of rewards and costs — material and non-material — which must be calculated in facing the agents of social control. The reverse convergence thesis of Dore, in which advanced industrial societies are supposed to move in the direction of Japan rather than that of the West, makes sense if one considers the highly-organised mechanism of social control as an index of development.[32] Japan may indeed be 'Number One', as Vogel claims, in having engineered highly-developed techniques of material, bureaucratic, and ideological manipulation.

Sources of conflict in the 'information society'. Some social consequences of technological change in Japan since 1973

Tessa Morris-Suzuki

It is no coincidence that the 1970s — a decade marked by widening international awareness of Japan's relatively advanced technological position — was also the decade that saw the export of one of the first Japanese-made pieces of socio-economic jargon: the term 'information society'. This concept, which originated in Japan in the 1960s, was by the late 1970s being quite extensively used by academics, bureaucrats and businessmen in Europe and elsewhere to analyse the social change accompanying the introduction of new information-related technologies such as computers, automated production systems and advanced communications networks.[1]

Since the appearance of the first Japanese writings on the information society, Japan's social and economic structure has undergone considerable changes. It is, therefore, an appropriate moment to examine some social developments in Japan during the past decade in the context of the predictions put forward by theorists of the information society. Such an examination would seem to suggest that, while their predictions have correctly drawn attention to important trends in the development of technology, their assessment of the social implications of these trends is open to question.

An issue of particular interest is the impact of recent technological change on the nature of social conflict in Japan. It is widely accepted that the shift in the economy's centre of gravity from older industrial sectors to the new information-based industries will alter the bases of work-related social conflict. The question to be considered is whether the emerging Japanese information society is characterised by a general decrease in the levels of economic and social conflict, or whether it is leading to the formation of new patterns and structures of conflict.

The term 'conflict', of course, is one which contains several layers of meaning. Dahrendorf has usefully distinguished between latent conflicts of social or economic interest, which develop between 'quasi-groups' consisting of people in similar social positions, and manifest conflicts — embodied in the activities of workers' organisations, protest movements, lobby groups etc. — which occur only where organised, structured conflict groups evolve out of the wider 'quasi-groups'.[2] My central concern here will be quasi-groups and latent conflict: in other words, the social stresses in the emerging information society which provide poential sources of overt conflict. But I shall also attempt to offer some brief comments on the ways in which these social stresses might be translated into more or less organised movements of manifest conflict.

The concept of the information society

The development and popularisation of the concept of an information society is closely linked with changes in the Japanese government's long-term industrial policy from the late 1960s onwards. The term 'information society' *(jōhōka shakai* or *jōhō shakai)* appears to have originated in the writings of Hayashi Yūjirō, a former Professor of Engineering at Tokyo University. Around 1969, it began to be taken up by governmental circles, inspiring the publication of a report entitled *Japan's Information Society: Vision and Tasks (Nihon no jōhōka shakai: sono bijion to kadai)* by the Economic Advisory Council, 1969,[3] and, three years later, the commissioning by MITI of an *Information Society Plan (Jōhō shakai keikaku),* prepared by the Japan Information Development Council and published in 1972.[4] Since the early 1970s the concept of an information society has gained widespread currency in the media, academia and the world of business, and has been further refined and clarified by numerous government reports and by the publications of such non-governmental bodies as the Information Society Research Council, *Jōhō shakai kenkyū kaigi.*

The concept of an information society clearly owes much to the images of post-industrial society created by American neo-conservatives such as Daniel Bell and Herman Kahn. Like the writings of Bell, Kahn and others, Japanese reports on the emerging information society present a picture of an economy in the throes of a fundamental change in technology and structure. In the newly emerging economy, by contrast to the hunter-gatherer, agricultural and industrial economies that have characterised earlier phases of human development, the principal element in the creation of wealth will no longer be direct labour or material inputs but 'information', 'knowledge' or 'technology' (the three words being used almost synonymously). As a result, in the information society, a declining proportion of the population will be employed in direct manual labour, and a growing proportion in service activities, particularly those associated with the generation of information. Because of the greatly enhanced productivity resulting from the application of new technologies, leisure time will be increased, and the consumption of material goods will become less important than the expansion and cultivation of leisure.

Writings on the information society differ from theories of post-industrialism mainly in the time span of their perspectives and the depth of their practical detail. Daniel Bell and Herman Kahn were essentially futurologists, sketching what they saw as the broad outlines of long-term human development. Many of the Japanese reports on the information society, on the other hand, have been policy documents concerned with the present and the immediate future: the *Information Society Plan* of 1972, for example, set as its preliminary target the year 1985. They have consequently been much more concerned than Bell or Kahn with the details of technological innovations which were either already applicable or were at least practicable for the immediate future.

At the same time, however, the concept of an information society in Japan has a highly utopian and ideological side to it. The writers of the *Information Society Plan* chose, as a brief description of the concept, the phrase 'a society in which intellectual creativity will blossom'. This description has been widely popularised and is incorporated into the definition of the 'information society' provided by that authority on fashionable terminology *Gendai yōgo no kiso chishiki*, a best-selling dictionary of terms in popular usage. Reports such as the English language document *The Information Society and Human Life* (published by the Economic Planning Agency in 1983)[5] recognise possible negative social effects of new technology: the report's authors list the dangers of producing a 'flood' of redundant, poor-quality or misleading information; the risks of invasion of privacy inherent in new information technology; and the problems of increasing computer crime. Such negative factors, however, are seen as being side effects of the information society which can be readily controlled by the introduction of relevant policies. As the introduction to the report states:

> . . . the discussions on which the publication was based were held on the premise that the various negative aspects which are likely to accompany the information society will be overcome by introducing appropriate counter measures.[6]

Assuming the existence of these 'appropriate counter measures', the report is then able to present the prospect of a community in which technology has virtually solved the social contradictions of alienation and exploitation inherent in industrial capitalism:

The promotion of corporate automation as a result of construction of the information communications infrastructure will lead to increased earnings and shorter working hours, and the duties performed in enterprises will involve more intellectual creativity. Relations between people will become closer as they are freed from restrictions imposed by time or distance, and an improvement will also be seen in other services such as social welfare, circumstances that will promote intellectual creativity even further.[7]

The ultimate test of the accuracy of these predictions clearly lies in the future. In the present, however, it is at least possible to consider the extent to which developments in Japan during the past decade have conformed to the outlines suggested by writings on the information society. Since the information society concept is not mere theory, but embodies the evolving strategies of business and government, it is not surprising to discover that certain recent economic trends in Japan have conformed quite closely to predictions set out in early reports on the subject.

The most significant of these trends is the growing importance of information as an element in production. The increasing ratio of non-material inputs (research and development, design, marketing, etc.) — sometimes referred to as 'soft' inputs — to 'hard' inputs of machinery and raw materials has been measured by Nagatomi Yūichirō of the Ministry of Finance. On the basis of his figures we can divide Japanese industry broadly into a 'soft' sector, where the value of non-material inputs account for more than 40 per cent of the total, and a 'hard' sector, where it accounts for less than 40 per cent. In 1970, 20.8 per cent of Japanese industry could be classified as being in the 'soft' sector, but by 1980 the figure had risen to 31.5 per cent.[8]

This trend has been accompanied, as anticipated, by a decline in the proportion of blue-collar jobs and an increase in the proportion of white-collar jobs in Japan's total employment. Between 1970 and 1982 the share of managerial, technical, clerical and sales personnel in the workforce rose from 35.1 per cent to 44.4 per cent. In industries where technological change has been particularly rapid, the shift has been even more striking. In 1970, for example, 60.7 per cent of the Toshiba Electrical Company's 74,000 employees were shop-floor workers, and 39.3 per cent were engaged in managerial, technical and office work. By 1980 the total work force had declined to 64,000, and of these only 40.8 per cent were shop-floor workers.[9]

The criticism to be made here, therefore, is not levelled at the predictions of technological development or of changing industrial structure contained in reports on the information society, but rather at the utopian images of human fulfilment and social harmony projected by these reports. I believe that these images arise from the information theorists' ideological orientation, from their constant tendency to blur the distinctions between the descriptive and the normative — between what is and what should be — and from the extreme technological determinism of many of their assumptions. To use Marxian terms, they assume that the evolution of the social structure is a direct reflection of changes in the mode of production (technology), without recognising that such evolution is also mediated by the existing relations of production, i.e. by the way in which industry is owned, controlled and operated. Like Daniel Bell's model of post-industrial society, the writings of Masuda Yoneji and others on the information society fail to distinguish clearly between the concepts of 'industrialism' and 'capitalism', and therefore fail adequately to identify those features of capitalism which will persist within the 'post-industrial' or 'information' society.[10] They see human fulfilment as being constrained primarily by technological limitations, without recognising that, within an economy dominated by competing private corporations, a crucial limitation will be the need to develop and apply technology in such a way as to maximise corporate profits.

In order to analyse the effects of changing technology on social relations and social conflict in Japan, it is necessary to redefine the 'information society' as 'a new stage in the development of Japanese capitalism'. This stage is characterised, not simply by the growing importance of information in the generation of profits, but by the fact that information comes to play a quite distinctive role in the total economic process. Whereas previously information entered into production only when embodied in labour (as skill) or in plant and equipment (in the form of inventions), now, more and more, it becomes a factor of production in its own right — as patented processes, software, etc. Ciccotti and others have observed that knowledge becomes a commodity: not merely any commodity, however, but one which makes a peculiarly central contribution to the self-expansion of the economic system.[11]

On the basis of this definition, it will be argued that the emerging information society in Japan, rather than representing the flowering of intellectual creativity, appears to be creating a system in which growing material productivity and technological potential are accompanied by alienation and insecurity of employment. To develop this argument, I shall look, not at those traditional areas of employment where automation and computerisation are causing long-term decline, but at some of the emerging and expanding forms of employment closely connected with new technology. In selecting this emphasis I am not denying the importance of structural unemployment and de-skilling in traditional areas of industry. On the contrary, these problems are crucial sources of potential social conflict in Japan as in other industrialised countries. Such problems, however, have already been the subject of quite extensive discussions and analysis. For present purposes, therefore, it may be interesting to consider sources of conflict inherent in the newly emerging employment structures of the information society.

Information production and the content of work — the case of the software industry

Superficially, the statistics would appear to support the view that Japan is moving towards Daniel Bell's model of post-industrial society, dominated by a class of professionals whose status is based on knowledge rather than wealth,[12] and that it has already begun to fulfil the prediction of information society theorists that

> . . . the proportion of intellectual labour will increase, compared with other types of work, and greater creativity will be called for, with an intensification of knowledge demand.[13]

But the concept of 'professionalism' or 'intellectual creativity' does not merely imply that labour is performed with the brain rather than with the hands. It also suggests a degree of control over the content of one's own work and an opportunity to perform varied, meaningful and coherent tasks. The problem here is that as information increasingly becomes a commodity, and as its production acquires growing importance in the generation of profits, so there is pressure to increase the productivity of the expanding intellectual work force by introducing an ever finer division of labour. The result is a process (in some ways similar to the transition from craft to factory employment in the Industrial Revolution) by which intellectual workers lose control over the product of their labour and are relegated to the performance of isolated and relatively repetitive mental tasks on the 'information production line'.

This process can most vividly be illustrated by examining the case of computer software production. The precise number of Japanese workers engaged in the design and production of software (that is, of programs for the operation of computers and computerised equipment) is uncertain but is unquestionably expanding in an almost exponential fashion. A Toshiba manager was quoted in 1982 as saying that

> . . . if we have to increase software engineers at the present rate, all the people on the planet will be turned into software engineers in a few years. This of course is impossible, for we have to develop new software technology to avoid this.[14]

The problems besetting software workers are not unique to Japan,[15] but they have become particularly evident in Japan because of the rapid expansion and intense competition that have characterised the Japanese software industry in recent years.

In the early stages of the software industry, individual workers operated very much on a 'craft' basis. In other words, they were responsible for the total production of a particular program. They therefore enjoyed a considerable amount of freedom in determining the methods for solving problems involved in their work and the ways in which they would structure their working day. As one software designer described it:

> About ten years ago, in my workplace, everyone worked independently. They wrote their own flow-charts, made their own programs and devised appropriate tests to check the results.[16]

But, during the past ten years, technological change and pressure for increased productivity have altered the content of work. In the first place, the shift from the punched card system, to the use of video display terminals VDT's for preparing and correcting programs has meant that, increasingly, the tempo of work is dictated by the machine rather than controlled by the programmer. Previously, each step in the software preparation process was a separate and self-contained one, and software workers could therefore divide their time amongst several tasks in the way that was most convenient and satisfying. With the introduction of video display terminals, however, control of the working day has diminished.

> With VDT's, there are many pauses while you wait for the computer's response, but generally the waiting time is too short to allow you to get on with other tasks, so all you can do is wait. A work rhythm of 'waiting — activity — waiting' is imposed by the system.[17]

Secondly, the desire to promote the productive efficiency of software workers has resulted in increased standardisation of tasks. Tests for the checking and debugging of programs, which were formerly independently devised by software workers on the basis of their own experience, came to be controlled by management. Guidelines and handbooks were compiled setting out standardised tests to be used in specified circumstances. While this may promote overall productivity, it has resulted in an increasingly routinised and uncreative relationship between the workers and their products.

> Previously, we ourselves would choose one of several possible methods of working, but later we began to say 'well, we might as well do it the way the company wants'. Then recently, people have begun — without noticing that there is anything inconsistent in this — to say 'of course we must do it the company's way'. Consequently, we have found ourselves in a systematised and computerised situation where everything is done 'in the prescribed manner'.[18]

Lastly, the desire to promote efficiency has also led to a division of labour, whereby the production of a single program has come to be subdivided between several specialised workers: commonly a planner, a programmer, and a person responsible for coding. The effects of this division, as described by an employee of another major Japanese software company, amount almost to a textbook illustration of the concept of alienation.

> To my mind it is like a factory. Particularly recently, when the number of people engaged in coding has increased, that feeling has grown stronger. In my workplace people seem to lack a feeling of wanting to make something whole by themselves. It's not that this feeling has disappeared entirely, but that when you are aware that you are responsible only for one part of the product, it becomes difficult to have a feeling that 'I made this'.[19]

Information production and the organisation of work — secondment and part-timers

The growing importance of information as an element in the creation of profit brings with it changes, not only in the content of work but also in the way in which work is structured. Here an important element is the apparent trend away from the patterns of lifetime employment and age-related promotions which have come to be regarded by some as characteristic of the Japanese enterprise.

This trend can be illustrated in a number of ways. One piece of evidence is the decline in the percentage of the Japanese work force employed in large firms. This is significant because, in practice, the life employment system has been mainly confined to such firms. Between 1971 and 1979 the percentage of the manufacturing work force in firms with over one hundred employees declined from 42.5 per cent to 38.4 per cent.[20] Another way of looking at the question is to consider the ratio of temporary to regular employees. Table 1 shows that, while the number of regular employees has been growing gradually in recent years, and that of day-labourers has been fluctuating irregularly, the number of short-time and temporary employees has shown a sharp rise, increasing by about one-third between 1973 and 1980.

To some extent these trends reflect the impact of the cyclical recession of the late 1970s and early 1980s, but there is reason to believe that there are also deeper-seated structural forces at work. A major reason for the initial introduction of the life employment system by large Japanese firms was their desire to reap the full returns of their investment in the training of workers. As Japanese industry expanded and developed, it was necessary for major companies to educate their work force in relevant skills. In order to prevent the workers they had trained from leaving to seek higher wages elsewhere, companies offered the promise of life-employment and regular age-related pay rises as incentives for 'loyalty to the firm'.

With the increasing rapidity of technological change, however, a situation has developed where skills may no longer be utilised for a worker's lifetime. Particularly in the relatively routine, semi-skilled areas of work related to information production, it becomes common for newly acquired skills to be obsolete within five or ten years. An example of this may be seen in the recent increase in the number of word processor operators in Japan. In the past two or three years several thousand Japanese workers (mostly young women) have been trained in a skill which is already being rendered obsolete as Japanese industry progresses towards the use of voice controlled word processing machines.

TABLE 1   TRENDS IN THE PRIVATE SECTOR NON-AGRICULTURAL WORK FORCE

| | (10,000) | | | |
Year	Regular employees	Short-time/ temporary employees*	Day labourers	Total
1973	3,269	189	127	3,585
1974	3,303	185	121	3,608
1975	3,327	174	116	3,617
1976	3,382	183	117	3,682
1977	3,406	208	124	3,737
1978	3,417	222	130	3,769
1979	3,485	233	128	3,846
1980	3,567	252	123	3,942
Percentage increase in 1980 compared to 1973	109.1	133.3	96.9	109.9

* Working less than 35 hours per week — including temporary and seasonal workers.

Source: Tokita Yoshihisa: *Gendai Nihon shihonshugi to rōdōsha kaikyū*, Tokyo, 1982.

In these circumstances, large companies have a decreasing interest in ensuring the lifetime loyalty of skilled and semi-skilled employees. Rather, they look for a 'disposable' work force which can be readily replaced by newly trained workers when its skills become outdated. Two methods for ensuring a supply of this disposable work force are the secondment *haken* system and the use of part-time workers.

The *haken* system is particularly characteristic of the newly expanding service areas of employment such as office cleaning and security, secretarial work, printing and copying, computer maintenance and software engineering. A growing number of large companies, rather than recruiting permanent employees to provide these services, hire workers on a temporary basis from 'secondment companies', *haken kaisha,* operating in a way rather similar to that of the secretarial agencies which have long been familiar in other industrialised countries. The advantage of this system for the corporations concerned is that it enables them to acquire workers relatively cheaply, without offering them the conditions of job security and fringe benefits associated with life employment.

A 1980 survey of data processing companies in the Tokyo areas found that 26.1 per cent of the 17,605 workers covered by the survey were working on a *haken* basis. For the great majority of these workers, hours and conditions of employment were determined by the corporations to which they were seconded, but almost 90 per cent of them were paid at rates determined by the *haken kaisha* which had recruited them: in other words, at rates below those of the permanent employees in the firms to which they were 'loaned'.[21]

Workers employed on the *haken* system are almost invariably non-unionised and are in a predictably weak position when it comes to bargaining over working conditions

> Systems engineer S. was sent to work on system development at an aircraft company. Together with twenty other systems engineers, he was on secondment from the computer manufacturer. He was working alongside several dozen programmers on secondment from a software company, as well as computer operators from a facility management company, who were responsible day and night for the actual running of the computer. In order to complete the system on schedule massive amounts of overtime were required, and it was not uncommon to be obliged to work all day and night for two or three days.
>
> S. took complaints about this to the aircraft company's union, but instead of his complaints being dealt with, an order arrived that S. was to be transferred to work on another user's project.[22]

The employment prospects of *haken* system workers as they grow older are in many cases unattractive. Those with obsolescent skills, and those engaged in areas such as data processing which involve irregular hours and demand prolonged concentration, are likely to be pushed onto the 'scrap heap' of increasingly low-skilled and low-paid work in middle age. (Software workers and computer customer engineers are generally regarded as being 'over the hill' after their mid-thirties.)

The second major source of 'disposable' labour is the female labour force, particularly the reserve of older, married women who form an important segment of Japan's part-time work force. It is interesting here to observe the intermingling influence of a number of contemporary economic currents. With the growing penetration of capitalism into the household economy (in the form of mechanised equipment for housework, commercial services such as *bentōya* etc.), more women have some time available for paid labour outside the home. At the same time, the coming of the information society, with its attendant pressures on the education of the next generation, creates added financial reasons for women to seek paid work. A survey conducted in 1981 showed that 12.6 per cent of women in part-time employment gave their main reason for working as being 'to cover costs of education for self or children'.[23] The flattening of the age-wage curve, associated with the weakening life employment system, is also an important motive for older women entering part-time work:

. . . although until recently male workers attained their top earning power in their 50s, now male wages have begun to peak earlier, in the 45-50 age bracket. 'My husband's earnings will peak when he's in his 40's — so I'd better go to work to help out the budget'. This sort of determination appears to be spreading rapidly amongst Japanese women.[24]

These financial pressures on women have conveniently coincided with the growing demand of companies for an educated but relatively cheap and, above all, flexible supply of labour. The result has been the widely-discussed phenomenon of the growth of women part-time workers — again a phenomenon not unique to Japan, but particularly clearly marked in Japan in recent years. As Figure 1 illustrates, the sharp increase in part-time employment in Japan during the 1970s was mainly accounted for by the rising number of women part-timers.

FIGURE 1   THE GROWTH OF THE PART-TIME WORK FORCE 1960-83

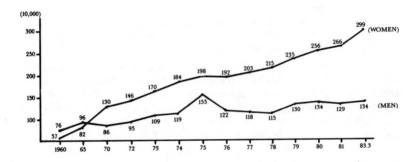

Source: Shibayama Emiko: 'ME kakumei to josei fuantei koyō no genjō'.

The growth of part-time employment has been particularly evident in the service sectors and in industries strongly affected by automation and computerisation. Consider, for example, the warehouse industry, which has experienced extremely rapid automation: a 1983 study by the Economic Planning Agency showed that, of eight major warehousing companies, four expected to increase their part-time work force in the next three years. None of the companies surveyed anticipated any increase in their full-time work force.[25] Part-time women workers in 1981 constituted 16.9 per cent of the work force in manufacturing, 21.1 per cent in transport and communications and 25 per cent in wholesale and retail trade.[26]

The rise of the woman part-time worker could be viewed in an essentially positive light. One might argue that the increasing participation of married women in the work force represents a step in the direction of sexual equality, and that the expansion of part-time, as against full-time, work is a sign of the promised coming of a society characterised by shorter working hours and increased leisure. In fact, however, neither of these arguments stands up to close scrutiny.

Part-time work by women may help to break down traditional social constraints against middle-class married women re-entering the work force, but it also helps to re-inforce the traditional sexual division of labour in which women are relegated to relatively insecure and low-paid areas of employment. Part-time work rarely provides any scope for promotion; and, incidentally, the participation of women in the paid work force seldom results in any equalisation of the burdens of housework.

There is also little evidence to suggest that the growth of part-time employment represents the type of job sharing which has been put forward by theorists of the information society as the ideal model of future employment patterns. Part-time work does not involve a sharing of the more prestigious, remunerative and creative areas of employment, but rather the growth of a new medium-skilled, insecurely-employed work force. Despite the label, so-called part-time workers do not even necessarily work short hours. Since there is no clear legal definition of part-time work, many surveys use the concept to cover all employees who work shorter hours than the regularly employed work force, or all employees whom management chooses to define as being 'part-time'. A recent government study showed that 24 per cent of so-called 'part-timers' were working seven or more hours a day.[27] At one big electrical goods plant in Fujisawa, 400 of the 500 workers involved in assembly and checking of products are 'part-time' women workers, most of them working seven to eight hours per day.[28]

The essential features of part-time work by women are most clearly captured in this statement from the viewpoint of management:

> Part-time work is . . . advantageous to the company employer. Part-timers are mostly women with previous work experience. Thus they already know the ropes. Moreover, they are patient because they are accustomed to domestic chores. The experienced and disciplined housewife is therefore ideally placed to give department store and supermarket customers good quality treatment and advice.
>
> The greatest merit of employing such housewives, however, is the lack of any need to pay them high wages. The company does not have to provide them with health insurance, pension or retirement allowances or other welfare benefits either. And most important, it can fire them in a recession.[29]

Conclusions

My object is not to offer a polemic against technological change, or to deny that current technological developments have the potential to free human beings from various forms of dangerous, dirty or dreary manual labour. What is suggested here is that technological change will not, by itself, solve the social problems of alienation, exploitation and inequality. The coming of the information society in Japan is not dissolving the contradictions and conflicts between management and worker or producing a utopia of increased leisure and human creativity, but rather sowing the seeds of new forms of social conflict.

The focus of this discussion has been a newly emerging group of workers mainly engaged in service sector activities and in areas of the economy where the current technological revolution is having its greatest impact. This group of workers is by no means homogeneous. It ranges from, at one extreme, the relatively highly-skilled, highly-paid and usually male software producers to, at the opposite extreme, women part-time workers operating supermarket cash points or supervising automated factory machinery. All members of this group, however, have certain features in common. Their work, though it may be identified as 'mental' rather than 'manual', tends to be routine, fragmented and alienating, and their employment patterns are characterised by insecurity and uncertain future prospects.

In many ways, their lives are well described by Andre Gorz's sketch of what he calls

> the post-industrial neo-proletariat which, with no job security or definite class identity, fills the area of probationary, contracted, casual, temporary and part-time employment . . . The neo-proletariat is generally over-qualified for the jobs it finds. It is generally condemned to under-use of its capacities when it is at work, and to underemployment itself in the longer term. Any employment seems to be accidental and provisional, every type of work purely contingent. It cannot feel any involvement with 'its' work or identification with 'its' job. Work no longer signifies an activity or even a major occupation; it is merely a blank interval on the margin of life, to be endured in order to earn a little money.[30]

The emergence of this group of workers with its common experience of insecurity and alienation provides only a potential root of conflict in the information society. The way in which this conflict becomes manifest will depend, as suggested in the introduction, on the ability of this 'quasi-group' to generate organisations which represent its interests.

As already indicated, traditional trade unionism has so far shown little ability to perform this organising role. Although there have been some attempts to develop unions for part-timers — for example, amongst supermarket workers — the great majority of those employed on the *haken* system or as part-time workers are non-unionised. This fact reflects both the practical difficulties of organising a fluctuating, impermanent work force, and a certain lack of political will on the part of enterprise-based unions to involve themselves in this new and difficult area.

To return to Dahrendorf's model, however, we may note that quasi-groups experiencing common work-related problems will not necessarily give rise to social movements which are simple and exact expressions of those problems. Where employees develop little sense of permanent interest in their place of work, and where labour organis-ations show little ability to represent their grievances, frustration and insecurity deriving from the work experience may come to be articu-lated through other types of organisation. Residents' groups con-cerned with local problems, citizens' movements demanding improvements in welfare, and women's groups protesting against in-stitutionalised inequalities have to some extent played this role in the past decade, and may be expected to do so on an increasing scale in the future.

The growth of an alienated and insecure non-manual work force forms a ready basis for the emergence of movements challenging the Japanese government's utopian images of the information society. The shapes which such movements may take will depend upon the ability of existing and emergent political groups to respond to the changing structure of work and of society in Japan. And it will depend, too, on their ability to take hold of the tools of the information society — the data collection systems, the personal communications networks, etc. — and to turn them into weapons, not only for the maximisers of cor-porate profits, but also for the opponents of corporate exploitation.

Educational democracy versus state control

Yamazumi Masami

Part One
Textbook revision:
the evolution of ultranationalistic textbooks

The two main forces behind the militarism and ultranationalism of prewar Japan were the army and the system of public education. If the former was the more direct cause of war, the latter was by far the more pervasive. More than 90 per cent of the children raised in this period received compulsory education at primary schools that were under strict government control. Textbooks, virtually the only teaching material allowed in the classroom, were subject to the strictest control.

When the national education system was first established in 1872, the government did not attempt to control textbooks, but instead left their preparation and publication in the hands of private publishers. The system changed in 1880, when the government moved to suppress the burgeoning freedom and people's rights movement. It first drew up a list of unacceptable textbooks, then the following year formulated rules for teaching, which textbooks were obliged to follow. The teaching of world history, with which educators had attempted to broaden children's horizons and diffuse modern ideas, was banned. Only Japanese history could be taught. In the government's view, the sole purpose of teaching history was to foster reverence for the emperor; teaching children about the French Revolution or America's Declaration of Independence, and thereby acquainting them with such concepts as freedom, equality, humanism and independence, could only work to the disadvantage of government. Other measures were taken to suppress the freedom and people's rights movement, such, as the

The initial version of this chapter was published in the *Japan Quarterly* vol. 28 (1981), pp. 472-478.

closing down of newspapers critical of government policy and the ban-
ning of political gatherings, but the government took the greatest
pains to control elementary education, for it knew this to be the most
effective method. This was the government's first assault on textbooks.

The second assault came toward the end of the decade, when the
government began promoting nationalism under the popular slogan
'increase the wealth of the nation and strengthen the army'. In 1886 the
minister of education stated: 'If Japan is a third-rate power let us strive
to be second-rate. If we are second-rate, let us strive to be first-rate.
Education can and must play a part in this process.' He then proceeded
to lay down guidelines for schools at all levels. Concerning the university he declared, 'If asked whether the university exists for the sake of
learning or for the sake of the nation, I would reply that it exists for the
nation.' A system for carefully screening primary- and middle-school
textbooks was established at this time. Furthermore, four years of
elementary education were made compulsory. In this way the government further strengthened its control over education. In so doing it
ignored demands from within the freedom and people's rights movements for the freedom to choose the content of education.

The third assault on textbooks came just before the Russo-Japanese
War (1904-05). In 1890 the government promulgated the Imperial
Rescript on Education, which was designed to bring to education the
same system of thought control that had been instituted in the army, as
a reminiscence of the prime minister at the time, Yamagata Aritomo,
makes clear: 'It seemed to me that education ought to possess an imperial mandate just as the military.' In this way education was made to
serve the interests of the imperial line. 'Should emergency arise, offer
yourselves courageously to the State; and thus guard and maintain the
prosperity of Our Imperial Throne.' It was to remain the guiding principle of education in Japan until 1945. Promulgation of the Imperial
Rescript on Education led to a lengthy discussion in the Imperial Diet
concerning textbooks. Members argued that the textbooks then in use
did not reflect the spirit of the rescript and they urged the state to take
over their preparation and publication. The chance to effect this
change came in December 1902, when, as a result of a scandal involving bribes by textbook publishers, a number of people were arrested
and the minister of education forced to resign. On the pretext of putting an end to the bribery problem, the government decided the following April to assume all responsibility for the preparation and
publication of textbooks. Indicative of the change in educational
policy, the minister of education, a former physicist, was replaced by

an army commander who, when hostilities with Russia commenced the next year, was appointed chief of general staff and sent to command the Japanese forces in Manchuria.

In the years that followed, textbooks were frequently rewritten to promote new government policies. The childhood of the renowned medical researcher Noguchi Hideyo (1876-1928) is a case in point. When Noguchi was one year old he burned his left hand so badly that it was deformed, and at school other children teased him about it. A passage in a 1937 ethics textbook reads:

> Hideyo began to attend school. As one might expect, the other children made fun of his hand. Though it saddened him he decided to ignore them: 'So what if my hand is deformed. If I study hard I can succeed in life — I'll show them!'

For the 1943 version, the passage was revised to read: 'So what if my hand is deformed. If I study hard I can do something great for my country — just wait and see!' The tide in battle had already turned against Japan and the citizenry had been mobilised; now children were expected to do their part as well, and toward this end the childhood of this historical personage had been rewritten. Revisions of this sort were common during the war.

Wartime geography textbooks, too, were heavily revised. They began by calling attention to the curved shape of the Japanese archipelago and its strategic location on the eastern rim of Asia. 'The shape of Japan is not without significance. We appear to be standing in the vanguard of Asia, advancing bravely into the Pacific. At the same time we appear ready to defend the Asian continent from outside attack.' Obviously this passage was meant to convince children that the location and shape of Japan indicated that Japan's mission was to rule Asia. It continued:

> Nurtured by the ocean from the Age of the Gods, we remain closely tied to the Asian continent, whence we imported so much of our civilisation. How appropriate our location is for fulfilling our mission, which is to extend over the continent and across the seas. And how symbolic the shape of our archipelago — as though stretching out its arms and legs in all directions! The location, the shape and the matchless natural beauty of our islands all indicate beyond doubt that our country was indeed conceived by a god.

The theory of Japan's divine origins was propounded most strongly in history textbooks. A 1943 edition began:

> The deep green of the pines within the Imperial Palace celebrates the prosperity of our emperor's reign, while the pristine waters of Isuzugawa speak to us clearly of Japan's primeval glory. Long, long ago in the Age of the Gods, the gods Izanagi and Izanami gave birth to these beautiful islands, which we now call the Eight Great Islands. These they arranged

like a great floating fortress to be caressed by the warm Black Current. Next they gave birth to a multitude of gods. Finally, the Sun Goddess was born as the rightful ruler of Japan. It is she who laid foundation of the Japanese state, she from whom our emperor is descended. The virtue of this most august of goddesses knows no bounds. As her name suggests, our country is awash with her blessings, which extend to the very ends of the earth.

The passages quoted above are by no means unrepresentative of wartime textbooks, which were consistent in their support for the mythological origins of Japan, impressing upon children how fortunate they were to live in the 'Land of the Gods'. Such was the final result of government-controlled education based upon the Imperial Rescript.

Postwar reform and the appearance of free textbooks
After accepting the terms of the Potsdam Declaration, the Japanese government repeatedly affirmed its intention to retain its national polity; however, from the late autumn of 1945 it stressed that the purpose of education was to promote world peace and the welfare of mankind. This was partly at the insistence of the Occupation forces, but another factor was pressure for democratic reform from indigenous groups kept silent during the war, including students.

There was no time to revise textbooks, so as a stopgap measure the government distributed old ones, after blackening out militaristic passages. Officials of the Occupation forces, however, decided the Japanese government efforts were inadequate, and, on 31 December 1945, forbade the teaching of ethics, Japanese history and geography and recalled all textbooks.

In the fall of 1946, the first new Japanese history textbook was published. Entitled *Kuni no ayumi (The course of our country)*, it was the first Japanese history textbook since the issuing of the Elementary School Regulations of 1881 that began with a description of the Stone Age instead of mythology. Moreover, it contained the fruits of prewar research into Japanese history, hitherto excluded from primary- and middle-school textbooks. The debate over *Kuni no ayumi* that followed its publication is also of great significance, since under the prewar system all criticism of textbooks had been stifled.

The Fundamental Law of Education was enacted the following year. At the time, approval of the Occupation forces was needed to promulgate all laws, but as statements of those involved in its drafting, such as Nambara Shigeru, president of the University of Tokyo, make clear, it was the product of independent discussion within the Education Reform Committee, which was formed in 1946. Its ten articles set a new guiding principle for education and educational administration. Especially important was the resolve expressed in its preface to realise through education the ideals of the Constitution: the sovereignty of the people, the basic rights of the individual and the renunciation of war.

> Having established the Constitution of Japan, we have shown our reso-
> lution to contribute to the peace of the world and the welfare of humanity
> by building a democratic and cultural state. The realisation of this ideal de-
> pends fundamentally on the power of education. We shall esteem in-
> dividual dignity and endeavour to bring up a people who love truth and
> peace, while education, which aims at the creation of culture that is both
> universal and rich in individuality, shall be spread far and wide. We hereby
> enact this law, in accordance with the spirit of the Constitution of Japan,
> with a view to clarifying the aim of education and establishing the found-
> ation of education for a new Japan.

With the Fundamental Law of Education as their guide, educators groped toward a new system of education, rejecting in the process standardised education. This is especially clear in the first Course of Studies drawn up in March of the same year. Attached to it was a proposal that schools themselves decide basic educational policy.

This new policy was realised most clearly in textbooks for the newly created social studies course. The desirability of a social studies course had been debated from 1945, and it had gradually taken shape along the lines of its American model. The first classes commenced in September 1947. For these classes the Ministry of Education had prepared eight textbooks. They differed greatly from the old geography and history textbooks, carrying such titles as 'Life in Olden Times', 'Land and Man' and 'Urban Life'. At the same time, their relative importance in the classroom was lessened, as is readily apparent from the instructions for teachers and parents contained at the end of each volume. The following are two typical examples:

> One must not assume that because a student has read and understood this
> book that he has mastered the social studies unit, or that you must force
> him to understand its contents before he can grasp the subject. Instead, you
> should consider this but one reference aid.

> The material in this book is not a collection of essential facts that must be
> taught to each and every sixth-grade student. To do so would be a biased
> approach both in terms of content and emphasis. You must not confuse this
> textbook with older ones. It is not meant to be systematically explained and
> committed to memory, nor should it be the only teaching material used.

Many teachers, used to relying solely on textbooks, had difficulty at first adjusting to the new policy. But before long, they were discussing local problems in class and using a variety of teaching materials.

The School Education Law, passed in 1947, re-established the textbook authorisation system. This returned the preparation and publication of textbooks to private hands, abolishing after more than 40 years the state-run system. Free textbooks were in use from 1949. Aware of the problems connected with textbook selection, the

Ministry of Education published a booklet on the subject in April 1948. School authorities, it said, were free, after consulting with teachers, to choose the textbooks they believed best for their schools. The prospectus for the 1949 textbook exhibition went even further: 'Within different classes at the same grade level, it is permissible to use different textbooks.' Teachers were thus given the greatest possible flexibility in their choice of teaching materials.

As for the ideological basis of militaristic textbooks — the Imperial Rescript on Education — at first the Ministry of Education maintained that it ought not to be abolished since it contained 'universal moral principles'. But it soon became apparent that it contradicted the spirit of the new educational policy. In June 1948 both houses of the Diet passed resolutions invalidating the rescript. Since these are extremely important historical documents, reflecting public opinion at the time, I shall quote the House of Councillors' resolution.

> In accordance with universal principles of mankind as expressed in the Constitution of Japan, we enacted the Fundamental Law of Education. In so doing, we solemnly proclaimed our intention to correct the past mistakes of our country's democratic system and to institute a democratic system of education capable of rearing citizens who seek truth and peace. The Imperial Rescript on Education, along with the many other imperial edicts that applied to the military and students, has already been nullified and is without power. But since there may be some who believe it yet to retain its original power, we hereby proclaim the Imperial Rescript on Education and the other imperial edicts to be null and void, and hereby direct the government to collect all copies of these documents that have been distributed. By so doing we affirm our intention to contribute to the dissemination far and wide of the educational concepts embodied in the Fundamental Law of Education, with which the people as one have established the true authority over education and promoted national morality.

It appeared that the new educational system based on universal principles would develop smoothly with the support of the people's elected representatives. International developments, however, soon caused politicians to retreat from their original stand.

The Conservative Party promotes textbook revision

In the opinion of the distinguished British Japanologist George Sansom, who visited Japan in 1950, one of the most encouraging aspects of the new Japan was its attitude toward public education. Regardless of the perils ahead, education, he believed, held great hope for the future of the Japanese people. He warned, however, of the likelihood of a revival of authoritarianism once Japan had regained its independence, in view of its lack of an indigenous tradition of respect for individual rights and the people's willingness to follow orders.

Sansom's fears were justified. The reverse trend began the very next year, when, amid growing US-Soviet tensions and the outbreak of the

Korean War, the peace and security treaties were signed in San Francisco, thus bringing the occupation to an end. In October the Advisory Committee for the Reform of Government Orders, which had issued reports on the depurging of war criminals, new economic and labor laws, and administrative reform, submitted a report covering education as a whole, entitled 'Recommendations Concerning Reforms in the Educational System'. While admitting that postwar educational reform had been useful in rectifying past mistakes and in establishing a democratic system of education, it said, 'By basing our system on that of a foreign country where conditions differ, and pursuing only ideas, we have incorporated in our system many undesirable elements.' It recommended among other things that members of local educational boards be appointed by local and prefectural governments rather than be elected, that vocational education be stressed and more vocational courses offered, especially at the junior-high level, and that the Ministry of Education once again assume responsibility for the preparation and publication of textbooks. The Japan Teachers' Union and textbook publishers objected so strongly to the final proposal, on grounds that it was a revival of the prewar system, that the advisory committee was unable to implement it.

In 1955 the ruling Democratic Party went on the offensive. In a booklet entitled 'Deplorable Textbooks', it harshly criticised the content of social studies textbooks. This was the first time the ruling party had resorted to such tactics and the public was understandably shocked. The booklet criticised the following four types of textbooks: those that supported teachers' unions and advocated their exercise of political power, those that depicted the life of workers as harsh and supported radical labor movements, those that praised the socialist systems of the Soviet Union and China while criticising the Japanese system, and those imbued with communist ideology. Once again the Japan Teachers' Union vigorously opposed what it regarded as an infringement on the right to free education, and it was joined by various educational and historical societies and the Science Council of Japan. They fought a losing battle, however, for with the merger of the Liberal and Democratic parties in the fall, the conservative forces gained a firm hold on the reins of power, and were able to consolidate their control over the educational system.

In 1956 two bills were introduced in the Diet, one to change the system for selecting members of educational boards from an elective system to an appointive one as suggested earlier and the other to tighten the screening of textbooks. These bills, too, raised a storm of protest that was not confined to members of the Japan Teachers' Union; ten university presidents, as well as the national federation for board of education members, denounced the bills. Only the first was passed, and only because the conservative party pushed it through the House of Councillors; in the process, several hundred policemen had to be called in to maintain order. The ruling party's drastic action in this case gives one some idea of its keen interest in controlling education. Although the bill on textbooks was tabled, the government accomplished its objective later that year by making administrative changes in the Ministry of Education, whereby textbook inspectors were placed within the ministry. To the previous five-man team, a sixth was added to inspect the new social studies textbooks. The last was notoriously strict.

The next year, the government attempted to break up the Japan Teachers' Union by instituting the Teachers' Efficiency Rating Plan, under which teachers were rated each year by principals. In 1958 it further strengthened its control by effecting a comprehensive revision of the curriculum. The proposal for textbooks attached to the Course of Studies drawn up in 1947, giving teachers free choice of texts, was abandoned. Furthermore, the new Course of Studies was published in the Diet's official 'Gazette', by which it acquired strong official sanction.

In 1963 the government passed the Law Concerning Free Provision of Textbooks in Compulsory Education. Both the constitution and the Fundamental Law of Education state that textbooks should be provided free; so long as education is compulsory this seems only reasonable. Until this time, however, the government had done everything in its power to subvert this policy, so, as might be expected, its motives in finally passing the law were not benevolent. For while it provided for the distribution of free textbooks, it also required textbook publishers to possess considerable capital. What is more, textbook selection was to be made at the municipal level, not by each school. These stipulations gave large publishers a distinct advantage. As a result, the number of textbooks available for selection was greatly reduced.

The change in the level at which textbooks were chosen had a more direct effect on education than did the strengthened textbook authorisation system. From then on few teachers attended the annual textbook exhibition; indeed, there was little point to it. The new system promoted standardised education while at the same time dampening teachers' enthusiasm. The latter effect was no doubt intended: spiritless teachers are tractable.

Government efforts to control textbooks are really but one part of a well-orchestrated, systematic plan to push the country to the right. While re-establishing its control over textbooks, the government has worked to rehabilitate the prewar national anthem, *'Kimi ga yo'* (The Imperial Reign), and the Rising Sun flag, to strengthen ethics education and to resuscitate the Imperial Rescript on Education.

Early in the century, the Christian leader Uchimura Kanzo (1861-1930) said that *Kimi ga yo* was not the national anthem. 'Its purpose is to praise the emperor. A national anthem ought to express the feelings of the people.' According to prewar textbooks it was a prayer that the emperor's reign last eternally, and it acquired unofficial status as the national anthem. Though it was discredited in the immediate postwar years, in 1950 the minister of education recommended it be sung at school gatherings on national holidays. In the 1958 edition of the Course of Studies for elementary schools, it was one of the songs in the curriculum for music class which all children were supposed to sing. Finally, in 1978, when the Course of Studies was again revised, *Kimi ga yo* was officially designated the national anthem.

But most disturbing are the government's attempts from the 1970s to revive the Imperial Rescript on ducation. In 1974 the prime minister, Tanaka Kakuei, wrote: 'Education today over-emphasises intellectual development at the expense of moral development. While we fatten children's intellects their morals starve.' Concerning the Imperial Rescript he has said: 'Much of it expresses universal moral principles. It has qualities that transcend its form, that speak to us today as then.' By 'form' he no doubt meant its designation as an imperial rescript. In his opinion, its form was irrelevant, since it contains 'universal moral principles.' His opinion is shared by many government leaders today.

Surely, in light of our experience, it would be a grievous mistake to reinstate the Imperial Rescript. All the virtues expounded in it were meant to strengthen the emperor's control over the nation. Even its seemingly universal concepts, such as conjugal harmony and trust among friends, cannot be considered outside their context. It is sometimes pointed out that Westerners have praised the Imperial Rescript, but their evaluations are based on translations, which are misleading. The word *kokken,* for example, has been rendered 'constitution' in English. Unlike Western constitutions, however, the Constitution of the Japanese Empire, promulgated along with the Imperial House Act, was an imperial edict. Such translations give the Imperial Rescript a specious modernity.

The question facing us today is how to avoid repressive government policies that stunt the individual's growth. We must help children to realise their full potential within their own districts, their own schools — where they live and grow. And by affording them contact with other cultures, we must endeavour to develop a Japanese culture that is at once universal and individual.

Part Two
Educational Reform*

I Background

Proposals for educational reform have an ominous ring. Japanese modern history is rife with precedents in which the fate of the country's education was determined by consultative organs on education reporting directly to the Cabinet. The three key precedents are the Special Education Conference *(rinji kyoiku kaigi)* of 1917, the Education Council *(kyoiku shingikai)* of 1937, and the Educational Reform Committee *(kyoiku sasshin iinkai)* of 1946. In view of the fact that the organ now being set up is to be known as the Special Education Council *(rinji kyoiku shingikai)*, which sounds like a combination of the names of the two prewar committees, one is bound to be suspicious.

If the Special Education Council now being promoted† were to make a mistake about the course to be charted for the future, the consequences for Japanese society could be disastrous, so it is necessary to reconsider what was accomplished by previous bodies of a similar character.

The Special Education Conference of the Taisho Period
Let us consider the advisory bodies directly responsible to Cabinet in prewar times. First, there is the Special Education Conference set up in 1917, at a time when circumstances both domestic and foreign combined to make such reform necessary. The experience of World War One underlined the importance of further advances in education, and of 'raising loyal subjects filled with patriotic spirit'.

The deliberations and proposals of this conference were respected and the function of the various academic institutions was changed in the 1920s in the following ways. First, as to universities, hitherto there had been only the imperial universities, but the number of those wanting to further their education had increased and industrial circles had been urging the cultivation of talents in order to cope with international economic competition. The Special Education Conference increased the number of universities by recognising public and private universities and colleges. To Article One of the Imperial University Edict — 'the Imperial universities have as their purpose to respond to the needs of the state by teaching science and the arts and by pursuing

* ' "Kyōiku rinchō" ni itaru chōryū — seiji to kyōiku', *Sekai*, May 1984, pp. 80-101. Translated by the editors. Professor Yamazumi's permission to translate, abridge, and publish in this volume is gratefully acknowledged.

† The bill for establishment of the Special Education Council passed both houses of the Diet and became law on 7 August 1984.

their deepest secrets' — it recommended addition of the phrase 'and they should pay attention to the moulding of character and the fostering of state ideology'. The reason for this was that scholarly research had advanced since the Meiji Restoration but spiritual education and moral education was thought to have declined, and the Great War in Europe showed that even if it were not necessary to set up deparments of morality it was necessary to educate students in this area.

The recommendations were adopted. In 1918 the Universities Ordinance was proclaimed. Private colleges like Keio and Waseda were recognised as universities, and thereafter greater attention was paid to 'guiding and thinking' of students. Steps were also taken to increase control.

So far as high schools, middle schools, and higher girls' schools were concerned, the implementation of national morality (or its cultivation in the case of middle schools) was added as a 'special' educational objective, while in higher girls' schools the cultivation of national morality was followed by 'due attention should be paid to the fostering of womanly virtues'. As for primary schools, the heading of a report of December 1917 set out their purposes as follows:

> In primary schools, national moral education should be pursued to the utmost and greater efforts should be devoted to strengthening the moral convictions of children, especially in the fundamentals of being imperial subjects.

The Conference moved to increase the number of schools at post-middle school level, and to increase the number of universities. It also recognised the importance of establishing a system in which the salaries of primary school teachers would be borne by the national treasury and accordingly in 1918 a law was drawn up to this effect.

However, as should already be clear, what was stressed above all at all levels of schooling was the strengthening of moral education.

The wartime Education Council
In 1937, an Education Council was established. Its basic character was clear. It was established five and a half months after the start of the Sino-Japanese war. Various measures were considered for improving physical education or the promotion of scientific and industrial education in order to establish a 'high-level defence state', with 'clarification of the national polity and the Japanese spirit' as the underlying premise. Virtually all problems of education were discussed at the Council, including the administrative and financial aspects of various kinds of schooling and social education. The main problem was how best to ensure that all education would be 'unified under the imperial way'. At the primary level, even the long familiar title of 'primary school' was abolished; instead the title 'national school' was adopted.

Although reforms which called for substantial financial backing were virtually impossible in wartime conditions, nevertheless various matters relating to the content of education were discussed. Some of these have a close relation to contemporary Japanese education, especially to the writing of historical textbooks. For example, in discussions over the change from 'primary school' to 'national school' the problem of aggression against various countries of Asia came up. At the tenth plenary meeting of the Council, in the preface to the 'Report on National Schools, Normal Schools, and Kindergartens', it was proposed that compulsory education be extended from six to eight years because the basic training of the people at a time when Japan was entrusted with an important mission in Asia and the world was a key national policy. Furthermore, the proposal went on to say that:

> Reforming the content of education, training the people by inculcating in them the imperial way, rousing the Japanese spirit, and planning the cultivation of the intellect and the improvement of physique is to cultivate the basis of industry and national defense. The implementation of these reforms internally will help cultivate the people of the great Japan of the future and demonstrate to the world the founding spirit of a united and harmonious world.

Postwar 1: The Education Reform Committee
This postwar Committee was quite different in character. Its immediate predecessor was the Committee of Japanese Educationalists (president: Nambara Shigeru) set up in February 1946 to cooperate with the American Educational Mission which came to Japan in March. Nambara's Committee presented a report to the occupation headquarters urging the abolition of the centralised, bureaucratic control of Japanese education, calling for the democratisation of education and the establishment of a child-centred educational process. This report was a major influence on the Education Reform Committee, which was set up in August of the same year as an advisory body directly under the Prime Minister and as a successor to the Committee of Educationalists. Usually, a body of this kind would engage in consultations and submit a report on items raised by the Prime Minister or Minister of Education, but the Education Reform Committee had to choose what were the matters of importance and to investigate and consult about them first, and then to advise the Prime Minister of the result of its deliberations. Response to specific questions was secondary. Its autonomy was respected.

Many reform proposals were drawn up as a result of three-sided cooperation between the Civil Information and Education Bureau of occupation headquarters (CIE), the Ministry of Education, and the Education Reform Committee. The Education Reform Committee carried out wide-ranging deliberations on educational problems, ranging from educational ideals (draft of the Fundamental Law on Education), primary education, middle education (middle school and high school), further educational institutions (universities), to training of teachers and educational administration.

Recent close study of original American documents shows that it was after November 1946 that consultations were undertaken with CIE and the Ministry of Education on the draft of the Fundamental Law on Education; delay on the part of CIE in responding to the Japanese side's work on the draft has been recognised.[1] It is clear that the Fundamental Law on Education, which spelt out the ideals of postwar educational reform, was drawn up by the Japanese side.

The Education Reform Committee was directly responsible to Cabinet, but it differed greatly from its prewar counterparts. The difference lies in the position *vis-a-vis* the supreme authority — in relation to the occupation forces, the supreme authority of the time, the Education Reform Committee was an autonomous Japanese body and it strove for independent reform particularly on the most important matters. This was of great significance for educational reform.

But the Education Reform Committee did not last long. Change began as soon as the San Francisco Peace Treaty had been signed (September 1951) and the US-Japan Security Treaty concluded. The Consultative Committee on Revision of Government Ordinances was set up in May of the same year. Just as the current 'Round Table Conference on Culture and Education' is a private advisory body of Prime Minister Nakasone, so this was a private advisory body of Prime Minister Yoshida. Yet 'private' bodies of this kind came to have an influence on the course of education. In November it submitted recommendations on the education system. As well as touching upon problems fundamental to postwar educational reform, such as the school system, the organisation of local educational administration, and the way of dealing with text books, it recommended that the various existing Councils should be combined and a single supreme consultative body set up to deal with the whole of educational administration.

Particularly noteworthy is its assessment that this body should be 'an organisation which can adequately reflect tendencies in society at large. For this reason, educationalists should make up no more than half of the members of such a body'. This was clearly a criticism of the Education Reform Committee (or Commission as it was known briefly).

Nambara Shigeru, Chairman of the Committee, stated that 'off the cuff, it is difficult to agree with this' and added that if a permanent council were to be set up centrally 'it should pursue its deliberations with great care, maintaining the basic spirit of the Education Reform

Committee'. The resentment of Nambara, who had worked without stint for the cause of postwar educational reform, is evident in these words. Nambara was ignored, and the Education Reform Committee abolished the following year. In its stead, the Central Council on Education Reform was set up in 1953 as an advisory body directly responsible to the Minister of Education.

Postwar II: Reforming away the postwar reforms
The 1917 and 1937 precedents show clearly what can happen in the case of organs directly responsible to Cabinet. An important reason for the establishment of such organs is said to be that a small-scale advisory body is no use. However, in 1956 the Diet rejected a bill for the establishment of an Extraordinary Council on the Education System, which had been proposed for just such a reason as a substitute for the Central Council on Educational Reform (established in 1953). The Council proposed in the 1984 bill sounds suspiciously similar in character to the one that was rejected in 1956.

What the government is advocating now is a re-revision of the education that was reformed after the war. From the autumn of 1955, when the Liberal-Democratic Party was formed by the fusion of the existing conservative parties, education was the number one item on its agenda for reform. (The situation in 1984 is similar. The LDP government has established a majority by embracing the New Liberal Club and has set its sights on educational reform as part of a comprehensive liquidation of 'postwar' survivals.)

In proposing his bill for the establishment of a Special Education Council in 1956, Education Minister Kiyose Ichiji said:

> the fundamental reforms of the education system carried out after the end of the war were epochal in the history of Japanese education and played a considerable role in educational development, but on the other hand, since these reforms were carried out hastily under the special conditions of occupation, there are quite a few points at which they do not accord with reality.

Exactly the same view had been stated in January 1953 by Education Minister Okano Seigo.

There were three points that Kiyose cited as needing reform. The first was to do with educational objectives: the Fundamental Law on Education listed eight objectives such as fulfilment of character, but other aims, such as 'loyalty to country' and 'feeling of family affection' were missing. Second was that the question of who was responsible for the content of education was not clear: while the Minister of Education drew up outlines for the guidance of study, he did not have the authority to supervise and see whether those outlines were implemented. Third was to do with the state of the universities following their rapid postwar expansion.

There were three educational laws at issue at this time: the bill for the establishment of the Special Education Council, a revision of the Boards of Education Law so that members of local Boards would be nominated instead of elected, and a new Textbook Law.

The hidden design of the second of these was the clarification of responsibility for the content of education. Under the changes to the Boards of Education Law it was planned to make the office of superintendent of education at the district or local level subject to the approval of the Minister of Education. Minister Kiyose, in explaining this, involuntarily let slip the word 'standardisation', although he quickly corrected himself so as to refer only to the 'maintenace of fixed standards'. Nowadays, in the context of the current strong demand in education reform for changes away from educational standardisation, it is worth reflecting on how such standardisation came about.

Because the Minister of Education could not afford to distance himself from the decisions of 'our party', hundreds of police were introduced into the Upper House in order to secure the passage of the bill to revise the Boards of Education Law.

The education in liberalism and respect for individuality that was promoted in the period of Taisho Democracy was later suppressed by state power, and education was changed in the direction of cultivating the 'loyal imperial subjects' prescribed by the Special Education Conference. Presumably the government will not be so foolish as to repeat this precise same mistake now, yet there is ample reason to fear that state intervention in education may be intensified.

II Nakasone's View on Education

Criticism of 'Piecemeal Improvements'
At a meeting of the National Policy Study Group held on 27 June 1981, Mr Nakasone, later Prime Minister, pointed out that, in postwar politics, international matters had generally been handled well, but at the level of domestic politics there had been little progress in the important area of administrative reform. He stressed that the Japanese people must have the spirit to complete the reform. Nakasone then suggested that the next phase following administrative reform should be a large-scale educational reform. He stated:

> The reform I have in mind is not a small-scale adjustment based on technical considerations such as has been discussed in the Central Council on Educational Reform organised by the Ministry of Education. We must launch a great educational reform which addresses the fundamentals of the overall educational system. Administrative reform is but a spiritual precursor to this.

In a discussion at about the same time with the political commentator Fujiwara Hirotatsu, Nakasone argued:

> After administrative reform, the focus should shift to education. For this purpose, a Special Education Council will have to be formed. The timing for overhauling the educational system is important; since in effect it means tackling the Constitution problem.

In this discussion, Nakasone went so far as to touch on the issue of the Constitution. The current law for the establishment of the Special Education Council contains the phrase 'on the basis of the spirit of the Fundamental Law on Education'. The preface to this law clearly states as its basic premise that the spirit of the Constitution is to be achieved through education, and obviously the educational reform committee should be so organised as to promote the spirit of the Constitution. Yet, from Mr Nakasone's remarks about 'tackling the *problem* of the Constitution' (italics added), the purpose of educational reform is obvious.

Over the last thirty years, the Liberal Democratic Party has on many occasions tried to carry out a reform of the postwar reforms. There are certain times when such moves are particularly apparent; in the educational sphere, it is whenever an organ directly reporting to the Cabinet is formed. In the present round, the strongest advocate of 'educational reform' is the prime minister himself.

In criticising postwar education, Nakasone argued in his book entitled *New Conservative Logic* published in November 1978:

> Only piecemeal improvements have been carried out within the framework of educational philosophy and institutions transplanted from abroad by the Occupation Authorities about thirty years ago.

The process may have been only piecemeal, but, while in Nakasone's eyes these 'improvements' look like so much temporising, I am one of those who believe that the immediate postwar reforms have bit-by-bit been worn away till in educational policy and administration their spirit has been lost. As early as 1971, soon after the Central Council on Educational Reform proposals were presented as a 'third educational reform', matching those of the early Meiji period and the postwar, Mr Nakasone stressed the importance of education reform:

> Despite the Central Council on Educational Reform recommendations, politicians tend to be evasive about education — do not wish to be bothered with it. Yet considering long-range planning for the nation, politicians must deal with education, even at the cost of one or two cabinets falling.

In Nakasone's statements about education, two points are clear. First of all, he attaches the utmost importance to educational reform, to the extent that it matters more than the collapse of cabinets. It is true that many people recently have come to wonder whether his position might not be just a device to prolong the life-span of his administration, since Japanese education is obviously rife with problems, and a political posture of deep concern with the problem might help his chances of re-election as head of the LDP. While this view may not be entirely wrong, one should bear in mind that Nakasone's interest in education has been consistent since the early days of his political career. This is evident in a booklet entitled *Ideals of Youth* which he published in March 1947 when he was just embarking on his political career. In this monograph, Nakasone referred to Fuchte's *Message to the Germans* and concluded: 'even in this period of extreme hardship, let us appeal to the public not to forget education since it is of such importance for the coming century of the nation'. His interest in education is not temporary but can be traced to his initial motive to become a politician.

The second point in Nakasone's educational philosophy is the importance attached to the tradition of the Japanese nation. In his *New Conservative Logic,* while criticising 'piecemeal improvements', he argued:

> Those educational policies introduced to Japan from abroad were filled with abstract idealism and universalism, splendid products of the history of mankind. However, education should not ignore the particular uniqueness, history, climate and social constitution of each nation. Abstract concepts may be fine in themselves without necessarily being suitable for a particular context.

In 1946, Shidehara Kijūrō, Tanaka Kōtarō and their associates emphasised the importance of the heritage of educational ideals with a universalistic and humanistic orientation. In 1956, Suzuki Yoshio stated in Parliament that it was important for the Japanese, as members of mankind, to pay due respect to what had been achieved as the result of mankind's bitter struggles over so many years. Nakasone, however, attempts to belittle the heritage of mankind and view it simply as 'abstract'.

After the establishment of 'Manchukuo' the Japanese puppet state created in Northeast China in 1932, the Japanese government constructed shrines dedicated to the Japanese imperial household. It was simply an attempt by the government to impose Japanese national Shinto upon other ethnic groups. The young Nakasone wrote in 1947 about this:

> It seems that they called these places by names such as 'house of founding gods of the nation'. I was appalled and sickened to read this report in the newspapers. The philosophy and policy of the Japanese Government at the time were mistaken to an astonishing degree.

Although this passage may sound like a criticism of militarism and ultranationalism, that certainly is not the case. Nakasone went on:

How could it be possible for Manchurians living in deserts and exposed to the red sun to understand the blessing of the Japanese imperial shrine? Because we belong to the nation abundant in forests, beaches and rice crops, we feel the urge to pay tribute at least once in our lives to the Ise Shrine where the ancestors of the emperor are venerated. Upon reflection, I must say that already at this time the basic causes for Japan's defeat in the Pacific War were maturing.

What Nakasone addresses is not the question of responsibility for the war but only that of the government's responsibility for the defeat. Furthermore, in this paragraph as well as in many of his statements, one can observe not only respect for the culture of the people but also the notion that Japanese culture is unique and probably superior to others. One is bound to wonder just what kind of education Nakasone would like to implement.

Nakasone witnessed Japan's defeat in the war as a paymaster lieutenant junior grade of the Japanese Navy in Takamatsu City. At the time, he felt 'a kind of public indignation at the way in which the very politicians who had been responsible for bringing the nation into the unfortunate war were coming back again to prominence'. This indignation is worth noting, because it prompted his resolve to plunge into the political arena in his twenties. At that time, he appealed to the people of Gunma Prefecture, saying that the new era must be one of democracy:

Democracy is like an orchestra where each individual part has to be fully developed to generate the proper sound. The quality of an orchestra depends on the richness of its various sounds. Japan has so far restricted the sounds and prohibited some. There was little freedom. Men and women were unequal. These are the circumstances which made Japan parochial and led her to tragedy.

This is a fine speech, which sounds as though it is based on the essence of democracy. It must have had a powerful appeal to a number of people in the climate immediately after defeat in the war. But words such as these are abstract, and one has to look at his subsequent words and actions to see what specific implications were to be drawn from them.

Nakasone's notion of devotion to the public

Those who attach great importance to education are concerned about the ways in which children and young people live their lives. There are two competing approaches: one encourages and expects youth to choose their own ways; the other considers it sufficient to educate them within the framework already established by adults. The latter approach is reflected in the *Image of the Person We Expect,* the document which the Council on Educational Reform published in October 1966. What is Mr Nakasone's position?

During a visit to China in March 1984, Mr Nakasone delivered a speech at Beijing University under the title of 'Towards the Twenty-First Century'. In a subsequent discussion session with students, he gave this answer to a question:

> The leaders of today's China devoted themselves to the achievement of their ideal, to the extent of enduring the great trials of the Long March. While I do not share their ideology I respect their way of life.

He then went on to say that the decline in the spirit of total devotion to a public cause in contemporary Japan was the thing which was of greatest concern to him and which he hoped to remedy by appropriate reforms. Granted that the statement was made for a student audience, it is an indication of his depth of commitment on this issue that Nakasone should speak of educational reform even while in China.

The problem is what Nakasone envisages as the spirit of public devotion and when and how he sees it as having been demonstrated in the past. The spirit about which he so often talks would appear to be quite different from that which was behind the Long March which the Chinese organised for the liberation of the nation.

The speeches delivered by Mr Nakasone directly to Japanese youth provide a clue to his real thinking. As the President of Takushoku University, he addressed the students on many occasions. When he assumed the presidency in September 1967 he made an inaugural speech entitled 'Message to Students'. In this speech, he stressed that every effort should be made so that innocent children never be sent off to the battle field. On the surface, the tone of his speech sounds very similar to the historic Japan Teachers' Union slogan of 1951: 'Never let our students be sent to the battle field again'. Nakasone made the point that the situation after World War Two was greatly different from that after World War One in the sense that the concept of 'peaceful coexistence' had gained currency; he stated that 'the greatest event in human history over the last fifty centuries is the emergence of the notion of peaceful coexistence'. It sounded as though he valued peace above all for the future of mankind.

However, Nakasone showed his true colours at the end of his speech. He referred to the kamikaze pilots who died towards the end of World War Two, while of about the same age as the students in the audience:

> Did these pilots die for the sake of self interest, or was it for the sake of vainglory or for imperalism? Or was it not rather that they set off on their mission with their hearts filled with pure love of their fatherland and their people? There is nothing more precious in any society than the voluntary abandonment of one's life for the sake of one's country and compatriots. I want you to bear in mind that those youngsters whose age was not much different from yours died just over twenty years ago for the sake of their compatriots.

Nakasone then ended his address saying that he had made 'all the key points' that he wanted to make. His concluding reference to the kamikaze pilots is of crucial significance.

In January 1968, President Nakasone addressed students on the theme of 'Bicentennial Ideal', on the occasion of the one hundredth anniversary of the Meiji Restoration and the commencement of a new century, asking the student with what ideals they were facing the next hundred years. After suggesting that there had been an ideal which had moved people over the previous hundred years, he suddenly raised the question of the kamikaze pilots again, saying:

> At about your age, these young student soldiers devoted their lives to the suicide mission. One does not yield one's own body to death except for an ideal. One could not go as far as to kill oneself only for the sake of medals or honour. Such an act becomes possible only when one finds something more valuable than self.

What Nakasone as president of the university was saying was that these students who died as kamikaze pilots shared a great ideal.

If we are to raise human beings who seek truth and peace in accordance with the spirit of the Fundamental Law on Education, such a statement must surely be seen as quite inappropriate. Wartime youth did not give up their lives for an ideal but were prevented from pursuing truth and reality. So far removed from peace were they that they could not even imagine what would happen when the war ended. And if some among these student soldiers believed that they were dying for the sake of a great ideal, what kind of education was it that indoctrinated them into such a belief? Mr Nakasone, who asserts that education is the key to the next hundred years of the nation, is obliged to elucidate on this.

III Problems in the Special Education Council

The current educational reform is being promoted by Prime Minister Nakasone. Those who have doubts about his views on education, or oppose them, cannot help feeling concern. They doubt whether these reforms are really designed to create a system of education in which children and young people can develop as human beings.

Treatment of the Fundamental Law on Education

The core issue in the planned educational reform is how the Fundamental Law on Education is to be treated. Mr Nakasone has long been an advocate of constitutional reform. As soon as educational reform came onto the agenda, he linked it with a solution to the constitutional problem. Therefore, it was only natural that when Nakasone became prime minister, his appointment should be most enthusiastically welcomed by those who had been publicly maintaining that the Fundamental Law on Education should be revised.

On 29 December 1982, the 'Association for the Protection of Japan' headed by fifteen representatives — such as Uno Seiichi, Kinoshita Nobutane, Yasuoka Masaatsu, the Director of the Agency of Shinto Shrines, the Chief Priest of the Meiji Shrine, and the President of Seichō no Ie — submitted to the new prime minister a document entitled 'Celebrating the Start of the Nakasone Cabinet — A Statement of Some Requests'. This association makes it a policy objective 'to promote patriotism and establish an ethical nation on the basis of the traditional spirit of Japan'. It has also campaigned vigorously to have the system of counting years in accordance with the reign of the emperor adopted as law.

In this document, the Association called for administrative reform, strengthening of defence forces, and revision of the Constitution. With respect to education, the Association maintained that the response of the Suzuki Cabinet to the textbook issue in 1982 had greatly harmed the prestige of the Japanese nation and hindered the growth of patriotism among the younger generation. Thus, they recommended, 'under the present circumstances, a fundamental reform in educational policy, including the revision of the Fundamental Law on Education, should be undertaken'.

The same document made reference to the prewar Imperial Rescript on Education and added that 'the government must make special efforts to promote the traditional moral principles, national consciousness and feeling of solidarity among the people as prescribed by the Rescript and to encourage the consciousness of being Japanese and the spirit of readiness to defend the nation'. These requests illustrate the warm expectation entertained by the Association of the new prime minister.

At the local level, the Gifu Prefectural Assembly passed a resolution in October 1980 demanding that the Fundamental Law on Education which had been enacted under the occupation be reformed to include points such as respect for traditional culture and the cultivation of a patriotic spirit. In March 1984, the Education Committee of the Nagasaki Prefectural Assembly, in the presence of its Liberal Democratic Party members only, carried a resolution presented by the Nagasaki Prefectural Branch of the Association for the Protection of Japan calling for reform of the Fundamental Law on Education. While such moves have not yet been widespread, the Association may start taking more active steps to promote this line in the future.

However the law governing the establishment of the Special Education Council stipulates in Article 2 that the Council's inquiry must be 'based on the spirit of the Fundamental Law of Education'. It is probable that the members of the Association for the Protection of Japan feel impatient about this phrasing and the soft line which Nakasone appears to be taking. In 1956, the reason given for the proposed Special Council on the Education System was that patriotism was lacking in the Fundamental Law on Education. The current Council contrasts sharply with this, although it may be merely that it was judged politically advantageous this time to adopt the framework of the Fundamental Law.

The real question is whether discussion will be carried out within the framework of the Fundamental Law and how its spirit will be construed. It has been said that the report of the 'Discussion Group on Culture and Education',[2] published on 22 March 1984, will provide the material for debate in the forthcoming Special Education Council and may form the basis of its recommendations. The section of general remarks at the beginning of this report reads: 'We have summarised our opinions without reference to the Fundamental Law on Education or any other particular views on education and have focused upon the desirable course of education in the future — particularly the necessity of educational reform and issues to do with it'. The major premise that the Special Education Council will be 'based on the spirit of the Fundamental Law on Education' is called into question by the adoption as a reference paper of a report which did not take that Law into consideration.

On 15 February 1984, Prime Minister Nakasone stated in the Budget Committee of the House of Representatives that 'my interpretation of the Fundamental Law on Education, which is also the interpretation of the Nakasone Cabinet, is that patriotism and filial piety must be taught as the goal of education'. This statement was perhaps an attempt to reassure those who were eager to revise the Fundamental Law. Those who are dissatisfied with the Law have been saying ever since the 1950s that patriotism and filial piety are missing from it. However, what is important here is the content of such ideas: the natural development of love of the nation in which individuals can voluntarily take part in making things better is one thing; enforcement of love of country regardless of circumstances is quite another matter.

Government Intervention in Culture and Education
Prime Minister Nakasone appears to be fond of the term 'culture'. Immediately after the war, both official and non-official circles put forward the notion of a 'cultured and peaceful nation' as the slogan of the new era. But it is necessary to consider whether the culture Nakasone is advocating is firmly tied to peace and consciously in line with this tradition.

The proponents of humanistic culture strongly oppose state intervention in culture. Education is the area where culture, including science and art, is transmitted to the younger generation, so that they in turn can become its propagators and creators. In answering questions in the Diet with respect to educational reform, Nakasone has stressed that 'state power will not be allowed to interfere with education'. But the recent series of cases involving the censorship of Professor Ienaga's history textbook is telling proof that his parliamentary statements are not reliable.

Intervention in the field of culture and education is most evident in the textbook trial. In January 1984 Professor Ienaga Saburo launched a textbook suit over the way textbook authorisation was carried out late in 1983. One item in his suit is the treatment of the Unit 731. In Ienaga's textbook there was the following account:

> A bacteriological warfare unit known as Unit 731 was set up in the outskirts of Harbin and for several years until the Soviet entry into the war atrocities such as the killing by various experiments of thousands of live foreign prisoners, mainly Chinese, continued.

The textbook authorisation official commented on this:

> Reliable academic studies, theses and books, as yet do not exist on this problem, and it is too early to treat this matter in text books. Please delete.

In other words the text would not be approved unless this passage was deleted. What is it if not intervention in scholarship, culture and education, for the Ministry of Education to judge whether various books or theses are 'reliable' or not?

It is true that there is no major work dealing with Unit 731. However, it is discussed in a book by Professor Ienaga himself, *The Pacific War*,[3] which in its translated version has been praised internationally. So the Ministry of Education is saying that Professor Ienaga's book cannot be relied on. Even if the last word in the academic debate remains to be written, it is the responsibility of adults to collect various kinds of evidence and write in textbooks about historical incidents which it is important to communicate to children and the young.

So long as such intervention by the Minister of Education in the Nakasone Cabinet occurs, the Prime Minister's statement to the Diet (denying that state power interferes with education) cannot be relied on.

Late in 1983, soon after he became Prime Minister, Mr Nakasone made reference on a number of occasions to a 'robust culture'. One is bound to wonder whether 'robustness' means intervention of this kind in education.

Current proposals of educational reform also have to be understood in the context of an attempt to reduce the amount of public assistance as much as possible.

Professor Kumon Shunpei's point deserves attention here. Kumon was a specialist member of the subcommittee which examined the goal of administrative reform. He was also a member of the subcommittee which explored ways and means to reduce governmental expenditure. Interestingly, Professor Kumon concluded his article entitled 'On Educational Reform Policy: What I Want to Assert', by saying that the most important way to reverse the present trend of decline in education is . . .

> through creative implementation of an education which, both in form and in content, is free and pluralistic.

The proposal to resist conformist education and to develop flexible and dynamic education is attractive indeed. However, in so far as Kumon's proposal rejects the idea that private schools should receive subsidies from the state treasury for performing functions in place of the state, it amounts to a measure for reduced government expenditure. It is a proposal to overcome uniformity and promote creativity and individuality without taking the steps necessary to achieve such ends.

Kumon's proposal is one of many which government-related organisations have floated with a view to limiting or scaling down public expenditures. Significantly, none of these proposals address the question of the urgent reduction of class size to the maximum of forty which so many primary and middle school teachers have been demanding. Those who have been trying to remove uniformity from education and practise education oriented to respect for individuality have come to believe that it is imperative to decrease the number of pupils per class.

In prewar Japan, the liberal and individualistic education initiated during the period of Taisho democracy was subsequently eliminated or suppressed by state power. Education was successively reorganised with a view to producing 'loyal Japanese subjects' such as the Special Education Conference had prescribed. One would hope that the present government would not repeat the same mistakes. With the implementation of education reform as planned now, however, there is ample reason to fear that state intervention in education may be stepped up and the chances of revitalising education be set back.

Class struggle in postwar Japan

Mutō Ichiyō

Introduction

Like a moth maturing inside a cocoon, a new political formation, with
the value system and institutions of totalitarianism, is growing under
the thin husk of Japan's 'peace' constitution. This progress has been
observable throughout the 1970s following the worldwide crisis of
capitalism triggered by the first oil crunch, but has gathered momentum in the last few years and accelerated since the rise of Nakasone
Yasuhiro. At least in appearance, the trend in Japan corroborates the
pessimistic thesis that the current crisis of capitalism leads to the emergence of right-wing regimes rather than to revolutionary upsurges in
the First World.

In the current march to the right, the Liberal Democrats, big business, and the ideologists and politicians of the right are fast losing their
inhibitions in advocating that Japan rid itself of the norms of 'postwar
democracy' — a historically specific political system that combines the
ideals of democracy and peace — and reform the state into a crisis
management system.

The late Prime Minister Ōhira, who, before his death in 1980 came
to be horrified at the desperate prospects of the world capitalist
economy, seized upon the notion of 'integrated security' which combines 'military security', 'energy security', and 'public peace' into a
single concept. According to this concept, 'energy security' — meaning
the security of nuclear power generation, crude oil supply and storage,
and LNG base building — is as important to national security as is
military preparation, and consequently opponents of energy security
projects should be regarded as 'security risks', almost traitors. The
Liberal Democratic Party in its 1981 statement declared that to maintain 'energy security', 'all opposition to nuclear power plants should be
crushed'. This sense of 'security' — defending the status quo against

This is an edited and abridged version of an article which first appeared in *Ampo*, vols
13, 4 (1981); 14, 1 and 3 (1982); and 16, 3 (1984).

'aliens' — is especially visible in the new penal code the Justice Ministry is planning. This new code would make 'leakage of corporate
secrets' a heavily punishable crime and legalise preemptive detention
of the 'mentally sick' who are considered potential subversives and
criminals.

Labour Front
The world of labour unions is now boiling, not with workers' struggles,
but with manoeuvres, secret talks and speculations among labour
bosses, and the formation and dissolution of coalitions and generally
deepening confusion among lower echelon union officers and activists.
The issue is 'unification of labour fronts' promoted by rightwing
unions.

The plan is to bind together major private industrial unions from
different and until now antagonistic national trade union federations
to form a new union centre around a hard core formed by the big
unions in the strategic industries — steel, automobile, shipbuilding,
and electrical. This federation, initially of private sector unions, is intended eventually to annex public sector unions — government employees and government corporation workers. The preparatory
committee for the envisaged national private industrial 'preparatory
council' (a looser form than a federation) was set up on 14 December
1981. The new federation ultimately aims at embracing all the major
unions from the private and public sectors.

To those who naively think that all workers should unite, this
strategy may sound innocent. But in the actual context, the emergence
of this new unified federation would begin a new, third, stage of the
postwar Japanese labour movement in which trade unions would cease
to be a progressive factor and become instead the most powerful organised force to support the capitalist regime in its time of crisis.

The most immediate result of this unification, if achieved, would be
the disappearance, sooner or later, of the 4.5 million-strong General
Council of Trade Unions (Sōhyō), the largest union federation known
as a progressive organisation. Of course, if final unification is
achieved, all of the participating federations will be integrated into the
new body and so cease to exist as such, but Sōhyō will be the only federation that will lose its identity and have to accept the others' principles of class collaboration.

The move for unification was first promoted by a six-man committee, which included a Sōhyō representative. In June 1981 the committee worked out a 'guideline', which it declared final, non-revisable
and to be accepted unconditionally by all the prospective participants.
The guideline proudly said that the Japanese economy had succeeded
in overcoming the two oil crises and was able to continue to grow on
a stable basis 'thanks mainly to the qualitatively superior and

quantitatively abundant labour force in this country' as well as to 'the (correct) attitude assumed by the union movement'. This statement could as easily have been used by a big business association like Keidanren (Federation of Economic Organisations). It says nothing about how millions of Japanese workers were expelled, overworked, transferred to irrelevant jobs, humiliated and driven to despair by the rationalisation drives Japanese capitalism undertook to 'overcome the two oil crises'.

But more ominous than the general guideline statement (which was drafted to gloss over contradictions) are the official policies of the major industrial unions which are to be the core of the unification program. Mr Nakamura Takuhiko, Chairman of the 400,000 strong Federation of Iron and Steel Workers' Unions (Tekkō Rōren), explained the goals of the unification as: (1) eliminating Marxist influence and the concept of class struggle from the Japan Socialist Party and turning the party into the Japanese counterpart of the West German Social Democratic Party; (2) promotion of nuclear power generation to save the nation from the energy crisis; (3) abandonment of the struggle against rationalisation and the 'industrial structural transformation' program (the government-business plan to relocate industries overseas); and (4) revamping the National Railways (the state-run railway corporation which is suffering from deficits) and other unprofitable public corporations through administrative reforms (meaning dismissal of tens of thousands of workers). Tekkō Rōren is still a member of Sohyo and is a trojan horse effectively disarming it from within. In fact, this union is one of the most powerful promoters of the rightist line.

Similarly, the Confederation of Shipbuilding & Engineering Workers' Unions (Zōsenjūki) in December 1977 sent an 'urgent recommendation' to the government that domestic production of weapons, especially warships and aircraft, be increased and speeded up. In the same year, the Matsushita Electric Union (National), the key union of the Federation of Electrical Workers' Unions (Denki Rōren), came out with a more explicit political program calling for a strengthened military alliance with the US, faster buildup of the Japanese military, promotion of nuclear power generation, and closer collaboration with the dictatorial Park Chung Hee regime, then in power in South Korea. The Confederation of Labor (Dōmei), the traditional rightwing union centre, and its political arm the Democratic Socialist Party, have fought against Sōhyō for decades, and together they are known as the most consistent champions of anti-communist drives in this country. Dōmei President Usami, when the historic uprising of Kwangju citizens in South Korea was suppressed by the Chun Doo Hwan junta, praised Chun as a 'great statesman' and went so far as to parrot Chun, saying that behind the Kwangju incident were the 'notorious Urban

Rural Mission (of the Christian Church) and Kim Il Sung'. These unions are the ones who are dictating the terms of unification.

It is important to note that the most active promoter of unification is the IMF-JC unions. These unions are affiliates of the International Metal Workers' Federation of the International Confederation of Free Trade Unions (ICFTU) who formed their Japan Committee (which is now called the Council of Metal Workers' Unions and has 1,870,000 members). The status of IMF-JC is unique in that it draws member unions from different existing federations. The 600,000-member Federation of Auto Workers' Unions (Jidōsha Sōren), led by Shioji Ichirō of Nissan, is an independent union unaffiliated with either Dōmei or Sōhyō. But the 540,000-member Federation of Electrical Workers' Unions (Denki Rōren) belongs to the Federation of Independent Unions (Chūritsu Rōren), while the 230,000-member Tekkō Rōren is a Sōhyō Union. The 170,000-member Confederation of Shipbuilding and Engineering Workers' Unions (Zōsenjūki) belongs to Dōmei. All these unions represent the export sector of the Japanese private industry whose overseas activities — exports, imports and capital exports — are a determining factor in the world economy today. The history and nature of this IMF-JC, the key to understanding the class situation in Japan, will be taken up later. The important point here is that unification was initiated by this wing of the 'union movement'.

Roughtly speaking, IMF-JC represents the business interests of the strategic export industries while Dōmei is a traditional rightwing union representing its own interests. Sōhyō, with its private industrial sector eroded and lost to Dōmei and IMF-JC, is being forced into an embrace with IMF-JC.

In this context another controversial issue is being raised in the context of the proposed merger: affiliation with the ICFTU. The assumption of the promoters of unification is that the new, unified labour federation should as a whole be affiliated with the ICFTU. Conscious of the delicate nature of this issue, the six-man committee made only an indirect reference to it in its guideline, saying that the Japanese labour movement should be united with its counterparts in the West where the labour movement is in a similar situation. But the implication of this goes beyond mere labour union solidarity. Mr Shimizu Shinzō, a longtime leftwing labour theoretician with Sōhyō, explained that this emphasis on joining the ICFTU reflects the need of the Japanese governmental and big business diplomacy to ease international economic frictions. The burgeoning export industries of Japan have caused, as is well known, serious friction with their West European and US counterparts, especially in the areas of automobiles, ships, and electrical goods, and this, coupled with the generally sharpening contradictions among imperial powers, are now only barely eased by occasional summit meetings. But the Japanese government feels uneasy about the future as the trade war intensifies. It thus wants the new labour federation, controlled by the big unions which serve the strategic export industries, to conduct its own 'labour diplomacy' with big Western unions to mitigate friction. The right-wing unions, eager to collaborate with their respective industries, are only too glad to play this role.

The rightwing unions are very strict about these conditions of unification and are not at all interested in getting all unions to come together in their new federation. Their goal will be attained if the main labour front in Japan is reorganised around them. They are averse to the idea of having to work with communist-influenced or leftwing unions unless they have been effectively disarmed in advance.

In December 1982 the process of unification of labour fronts entered a new stage with the official establishment of the National Private Sector Union Council (Zenmin Rōkyō), embracing five million members. Although the Zenmin Rōkyō unions are still members of Sōhyō and other original federations, the establishment of this new council has practically shorn Sōhyō of its power in the private sector.

The government is now engaged in a concentrated assault on public sector unionism which, under Sōhyō, retained shopfloor militancy until recently. In its administrative reform program, the government has chosen the National Railway as its target, deprived its shopfloor union units of their power to negotiate and settle on working conditions and, threatening to cut up the railway corporation into a few private firms, has successfully driven the workers into drives to 'save' their corporation. This tactic is also being employed against other public corporation workers, setting postal workers against private parcel delivery services and generally forcing public workers to emulate the efficiency of private industrial workers. The Sōhyō-affiliated public workers' unions, despite their supposed strength, have failed to make effective counterattacks and are being driven into the same path of corporatist unionism.

The new corporatist force thus emerging has no interest in workers' shopfloor power. Numerically large, the movement hopes to function as a pressure group on national policy-making to modify in its favour labour-related state institutions. Its leadership is too deeply committed to productivity principles to confront management or government. Rather they hope to be represented in government consultative councils dealing with the question of 'institutional reform.'

The fundamental spirit is that of commitment to *gōrika,* a word which may be translated literally as rationalisation but which conveys in the Japanese context a peculiar degree of thoroughness, intensity, and refinement whereby the buildup of new production capacities, application of new technological methods, restraints on organisation of labour, and enforcement of new kinds of labour control devised to preempt and decimate workers' power are organically linked. The members of the new labour front will collaborate with, or promote, further *gōrika* and will try to obtain some gains in exchange for their collaboration.

In the same spirit, they will champion the Japanese 'national interest'. Here, however, their position is delicate. They are afraid, as are the government and big business, that too extreme *gōrika* leading to too great competitiveness of Japanese goods may dangerously aggravate relations with the United States and Western Europe. The corporatist union movement can here extend a helping hand to the government and big business by volunteering to be labour diplomats to assist the solution of issues with their working brothers and sisters in the West. Partly from the same considerations of smoothing relations with the US and also increasing the pie they share, the corporatist union movement is likely to press for a hardline foreign policy (anti-Soviet and pro-South Korean policy, for instance), for accelerated military build-up and for expansion of the defence industry. Some major unions, including the shipbuilding union, have begun to do this.

Ideologically, the new unionism endeavours to clear the working class of the concept of working-class and class struggle, let alone 'revolution'. As Miyata Yoshiji, Chairman of Tekkō Rōren stated, 'Trade unionism negates revolution and class struggle. Respecting parliamentary democracy, it aims to build a welfare society through reforms in capitalist society'.[1]

The ideal of this viewpoint is a society without serious dissent and antagonism. The result can be an enlarged replica of the company world where cost-efficiency rules at the sacrifice of such considerations as human dignity, class identity, and equality.

The Liberal Democratic Party in its paper's 1982 New Year editorial mapped out its perspective for a '1985 System'. According to the party, Japan historically has experienced a major political institutional change every 30 years. Though the editorial's references to history are poor and arbitrary (World War Two is not mentioned), it sufficiently conveys the party's wish to replace the '1955 System', which offered a viable superstructure for the whole period of prosperity and growth, with a new corporatism. The LDP editorial refers to the 1985 system as 'fully integrating the trade union movement with the ruling party' which will 'directly absorb the voices of the urban communities, consumers, and the aged'. The LDP considers that the ruling party that will integrate all these mass movements will be the LDP. But a more likely political outfit for this function may be a coalition government between the LDP and the so-called middle-of-the-roaders. However reformist, the Communist Party will be excluded, but the Socialist Party, losing its mass basis in the Sōhyō movement and plagued by internal division, is approaching a middle-of-the-road position at a visibly quickened pace.

But in the dialectical process of history things are often turned into their opposites, and a triumphant rightwing push, shaking the traditional set-up of labour bureaucracy and creating a new dynamic, could be the beginning of a positive process — the emergence of a new, radical, and anti-imperialist labour movement. The Communist Party-influenced Sōhyō unions (the Day-Labourers' Union and several other national unions), criticising the unification plan as class-collaborationist, have formed their own semi-independent liaison centre called Tōitsu Rōsokon and declared that they would not go along with any unification.

Sōhyō's top leaders, especially Chairman Makieda (from the Japan Teachers' Union) and Secretary General Tomizuka (National Railway Workers' Union), are desperately manoeuvering to talk all members into the merger line, but a few major unions other than Tōitsu Rōsokon, too, have begun to express either doubts or opposition.

Partly allied with these critics is the radical wing of the labour movement, loosely represented by the Rōdō Jōhō (Labour News) started in 1977 at a national congress of workers in Osaka. This trend inherits the worker radicalism that exploded in the anti-Vietnam war struggle in the late 1960s, and comprises the long-struggling metal workers of Osaka and a network of radical workers' groups and individual unions in Sōhyō as well as in enterprises controlled by rightwing unions. These groups share a desire to push the situation further than simply defending the Sōhyō tradition. The collapse of the existing labour establishment offers an opportunity for them to make alliance among genuine unions loyal to the class struggle in order to remake the Japanese labour movement totally into a worker mass-based (not big enterprise-based) anti-imperialist movement.

The present is regulated by the past, and the immediate past that regulates Japan today is the whole era of what is called 'Postwar Democracy'. This is not a term referring to Japanese bourgeois democracy in general, but is a specific historical concept comparable to 'Weimar Democracy' which describes post-World War One Germany. The term Postwar Democracy, however, does not include the turbulent years immediately after the war.

It is generally acknowledged that Japan's Postwar Democracy as a stable system of domestic rule finally emerged in 1955, the year in which several significant events converged to announce the arrival of a new era. These were:

(1)   The recovery of the Japanese economy to its prewar peak level.
(2)   The merger of the two conservative parties (Liberal Party and the Democratic Party) into a single conservative Liberal Democratic Party, which became Japan's permanent ruling party. In the

intervening years, it has never handed political power to, or shared it with, another party.

(3) The unification of both the left and right Socialist parties to form the Japan Socialist Party (JSP), which came to be the main opposition to the LDP government.

(4) The unification of the Communist Party (JCP) through a compromise reached among its feuding factions, entailing the party's choice of a parliamentary course.

(5) The establishment of the Japan Productivity Centre to promote thorough-going rationalisation drives in all industries.

(6) The launching of an annual Spring Campaign *(Shuntō)* for higher wages by Sōhyō's new leadership.

(7) The emergence of a broad popular movement against nuclear weapons based on the Hiroshima and Nagasaki experience and triggered by the 1954 US hydrogen bomb experiment in the Pacific which victimised Japanese fishermen.

These events are important indicators because they represent the socio-political factors whose specific combination would characterise the coming decades.

Politically, the pattern of confrontation that emerged pitted the LDP, as the ruling party with a majority of seats in the Diet, against the Socialist Party, allied with Sōhyō and in unstable collaboration with the Communist Party, a combination which came to constitute the main opposition force to the LDP. The Socialists, Communists, and Sōhyō, joined by progressive intellectuals, formed the so-called 'progressive camp'. The LDP with its vast pool of rural and urban clients formed the 'conservative camp'.

The issues that divided the two camps politically centred around the questions of peace and democracy. The conservatives favoured alliance with the US while the progressives opposed it on the grounds that the military alliance and presence of US military bases might at some point involve Japan in another war. The conservatives advocated strengthening the Self-Defence Forces, asserting that Japan should possess the means to defend itself, while the progressives warned that a Japanese military was unconstitutional and could give rise once again to militarism. The conservatives did not like the democratic rights and peace clauses of the Constitution, nor for that matter were they happy with the postwar Constitution itself. The progressives, however, pledged to defend both democratic rights and the Constitution. The JSP slogan was 'unarmed neutrality' whereas the LDP claimed that peace was bought at a price: Japan- US military alliance backed up by the Japanese Self-Defence Forces. The JCP took a somewhat different view of the Constitution. It accepted in principle the notion of national self-defence and for this reason did not support Article 9 of the Constitution. The party also stood opposed to the Emperor system, which was preserved in the Constitution if in a benign form. However, the party consistently sided with the JSP in resisting LDP attempts to revise the Constitution. The conservatives sought to enhance the role of the Emperor on every occasion, and the progressives interpreted each new ploy in this direction as further proof of the LDP's intention of setting the clock back to the prewar days.

Since each of these issues was fundamental, the gap between the two camps appeared unbridgeable. When blatantly bellicose and antidemocratic measures were taken by the government, as for example in 1960, the progressive camp was able to mobilise millions of people and deliver LDP designs a serious blow.

But the decisive factor shaping this period of Postwar Democracy was the continued, rapid growth of capitalism, which promoted and rapidly diffused the myth that well-being was the result of high industrial growth and economic progress. As this myth established its grip on the minds of workers, labour was induced to think that it had better be content with sharing the fruits of growth with capital in the form of higher wages. This gradually disarmed the working class and weakened its determination and ability to resist incessant rationalisation drives.

In fact, the prevailing atmosphere of the early period of Postwar Democracy was one of general buoyancy and great expectations. People looked back with bitterness on starvation, homelessness, unemployment, rampant inflation, and the cruelty of the war they had experienced a few years earlier. This atmosphere sustained the JSP's pacifist slogans, but at the same time heightened expectations that better days lay ahead if only economic growth could be maintained.

Insulated from the turbulent postwar experience and accepting the basic premises of capitalist development (although the JSP superficially upheld the socialist cause), the progressive camp as a historical formation could react to the political situation only defensively when and where it felt the values of peace and democracy were jeopardised.

In most Japanese writing on the subject, right or left, the era of Postwar Democracy is generally referred to as a period of ultra-rapid economic growth and a period of heavy and chemical industrialisation. It is rare for a nation to define an entire period of its history in such economic cliches. That the Japanese do so points to the special role of economic factors during that period. Hitherto, historical eras had been demarcated by the wars Japan fought, but the character of the new era could only be expressed by giving it an economic name. It may be that in this period of Japanese history, capitalism and its immanent fetishism — undistorted by extra-economic factors such as a 'crusade for freedom' or 'Imperial Japan's sacred mission' — found the purest expression it has achieved anywhere in the world. This purified spirit of capitalism could flourish, as we saw already, thanks to the 'complementation arrangement' with the United States.

In this sense economic growth was myth as well as fact. And this myth, or ideology, helped accelerate the pace of the growth of capitalist production, while the fact of growth in turn strengthened the myth. But of course it was the objective side of reality that was the main factor.

Company world

In the 1960s workers' power on the shop floor was eroded. Such existing industries as steel and automobiles expanded rapidly, and petrochemical, electronic and other new industries were created, sharpening competition among giant enterprises on the one hand and making the labour supply tight on the other. This latter factor offered a favourable environment for Sōhyō's wage increase campaign, although in most years annual wage increase rates lagged behind productivity growth rates. Sōhyō and the Socialist Party, in loose alliance with the Communists, still were pledged to the cause of peace and democracy, and at times did mobilise the masses in political campaigns on the issues of military bases, the military buildup, and various reactionary measures. However, beneath the facade of successes in the wage struggle and the occasional political mobilisations lay the stark reality of Sōhyō's loss of one private sector union after another to the rightwing collaborationist Dōmei. The gap between Sōhyō's apparent strength in terms of mobilisation and its receding influence on the shop floor in key private industries continued to widen throughout the decade.

The massive accumulation of capital during this period was largely due to this overthrow of workers' power on the shop floor. To the degree that management succeeded in preempting workers' resistance in the plants, it could feel free to implement technological innovations, expand the scale of production, and thus obtain special surplus value for reinvestment. And conversely, this technological innovation and work system rationalisation tended to further disintegrate working-class solidarity.

Central to the understanding of this process of atomisation of the working class is the formation of what may be termed the 'company world', a phenomenon which is the key to an understanding of postwar Japanese capitalism.

The 'company world' is an institutional-*cum*-ideological device used to translate inter-enterprise competition (which was always sharp) into inter-worker competition. The big company is structured into a world within which the workers are coerced into sharing the fate of the company. Once workers are integrated into this 'world', they are forced to compete with one another to achieve the goals set by the company.

While many western observers ascribe Japanese workers' 'loyalty' toward management to what they call traditional Japanese 'submissiveness' to the authority or to traditions of 'collectivism', the truth is that this apparent 'loyalty' is the result of highly individualistic competition based on economic motivation and has little to do with cultural traditions or 'collectivism'. On the contrary, this 'loyalty' has emerged from the debris of the worker collectivism which Japanese labour so forcefully displayed in the struggles of the postwar era. In fact, it took violent repression from the occupation authorities and the Japanese government to conquer this worker collectivism.

The concept of the 'company world' requires some explanation. Inter-company competition, which was very intense during the period of resurgence of capitalism in postwar Japan, is one kind of competition and depends mainly on the commodity market situation. Inter-worker competition is, of course, another, but in it the determinants are labour market factors. The Japanese bourgeoisie has managed to combine these two different kinds of competition by herding workers into pens sealed off from the general labour market as well as the general relationship of class forces, in which they are motivated to fight each other to attain the company goal. In order to hold the workers in this secluded 'world', the company needs a wall to demarcate the arena within which this inter-worker competition takes place. The well-known 'seniority wage' system coupled with the 'life-time employment' system served this purpose well. The latter applies only to the regular employees of big companies, who account for less than one third of the Japanese industrial labour force, and has the effect of distinguishing between the privileged citizens of the 'company world', its lesser-status inhabitants, and outsiders. Moreover, 'life-time employment' is a misnomer, for it has never meant 'life-time' employment but rather compulsory retirement at the age of 55. Nor did it mean 'guaranteed employment', life-long or otherwise. In fact, as we will see later, hundreds of thousands of workers assumed to be protected under this system were kicked out, the older ones first, when the capitalist crisis of the 1970s arrived. This system nonetheless served its purpose as a fence surrounding the 'company world'.

The various 'intrafirm benefits' such as company houses, company loans, company gyms or company-sponsored 'cultural circles' were so many bricks in the 'company wall'. The wage systems which became increasingly complicated were also made to make the 'company wall' sturdier. Instead of being a simple seniority wage system under which the wage rises with the age of the worker, the actual wage systems made the wage more and more subject to the capacity of the worker and evaluation by management. The wage scale is peculiar to a given company and there is no scale common throughout a particular industry. Individual workers have very little idea how much they will get even after a wage increase is agreed upon, since so much of their pay is based on evaluation according to various standards of which they are kept ignorant.

The standardisation of the work process is also carried out in a fashion peculiar to the enterprise, thus depriving the worker of the universal applicability of his/her skill — another factor that keeps the worker inside the 'company world'.

These and other artificially created systems worked effectively to maintain the big company 'enclosure'. Watanabe Ben, a left labour leader of the Sōhyō-affiliated General Workers' Union, has said that the company home-loan system alone would be enough to destroy the militancy of Japanese big enterprise workers:

> An employee of a big private company can borrow money from the company to buy a tiny house on the condition that he repay it with his severance pay at the age of 55 when he has to retire. This agreement ties his fate to that of the company. If he should resign prematurely, his severance pay would be much less than his debt to the company. For a worker, being hired by a big company is like mortgaging his whole life; also the company housing loan is usually not enough to enable a worker to buy a house, and so he borrows from other sources as well. If the company should go bankrupt, he also goes bankrupt, as he cannot repay his debt to the private housing company, and his house will be confiscated.

The 'seniority wage system' works similarly. If a worker is in continuous service with the same company for 20 years, his salary goes up, and his life style and local status improve accordingly. But if his company goes bankrupt, he can hardly get a new job at a comparable salary and maintain the same living standards. For one thing, his skill has been shaped in accordance with the particularised systems of his company and often has little universal value. Even if his skill has a universal value, his social value does not.

The 'company world' is thus held together by means of intimidation, and this intimidation is substantiated by real and objective systems enmeshing all aspects of a worker's life. Once a worker is trapped in this 'world', he or she (mainly he) begins to compete with his fellow workers in order to survive and to climb the ladder of intra-firm status and wage promotion. The 'company world' might better be called a 'company country', for the partition by the 'company wall' resembles the division of the world's working class into separate nation-states, which enables the state to channel the discontent of local working people into outbursts of national chauvinism in the context of nation-to-nation competition.

The 'company world' is the key to the understanding of postwar Japanese capitalism, with its peculiar hyper-accumulation. It is in fact the citadel of the Japanese bourgeoisie. Pushed into this 'world', a large (privileged) segment of the Japanese working class has taken up inter-company competition as its challenge without, however, fully believing in it.

The 'Spring Struggle' tactic, for example, was never able to challenge the root problem of workers in the 'company world', for its sole aims were an increase of the absolute level of wages, and intra-firm welfare. The absolute level could be, and in fact was, raised when the big enterprises were expanding and prospering, but the acquisition of a higher absolute level of wages and welfare, when purchased at the cost of permitting unrestricted technological and management system rationalisation, only helped to strengthen the 'company wall'. This development eventually placed limits even on Sōhyō's capacity to win higher wages.

QC Drive and Small Groups

Throughout the 1960s and 1970s, the period of the formation of the 'company world', the major struggle inside big companies was over the question of which side would organise workers — management by infusing them with its own ideology, or the workers themselves, on the basis of their independence. Among the diverse methods used by management to organise workers on its own terms, the 'small group' formation, coupled with 'quality control', emerged as the most effective institution for cooptation.

The concept of 'quality control' originated in the United States but was brought to Japan in the late 1950s by the Japan Productivity Center. There it was wedded to the 'small group' concept, and by the early 1960s played a major role in both integrating labour and controlling the production process. The Zero Defect (ZD) drive, begun in the US missile industry to eliminate defective components, was first applied in Japan by the Nippon Electric Corporation in the early 1960s, and underwent similar modifications. These models were incorporated into the 'small group' activities, or 'workers' self-management,' as it is called at Nippon Steel Corporation.

Under this system, workers at big enterprises are 'voluntarily' organised into small groups, called QC circles. Here they study the work process, invent new work methods or develop improvements to the existing ones, and propose them to management in order to promote higher product quality and productivity.

Gōrika, the Japanese adaptation of Taylorism, having fully evolved on its new soil, became transformed in a way that Taylor could not have imagined — the application by workers to workers themselves. At this stage, worker collectivism is seemingly revived, but as its zombie. Webster defines a zombie as 'supernatural power through which a corpse may be brought to a state of trancelike animation and made to obey the commands of the person exercising the power; or a corpse so animated'. The vulgar, widespread stereotype of management-loyal and work-oriented Japanese labour mirrors nothing but labour in this state.

Each workshop is supposed to have at least one QC circle, and the group meets usually once or twice a month, more frequently in some enterprises. These meetings are held after the day's work is finished, and in most cases the participants are not paid overtime. Often, these 'circles' are structured horizontally at the factory level, and then at the company level. The main organisers are foremen or superintendents, and the circles discuss a wide variety of work-related subjects. Each individual and each group is encouraged to make proposals, and if management finds a proposal excellent, a prize is awarded. The prize winners have the privilege of attending a higher level QC presentation session, where the best of them is rewarded with, for instance, a trip to the US.

Participation in these circles is assumed to be 'voluntary', but actually it is hard for workers not to participate, since their pay and promotion depend on evaluation by management. Participation or non-participation in the QC drive is considered an important factor in evaluation.

According to a 1976 survey by the Japan Productivity Centre, 71.1 per cent of Japanese enterprises had QC circles. Among big enterprises with 10,000 or more employees, the figure was 91.3 per cent. Take the steel industry for instance. Nippon Kōkan (Kawasaki Mill) and Kobe Steel (Takasago Mill) implemented QC drives as early as 1963, and Nippon Steel (then Yawata Iron and Steel Co.) followed suit in 1966. Now 30,000 QC circles are operating at 169 mills, factories and offices in the steel industry, involving 230,000 workers, or 83 per cent of the total steel work force.

'To give workers something to live for' was the formulation of the QC campaign's purpose at Yawata Iron and Steel when it began.

> One of the most serious problems facing modern industry is how the prosperity of the company and human satisfaction of the workers can be made compatible. These seemingly contradictory requirements — higher efficiency and regained humanity, must be met simultaneously. The solution is to create a system that links together the hearts and minds of workers as human beings and helps them to display their respective capacity and creativity to the fullest.

This lofty pronouncement was more realistically expressed by Nikkeiren (Japan Federation of Employers' Associations), when it said, 'The sense of belonging to a small group will give workers more satisfaction and lead to higher efficiency'.

Though QC drives take diverse forms they generally have the same basic purpose: (1) making the workers think on behalf of management, or penetrating the inner world of individual workers with management ideology, thus preventing them from having their respective independent inner worlds beyond the world of the work place; (2) alleviating the sense of isolation workers suffer in the wake of technological innovations; (3) spurring competition among the workers to emulate the achievements of others; (4) placing workers under minute and constant control with regard to their ideology and behaviour; and (5) improving efficiency and raising the level of product quality.

In many cases, the primary emphasis of the drive is on the first goal. In the 'company world', the workers are no longer allowed to do just what they are told to do, but are supposed to contribute positively to the company out of a feeling of 'voluntary participation'. But participation is not in fact voluntary since the demand for it comes from the top. At Nippon Steel, the management in 1978 declared that the company should be totally structured so that it could operate without suffering a loss even if the operation rate of the mills should drop to the 70 per cent level for an extended period. This grand strategy was conveyed to each QC circle, which was then urged to help make it concrete. The group's duties were (1) to select a specific area in which it could make contributions to the company, (2) to analyse the situation, (3) to set a target, (4) to effect improvements for achievement of that target, (5) to confirm the effects of these improvements, (6) to standardise the results of the improvements so that other workshops could implement them, and (7) to draft reports about the whole process. Through these efforts, the company claimed that 17,000 proposals made by QC circles were implemented to solve problems of energy conservation and cost reduction, resulting in a 35.6 per cent cut in oil consumption by 1980.

This process shows an incredibly high degree of organisation of workers by management. Workers have to work during their regular hours, put in overtime, and then contribute to productivity and efficiency by studying the work process, gathering data, and writing reports. Even if there is a genuine union in the workshop, there is no room left for union activity since all the available time and energy of the workers is absorbed by the company. Quoting a socialist worker who was once secretary-general of the union at the Hirohata Mill of Nippon Steel, Watanabe Eiki writes that the management's success in organising the vitality and energy of the workers has eroded what had once been considered the union's proper function.

> Nowadays, young workers know how to speak in public because they have to attend so many QC sessions and report on their activities. Formerly, workers used to become good speakers through union activities. QC circles have usurped the role of workers' activism from the union.[2]

After the Yawata and Fuji iron and steel companies merged in 1970 to become the world's largest steel giant, Nippon Steel Corporation, the management gave this process an ironic new name — 'workers' self management' *(Jishu Kanri)* or 'JK' campaign.

Do workers self-manage? Do they participate in decision making? The most tragic aspect of this JK campaign is that it resembles self-management and participation as closely as a glove turned inside out resembles the original glove. For, in nine out of ten cases, 'self-management' results in increased work intensity and strengthened exploitation at the cost of workers' interests. Kumazawa Makoto, a labour researcher who divides QC activists into 'doves' and 'hawks' (the doves tending to take up subjects not leading to direct intensification of work), cite a case of 'hawk' QC elites at the Toyota Motor Kariya plant.[3]

The QC circle in question consists of 14 workers who perform the final painting of car bodies. They are said to have done an 'exemplary' job of 'improving' the work process. According to their report, the purpose of the improvement is reduction in worker-days required for the blacking-out process.

> Our purpose was to concretise the policy of our section to fight increases in manning and material costs. When we proposed reducing two men to one, complaints were heard that cutting personnel in half would be too much and that it would result in intensification of work. People also asked us where the surplus men would be transferred.
>
> But we persuaded these dissidents, saying that by studying industrial engineering methods we would find ways to hold down our work load even if our personnel were cut by 50 per cent. We also pointed out that Mr. H, who is a seasonal worker, is resigning soon.
>
> Our member U, who had undergone training at another firm recently, came back and reported that there they were doing twice as much work as we do here.

Thus, the group studied industrial engineering methods thoroughly and reviewed all the operations so that one man could do the work of two. The target was to reduce the required work time from 302 DM (deciminutes) to 160 DM. The 'improvement' finally reduced the work time to 155 DM.

Professor Kumazawa, analysing the 'improvements' thus made, points out that not only was one out of two workers phased out as if by magic but also that any remaining relaxation time during work was completely eliminated because of the 'improvements'. All waiting time and time to change tools was cut, and the workers now have to chase the car body as it moves past them, instead of waiting for it to reach them.

How coercive this type of 'small group' control can be was dramatically shown at Sony, now known around the world as Japan's archetypal electrical manufacturer. Despite the shining image it carries, the Sony world is unlivable for workers.

In the early 1960s, when this young company was becoming a major television set manufacturer, its founder and president Ibuka Dai hired

Kobayashi Shigeru, a semi-professional union buster, to crush the Sony union, which was becoming militant. The management declared that all its employees would soon be made submissive and those who refused to surrender would be eliminated. This promise was kept. Union activists were physically attacked, general secretaries of union branches fired, union executives given punitive transfers, and many members given disciplinary wage cuts. A company union was created in the spring of 1961, causing the original union to lose more than half its members in a few months.

It was in this belligerent atmosphere that Kobayashi was appointed director of the Sony factory at Atsugi, then the company's brand new main plant making transistor radio sets and integrated circuits. The overwhelming majority of the workers at the plant were very young girls just out of junior high school who came from farming families in northethern Japan. It is upon these 15-16 year-olds that Kobayashi imposed his 'small group' system. In his well known book of self-praise, *Sony Makes Humanity*, he later explained this system as one of giving a sense of purpose and meaning of life to workers. Strangely, he chooses to take his terminology from the Communist vocabulary, so that the small groups he organised were called 'cells,' and the factory became a 'workers' school.'

Sony Atsugi in fact had a school, Sony Gakuen High school, integrated with the factory. The factory, the school and the dormitories were in the same compound located in a newly-opened industrial area 50 kilometres west of Tokyo still surrounded by farmland. All the young workers had to live in the dormitories, and Sony granted them the opportunity to continue their studies.

The worker-students got up at 4.45 a.m. and started work at 5.30 a.m. After working for one hour and 45 minutes, they had breakfast from 7.10 to 7.35 a.m. and then resumed work which lasted until 1.15 p.m. After lunch, they went to school and studied from 2.20 p.m. to 5.30 p.m. They then returned to the dormitory. This was for the morning shift. The evening shift workers would go to school in the morning, begin work at 1.10 p.m. and work until 9.55 p.m.

They were organied into 'cells' each consisting of five to eight members with a 'leader' and a 'subleader.' The leaders were 'sisters' who had been with the company for more than four years. They would 'take care' of the young girls, intervening in every aspect of their personal life. Love affairs had to be confessed to the 'leaders' and if they had any complaints, they had to tell them first to the 'leaders'. But the main purpose of the 'cell' was to make the young girls work harder. The 'cell' met two or three times a week, and each member had to report to her colleagues her renewed work target. If she failed to achieve it, she would be humiliated in front of her colleagues. Naive and helpless young girls from villages were removed into this strange environment.

They had no alternative but to accept what they were told. Competition within this framework, established by the company but ostensibly created by the workers themselves, escalated without limits. According to Saitō Shigeru, who recounted the stories of these isolated girls, most of the workers would arrive at the factory at 5.00 a.m., half an hour earlier than the official starting time and begin to work.[4] Otherwise, they could not fulfil the targets they had set themselves. The girls had to submit their self-critical personal reports (about what they did and thought) to the 'leader' and the 'leader' would check them and criticise them if necessary. The targets were thus 'voluntarily' raised gradually, and those who attained the target were given a plastic 'OK' mark which was tagged to their work tables.

Nor were they free from company control after they returned to their dormitory rooms. Four to six workers were packed into a room with double bunks, and TV sets were prohibited. From 7.30 to 8.30 p.m. the residents had to observe a 'silent time'. They were supposed to meditate, criticising themselves for weaknesses that might have caused the company trouble.

For three months after they joined the company, they were prohibited from having any visitors, even their parents. The dormitory had its 'mother' who would tell the girls, 'If your parents come and see you, others whose parents could not come would be hurt'. The 'mother' is the almighty supervisor. She would come into the room at any time to check the books on the shelf, for the sake of 'protection.'

But the 'protection' turns to repression the moment workers assert themselves. Electronics work is highly injurious to the eyes, the organic solvent used in the process is often lethal, and the ever-increasing speed of the assembly line often caused chronic or acute troubles in the workers' hands and arms. The Sony management is unresponsive to complaints about industrial diseases, and without union support workers who want to protect themselves have to fight individually or in small groups. The Sony 'world' has its hospitals and clinics where doctors conceal the real causes of industrial troubles, and protests are met with job transfers and, ultimately, violence.

In this tightly organised pen, resistance required a great deal of personal courage and spirit, which some brave Sony workers in fact displayed, as the following story of the struggle of three women workers on behalf of their co-workers as well as themselves illustrates. Hired in 1969 by Sony's Shibaura plant, they soon saw the speed-up of the line causing physical troubles for many of their colleagues. They themselves soon began to feel acute pains in the arms and hands and so decided to demand that the conveyor speed be slowed down. This was an outrageous demand, coming from ordinary workers. Management immediately started to harass them, but they did not yield. Management ultimately ordered them transferred to other lighter jobs but they took the principled position that transfer would not solve the problem and refused. Wearing slogans on their jackets, they stayed in their original workshop and continued to work. A violent confrontation developed and security guards were finally mobilised to beat them up and throw them out.

Better known is the case of Naganami Inakichi, a temporary worker at Sony's Shiogama plant. Forced to inhale a toxic organic solvent on the job, he developed complex liver troubles and died in 1974. The company denied responsibility from the beginning despite a clear relationship between his symptoms and the toxic vapors. He died cursing Sony. His family and his supporters have continued his struggle by suing Sony.

Competition — wage and status

The type of labour control used at Sony's Atsugi plant in the early 1960s cannot be seen as typical for all of industry, since the inner worlds of big corporations differ from one to another. However, there are some striking basic similarities among all major private companies: (1) thorough organisation of the employees into company interest-oriented groups; (2) hierarchical structuring of the workers designed to divide them by giving a sort of sense of privilege to one group of workers over another; (3) artificially organised competition among individual workers; (4) quasi-collectivism, a distorted copy of worker collectivism; (5) intimidation and ostracism, and ultimately the exercise of physical violence against dissidents (either by company guards, union goons or the police); and (7) a 'union' which serves as the most effective, and, often, the most violent, protector of the whole system. Of these, competition is the core around which all the other institutions have been organised.

The wage system coupled with the 'ability evaluation' concept is the main means by which workers are divided and made to compete with one another. The 'ability-ist' *(nōryoku-shugi-teki)* labour control principle was proclaimed by Nikkeiren (Japan Employers' Federation) in 1969 in a 600 page handbook written on the basis of a 1965 resolution. The guideline set out in this policy paper reflected a process that had already been under way for years, a shift from the traditional form of the 'seniority wage' system, under which age was the most important wage determinant, to a modified system, which used the workers' ability as the primary consideration. It also recommended a shift to an elitist labour force, rather than a mass labour force.

Under the traditional 'seniority wage system', the employees were divided into two major categories according to education — workers and officers. Workers, as they accumulated seniority and their skill increased accordingly, could be promoted to supervisory jobs, but not to officers' positions. There was general correspondence between age, skill and wage levels. This traditional system started to erode due to the postwar super-growth of the economy. As has already been described, the factor of skill was the first to be undermined. The formation of work-teams around older, skilled, and relatively highly-paid workers, was eliminated as part of the process of technological innovation and work standardisation. Instead of age and skill, 'ability' — (i.e., each individual's contribution to the company's interests) became the major factor for determining wages and promotions. The wage and promotion systems were rapidly reorganised in the 1960s and 1970s in accordance with these 'ability-ist' principles.

Consider Nippon Steel's Hirohata mill. There, a 'hierarchical job duties' system was introduced in 1967, dividing workers into five — later seven — categories with sizeable wage disparities between them. Once workers were promoted out of the bottom rank, they entered the realm of high-status titles: 'deputy secretary', 'secretary', 'deputy councillor' and 'councillor.' These people are all blue-collar workers and not officers. In effect, they are industrial non-commissioned officers who are above ordinary workers, or soldiers. The 'soldiers' were also subdivided into several status/wage groups. The 'basic wages' are linked to these categories, and when the average basic wage is raised the higher status workers or officers are given larger increments.

Moreover, the wages for workers of the same status are not the same, as a large part of their pay is subject to evaluation by management. When the wage is increased, 20-40 per cent of the wage increment is determined by how the worker's work is evaluated by management. At Sumitomo Metal Industries, for example, the evaluation-development portion is 45 per cent. At Nippon Steel, while the average wage increase in 1980 was 3,000 yen, those workers who got the highest evaluations obtained 6,600 yen raises and those with the lowest, 2,500 yen. Those who were 'highly evaluated' and promoted to 'secretary' were paid around 2 million yen higher a year than their colleagues of the same age and with the same period of service who had failed to be promoted.

A more extreme case of arbitrary evaluation is seen at Nissan Motor, where only 13.5 per cent of the wage is the 'basic wage' and 72.9 per cent is a 'special allowance' largely determined by management's evaluation.

Though evaluation is supposed to be based on 'ability', in actual fact loyalty to management is the most important criterion. In interviews with applicants for a higher status, the examiner asks few questions about their jobs. According to Watanabe Eiki who interviewed Nippon Steel workers, the most frequent questions asked are 'Do you know the difference between Sōhyō and Dōmei?', 'What do you think of strikes?' and 'What do you think about trade unions?'

At Nippon Kōkan company, promotion is based on regular exams. There are four statuses among blue-collar workers in the company, and, according to Watanabe, the examination for promotion from the first to the second status is extremely difficult.

> Workers are not allowed to take the examination without the permission of their superintendent. The results of the evaluation are secret and not disclosed to the workers involved. The examinations are graded according to such general and vague criteria as collaboratory spirit.

Under these circumstances, favourably impressing superior officers naturally becomes the shortcut to promotion. The easiest way is flattery; the next easiest is to display extra dedication and enthusiasm. One worker told Watanabe,

> (Work intensification is) tremendous. You know overtime is regulated, and the company management highly values those who can finish their work quota within the stipulated overtime. So, workers would not apply for overtime pay even when they work beyond the limited time . . . This is because they want to be considered specially capable.

Hierarchy — subcontract workers
The 'company world' is the summit of Japanese society where the power of the bourgeoisie is concentrated. Each 'universe' thus stands at the top of a pyramid consisting of a vast number of medium, small, and tiny enterprises. In some extreme cases, giant companies, like Toyota Motor, Hitachi, Kawasaki Steel, or Chisso Corporation, subjugate whole towns in which their main plants are located. In such company towns, the majority of municipal assembly representatives are spokespersons for, or agents of, their corporate masters and they manipulate city politics in the latter's self-interests. Since the whole town feels that it is dependent upon the company, dissidents are threatened with ostracism. The magnitude of the company power can be measured by the fact that the Toyota family, which started a textile machinery business at the turn of this century in Omoro City, succeeded in getting the name of the city changed to Toyota after Toyota Motor became one of the world's largest automobile manufacturers. Kawasaki Steel is the master of Chiba City. There, dissident citizens fighting against pollution from the company steel mill are harassed and threatened. Likewise, Minamata in Kumamoto Prefecture, Kyūshū, is known as Chisso's town, and challenging Chisso's authority was almost a blasphemy. This is why this murderous company could keep killing and maiming thousands of fisher-people on Minamata Bay for more than 10 years with organic mercury pollution. Chisso knew that the mercury it was discharging into the sea was the cause of Minamata disease but suppressed this information and denied

responsibility by using its mafia-like power over the local administration, hospitals, and communities.

But company towns are not the only form of corporate domination. All major companies subjugate a vast number of subcontract firms which exist to supply parts and/or components, or to render services for the main companies. Though the subcontract firms maintain formal independence, they are virtually branches of the giant firms. One big company often turns hundreds of such smaller firms into vassals, telling them what to make, unilaterally deciding the prices of products they deliver, demanding highly punctual delivery, imposing high quality requirements, and dictating precise technological innovations at the latter's cost. The subcontracting firms are not all the same either. Smaller ones are subjugated by larger ones and, in many caes, the actual manufacturing is contracted out to poor families where housewives do the assembly work at incredibly low piece-work rates. Typical of this kind of structure is the automobile industry. The nine main car manufacturing firms that are assemblers 'outsource' 75 per cent of their work to these primary, secondary, and tertiary subcontractors. The comparable ratio in the United States is 50 per cent. Thus, the eight major car manufacturers directly employ only 200,000 out of the 600,000 auto workers. The wage and other working conditions decrease toward the bottom of the pyramid. The wage level for tiny subcontract firms with between one and three employees each was 19.7 as opposed to 100 for relatively large subcontract firms making parts. The wage gap between top and bottom was widening year by year.

Even inside the 'company world' itself there are second and third class citizens along with 'full members,' i.e., the regular employees. They are discriminated against both in wages and other working conditions, and are denied the benefits given the regular employees. They include the so-called 'outside workers' or 'collaborating workers', who are employed by subcontract firms, but work inside the factory of the main company. In some cases, they are assigned to work in the same jobs as regular workers but are paid less. In other cases, they are assigned to do the 'dirty jobs' or subordinate jobs that regular workers do not do. In still other cases, they work under the supervision of their 'subcontracted' employers, rendering such services as plant cleaning, disposal of wastes, maintenance, or transportation inside the plant. Subcontractors are often mere hiring agents with a small office, a telephone, and a clerk. They recruit workers on the day-labour market, send them into the main company, and take 30 per cent or so of the wages paid in a lump sum by the main company. In extreme cases like the 'labour dormitories' of northern Kyūshū, gangsters are involved to keep the workers from running away. In any event, the 'outside workers' are hired not by the main company but by the subcontractors, and so the management of the main company refuses to negotiate on their working conditions.

Other categories of workers discriminated against in the 'company world' are temporary workers who can be fired at will, seasonal workers, or farmers who come to urban areas to work for a certain period of the year, and 'part-time' workers — overwhelmingly women, mainly elderly housewives, — who, despite the label, often work for eight hours a day.

The major industries, such as steel, shipbuilding, automobile, and construction, rely heavily on these underprivileged workers. The larger the enterprises, the more heavily they depend upon them. Approximately 12 per cent of the work force employed by large companies with 500 or more employees were workers in this category, while at enterprises with between 30 and 99 employees, the figure was only 2-3 per cent.[5]

The rate of dependence on outside workers is exceptionally high in the steel industry. The five major steel firms in 1973 had as many as 154,999 outside workers in their employ (46.9 per cent) as compared with 175,675 regular employees. The percentage rose to 58.9 per cent in 1976. Shipbuilders are next in their degree of reliance on outside workers (though many of them were laid off during the 1974-76 shipbuilding slump), while the auto industry favours seasonal workers and 'outsourcing'.

A survey of the Kimizu steel mill of Nippon Steel shows that the highest paid of the outside workers, those doing the same jobs as regular workers, were paid approximately 70 per cent of the regular workers' wages.[6] They are also supervised by regular workers, often a humiliating experience. Regular workers behave in a superior and authoritarian way toward the lower-status workers, thus reproducing in this relationship exactly the relationship they have with their own superintendents. This is a well-developed divide-and-rule policy that creates for the lowest echelon regular workers a still-lower status of people to look down upon.

Controlling a labour force organised into such a hierarchy is easy for management. When subcontract workers are organised into a genuine union, management can discontinue the contract with their firm. Threatening to do so is enough to deter subcontract workers. This happened at the Tokyo No. 2 factory of Ishikawajima-Harima Heavy Industries with 50 subcontract firms. Subcontract workers employed by one of the subcontracting firms in 1972 organised themselves, trying to establish their right to negotiate with the IHI management, which is practically their direct employer. The subcontract with the hiring agent was terminated. Similarly, when a bus company providing transport services for Nippon Steel's Tobata mill was organised, the bus company itself was kicked out.

Discrimination and competition are the two principles governing this pyramid. Subcontracting firms compete with each other, and their workers, in order not to lose their jobs; they have to compete to keep their company in the big firm's good graces. This system of dividing the working class by stratum and setting one segment against another assumes a horrendous dimension when Japanese big companies go abroad, especially into Third World countries with dictatorial governments.

The reality of enterprise unionism

Kawanishi Hirosuke

In recent years 'Japanese labour-management relations' and 'Japanese labour unions' have received increasing attention for their role in sustaining the country's phenomenal economic growth. Outside Japan, Japanese labour unions have been thought to be based on individual companies ('enterprise unions'). The enterprise union is a union organised within an enterprise and consisting of all employees, including blue collar and white collar workers. Furthermore, a worker automatically becomes a union member when he or she joints the enterprise. Thus the enterprise union is based on the principle 'one enterprise — one union' and belongs to the type of 'all-entry' labour unions.

But this view does not accurately explain what the unions are like and how they operate in Japan. This essay, based on empirical research, attempts to show that the Japanese enterprise unions have failed to improve satisfactorily workers' living conditions.

The first empirical study of Japan's labour unions in the post-war period appeared in 1950.[1] On the basis of the results of the surveys Ōkōchi Kazuo first formulated the theory of the 'enterprise union' in Japan.[2] Ōkōchi defined the enterprise union as a labour union organised within the confines of an enterprise. He further asserted that Japanese migrant workers from rural regions (temporary rural workers who were employed in urban areas on an unstable basis and who subsequently returned to the countryside) contributed to the formation of enterprise unions, because individual companies procured their own labour force, and the Japanese market was structured on the basis of individual enterprises. Lastly, Ōkōchi painted a pessimistic picture about the 'negative' function of the enterprise union, especially

An earlier version of this chapter was published as an occasional paper of the East Asian Institute of the Free University of Berlin.

in this period after 1950 when the labour movement declined. He argued:

(a) An enterprise union is egotistic in nature, since union members, blue collar and white collar workers, with no fixed employment duration but employed on a lifetime basis, seek improvements of working conditions and security of job status only as employees of the company.

(b) Under such circumstances, it is evident that the interests of the working class as a whole are ignored. Moreover, the interests of temporary workers of the same company are also disregarded.

In this way, Ōkōchi dealt with a fundamental question of the enterprise union, pointing out that it easily becomes a 'yellow' union — a weakness not apparent in American and European trade unions.

Recently a new version of the established theory has gained currency among researchers on Japanese labour problems, supplanting Ōkōchi's original version. It is an enterprise union theory based on an 'internal labour market' and is advanced by such researchers as Shirai Taishirō[3] and Kōshirō Kazuyoshi.[4]

Ever since Ōkōchi's studies, the organisational form of a labour union has been thought to be determined directly by the structure of the labour market. Ōkōchi argued that the labour market was of a closed nature based on an individual enterprise. According to the theory of the 'internal labour market', with the development of advanced capitalism there is an increasing necessity to prevent the transfer of the labour force and to balance supply and demand of labour within an enterprise. The labour market, therefore, becomes an internal one. This theory says that consequently the organisational form of labour unions will necessarily be an 'all-member-entry type enterprise union' (union shop) — a phenomenon common to highly developed capitalistic states.

Koike Kazuo, for one, based on an international comparative study of his own, argues that employees' organisations in the advanced countries of Europe and America substantially resemble Japanese enterprise unions.[5] Taira Kōji goes a step further to say that Japanese enterprise unions are best suited to highly developed capitalistic societies and that their organisational forms will become excellent models for unions in other advanced capitalistic countries as well.[6] According to Koike and Taira, all-member-entry type enterprise unions may be expected to increase in Japan, and there seems to be virtually no possiblity of such unions being displaced by other forms.

Looking next at the functions of an enterprise union, many of those advocating the 'internal labour market' theory, unlike Ōkōchi, take a positive view of enterprise unions and even commend them. Shirai Taishirō, for example, praises the function of enterprise unions because of what he sees as their contribution to Japan's rapid economic growth. His arguments in summary are as follows: (1) Enterprise unions have promoted technical innovations and changes in industrial structure. (2) In the period of Japan's rapid economic growth, enterprise unions achieved remarkable results in improving wages and working hours: nominal wages for Japanese workers surpassed those of British, French, and Italian workers. (3) When economic growth declined after the first 'oil shock', enterprise unions helped to brake inflation by agreeing to low wage increases. They also helped management adjust to the adverse economic conditions after the oil shock by co-operating in employment adjustments (by not filling vacancies, voluntary retirement, shifting of employees, and temporary transfers), and thus prevented the occurrence of massive unemployment. (4) Enterprise unions have come to have a greater say in decisions on employment and working conditions through an improved participation. (5) Enterprise unions are more democratic than trade unions in the US and Europe.[7]

In my opinion, such a view confuses recognition of the fact that there exists a *basis* for enterprise unions to come easily into being in Japan with the evaluation of the *actual functioning* of such unions. It often conceals various defects inherent in enterprise unions and leads to simply praising the status quo.

As regards the organisational form of an enterprise union, the established theory ignores the fact that there are three types of labour unions in Japan. These are: the 'all-member-entry type', the 'plural-type' (two or more unions coexisting within an enterprise), and the 'new-type' labour union. It is true that in Japan at present the 'all-member-entry' enterprise unions are the most numerous, but the established theory's prediction that these unions will greatly increase in number in the years to come is unsound for two reasons: first, the theory ignores the existence of 'plural-type' enterprise unions within many enterprises; second, contrary to the established theory, in Japan labour unions of a type different from the traditional enterprise unions (which we may term 'labour unions of a new type'), are being created and continue in existence.[8]

In large private sector corporations, the 'all-member-entry' enterprise unions no doubt predominate in number and constitute the core of Japan's labour movement. This basic type of enterprise union has, however, often stimulated the emergence of its opposite, the 'plural-type union' (consisting of a majority union and a minority union). The postwar labour movement in Japan contains innumerable examples of splits which occurred at the time of decisive events in important unions.[9] Most of the minority unions born after the splits have survived. Because analysis of Japanese labour unions has long been plagued by the established theory, which proclaimed that they exist as enterprise unions of the 'all-entry type', cases of 'plural-type' unions are almost completely neglected, and quantitative trends go undetected. Yet, from various surveys now available on private sector corporations, it seems that there are many plural-type unions today.[10]

According to reports of the Ministry of Labour, plural-type labour unions came into being at the rate of some 300 each year during the 1960s,[11] and such unions account for about 12 per cent of the enterprise unions belonging to *Sōhyō* (General Council of Trade Unions of Japan).[12] In 1982 Sōhyō claimed that there were 768 plural-type company unions within its organisation. The Japan Federation of Employers' Associations (Nikkeiren) said in its survey that such unions account for 15.1 per cent of corporations affiliated with it (1980). Table 1 reveals that some 41 per cent of labour dispute cases in the private sector handled by the Central Labour Relations Committee *(Chūrōi)* concern plural-type labour unions.

TABLE 1 NUMBER OF PRIVATE SECTOR LABOUR DISPUTES HANDLED BY THE CENTRAL LABOUR RELATIONS COMMITTEE (CHŪRŌI)

Year	Total number of disputes	Disputes in plural-type labour unions	Percentage
1967	509	219	43
1968	503	212	42
1969	489	229	45
1970	513	236	46
1971	495	219	44
1972	650	307	47
1973	564	244	43
1974	625	263	42
1975	745	268	36
1976	675	228	34
1977	615	213	35
1978	634	262	41
1979	529	222	42
Yearly average	580	240	41

Source: Annual reports by the Central Labour Relations Committee cited in Kawanishi, 1981, p. 7.

These surveys indicate that plural-type unions are no longer negligible in the private sector. Furthermore, plural-type unions are more evident in the government and public employees' sectors: there are six unions in the Japanese National Railway, four in the Ministry of Posts and Telecommunications, and eight among teachers.

Contrary to the established theory, there is a growing tendency toward formation of 'new-type' labour unions that may undermine existing enterprise unions. This tendency is particularly conspicuous in medium, small, very small companies — the 'periphery' of the labour movement.[13] A trend to the formation of craft (horizontal) unions, temporary workers' unions, and part-time workers' unions is also apparent. Further, there are moves to organise labour unions for the mentally ill and physically handicapped, for those above 50 years of age (as employees in this age-group are vulnerable to dismissals, they seek greater security of employment), and for female and jobless workers. These labour unions, with organisational forms and a consciousness which transcend the scope of an individual company, adopt a keen stance of opposition toward discrimination and assert independence and autonomy vis-a-vis the 'core' workers. This new labour movement tends to organise workers at small and medium-scale companies first, then the stratum of 'non-elite' workers in large corporations. New-type labour unions thus exclude only permanent elite-workers (male employees on the regular payroll of private large corporations).

The established theory of Japanese labour unions deals only with a minority of workers, i.e., those employed on a permanent basis. Even within this stratum of elite-workers, many belong to plural-type unions ignored by established theory; thus the established theoretical framework takes even less than the organised 30 per cent of the labour force into account. In short, the established theory, which seeks to comprehend the total situation of Japanese labour unions by means of the single concept of the all-entry type union, is inadequate.

Are the effects of enterprise unions really as positive as the established theory maintains? The advocates of the enterprise union cannot draw upon empirical studies to prove their contention.

Empirical studies on enterprise unions in those key industries which contributed to Japan's rapid economic growth have been conducted by Yamamoto Kiyoshi for the automobile industry,[14] Matsuzaki Tadashi for the steel industry,[15] Inagami Takeshi for the steel, telecommunications etc.,[16] and Kawanishi Hirosuke for the electric machines and chemical industries.[17] Only Inagami presents a positive view of the function of the enterprise unions. But his survey, based simply on a large-scale questionnaire, is limited to an investigation of workers' consciousness. He conducted little in-depth analysis on whether enterprise unions contribute to the preservation and improvement of labour conditions of workers on the shop-floor.

Yamamoto, Matsuzaki, Kawanishi and others who have carried out detailed survey research on enterprise unions, employing intensive survey methods, arrived at conclusions which are critical of the enterprise union's effects. Their findings were, first, when we inquire whether enterprise unions have contributed to the workers' wage increase, the answer is no. Table 2 shows the rate of increase of real wages in large corporations during the period of rapid economic growth. It is true that Japan's wage levels rose steadily throughout the postwar period. But the wage increase rate in the period of rapid economic growth cannot be regarded as very high when compared with that during the years of reconstruction (1952-54).

TABLE 2   AVERAGE LABOUR INCOME (LABOUR SHARING RATION) AND INCREASE IN PRODUCTIVITY AND WAGES (YEARLY AVERAGE)

Size of enterprise		Period					
		I	II		III		IV
		1951-1954	1955-1959	1960-1964	1965-1969	1970-1973	1974-1979
More than 1,000 workers	Labour income ratio	39.1	37.6	31.4	31.7	32.9	38.3
	Rate of increase of value-added labour productivity	12.0	9.5	10.1	13.4	7.0	4.9
	Rate of increase of cash wages per worker	13.8	5.4	8.3	10.6	11.5	5.8
'A' auto company	Labour income ratio	70.5	38.4	20.9	30.4	37.9	55.2

Source: Yamamoto, 1981, p. 114; 1982, p. 17.

Japanese workers' wages rose 13.8 per cent annually during 1951-54. They increased 5.4 per cent in the first half (1955-59) of the initial period of rapid economic growth, 8.3 per cent in the second half (1960-64); 10.6 per cent in the first half (1965-69) of the second period of rapid economic growth and 11.5 per cent in the second half (1970-73). From these figures it is apparent that the wage increase rate in the rapid economic growth period levelled off or declined slightly when compared with the years of reconstruction. When both the bargaining strength of labour unions and productivity growth are taken into account, the wage increase rate is seen as relatively higher in the 1951-54 period than in later years. In other words, the bargaining strength of labour unions was stronger in the period 1951-54. In 1955, the Japan Council of Metal Workers' Unions (IMF-JC) assumed the leadership of the big company enterprise unions. Since then, the rate of wage increases has slowed somewhat. The sharp rise in wage levels after 1970 was only a reflection of 'labour force shortage' accompanying the overheated Japanese economy at that time.

It is the labour income ratio[18] which shows the labour unions' bargaining strength. Table 2 shows that the labour income ratio tended to decline, registering 39.1 per cent from 1951 to 1954, and 32.9 per cent from 1970 to 1973. The lowest labour income ratio of 31.4 per cent, from 1960 to 1964, reveals that out of eight working hours a labourer worked 2.5 hours daily for his wage and 5.5 hours to produce company profits. We may therefore conclude that during the period of rapid economic growth the workers' relative position versus capital deteriorated; the bargaining power of labour unions weakened.

The automobile industry is a typical area sustaining Japan's rapid economic growth. Let us consider 'A' (employing 57,800 workers) as representative. At 'A' corporation, the leading automaker in Japan, the labour income ratio reached the high level of 70.5 per cent in the 1951-54 period, when its labour union was said to be one of the most powerful in Japan. But the ratio declined markedly, dropping to 20.9 per cent at the lowest point in the second period, when a rightist second union assumed the leadership. According to a calculation by Yamamoto Kiyoshi, the corporation's labour productivity rose at a yearly average of 15.6 per cent in the preceding 18 years, and gross profits rose an extraordinary 24.6 per cent whereas during the same period real wages increased by a mere 4.5 per cent.[19] These figures demonstrate that 'A' corporation's labour union was unable to exert much pressure for wage increases during the rapid economic growth period.

From this we may safely conclude that wage increases in the period of rapid economic growth were not brought about by the labour union's bargaining strength, but merely through the 'enlargement of the pie' resulting from rapid economic growth and shortage in the available labour force. Labour unions' bargaining power over wages was reduced even further when economic growth slackened.

From 1974 to 1979 labour income rate rose somewhat, but the rate of wage increase declined to only 5.8 per cent, about half of the rate prevailing during the period of rapid economic growth. This means that the growth in the labour income rate was not a result of the bargaining strength of labour unions but simply a result of productivity decline ('shrinkage of the pie').

Did the enterprise union contribute to the maintenance and expansion of employment? There are no grounds for assuming so.

It is true that there was an overall increase in the number of workers employed in the period of rapid economic growth. But to know whether or how much the unions contributed to this expansion of employment we have to examine the content of the increase in different categories of employment. Since, in substance, the employment increase occurred in the strata of those workers who were not allowed to enter the enterprise union, it is unreasonable to conclude that enterprise unions had anything to do with it. The most important industries that sustained Japan's rapid economic growth were automobile, steel, shipbuilding, and chemical. The data (Tables 3 and 4) show a remarkable increase in employment in each of these industries. But, with the exception of the chemical industry which is an equipment industry, employment increased substantially only for temporary workers and subcontracted workers while the expansion rate for regular workers was negligible. In the automobile industry, for example, against the base index of 100 for the period from 1952 to 1954, the number of regular workers declined slightly to 99 from 1955 to 1959 and rose to 125 from 1960 to 1962. In contrast, the contingent of temporary workers grew tremendously, with the index registering 307 for the 1955-59 period and 487 for the 1960-62 period against 100 for the 1952-54 period.

TABLE 3   INDEX OF DISTRIBUTION OF REGULAR AND NON-REGULAR WORK FORCE

	I	II	
	1952-1954	1955-1959	1960-1962
Automobile industry			
Regular workers	100	99	125
Temporary workers	100	307	487
Total	100	109	174
Shipbuilding industry			
Regular workers	100	101	104
Temporary workers	100	187	124
Subcontracted workers	100	236	237
Total	100	126	123
Steel industry			
Regular workers	100	102	133
Temporary and daily workers	100	129	163
Total	100	105	136
Chemical industry			
Regular workers	100	131	136
Temporary workers	100	95	45
Total	100	125	112

Source: Yamamoto Kiyoshi, Nihon rōdō shijō no kōzō (Structure of the Japanese labour market), Tokyo 1967, pp. 72-73.

TABLE 4   DISTRIBUTION OF REGULAR AND NON-REGULAR WORK
FORCE (1960-1962 AVERAGE, IN PER CENT)

	Regular workers	Temporary workers	Subcontract workers	Total (numbers)
Automobile industry	63.3	36.7		100.0 (36,312)
Shipbuilding industry	66.8	8.5	24.8	100.0 (107,404)
Steel industry	87.2	12.8		100.0 (204,572)
Chemical industry	93.9	6.1		100.0 (36,946)

Source: Yamamoto (1967).

The shipbuilding industry shows a similar pattern. The index for regular workers recorded 101 for the 1955-59 period and 104 for the 1960-62 period against 100 for the 1952-54 period. But the index for temporary workers jumped to 187 for the 1955-59 period and to 124 for the 1960-62 period. In the case of subcontract workers, the increase is even higher: the index shows an extraordinary expansion of 236 for the 1955-59 period and 237 for the 1960-62 period.

Hence the employment expansion in the early period of Japan's rapid economic growth meant, in reality, increased job opportunities for temporary workers and subcontract workers who were beyond the orbit of the enterprise union. Certainly, in the last stage of the rapid economic growth, some temporary workers and subcontract workers became regular workers. Yet this occurred only in a situation in which the corporations, faced with a severe labour shortage, could no longer hire temporary and subcontract workers. The rise in employment for some 20 years until the first oil shock, therefore, was not a result of the bargaining strength of the enterprise unions.

Nor can one say that the enterprise unions exerted any efforts to maintain employment when they were confronted with recession after the oil shock. On the contrary, the enterprise unions in several industries actively co-operated with management in implementing massive lay-offs. In the shipbuilding industry, for instance, 30.6 per cent of the staff (white collar), 36.7 per cent of the regular workers, 44 per cent of the temporary workers and 52.8 per cent of the subcontracted workers were laid off (see Table 5).

Minority labour unions (Sōhyō-affiliated) opposed the cut-backs, but Dōmei-affiliated majority unions backed management. Many majority unions even took the initiative and advised the management to reduce the work force. One example is the enterprise union of Sumitomo Heavy Machinery Industries. This company, with 12,409 employees, had its work force reduced by 31.3 per cent, or 3,878 workers, from 1977 to 1979. (During the same period, the six major Japanese shipbuilding companies slashed their work force by 22.7 per cent or 44,259 workers in total.)[20] In implementing the dismissals, Sumitomo set a standard for 'voluntary retirement', which meant that either husband or wife (when both were employees), older workers, and union activists were fired. Moreover, 17 members of the minority first union (affiliated with Sōhyō) were fired for political reasons. The majority second union (affiliated with Dōmei) actively supported these dismissals. Members of the second union and non-unionist company executives too applied pressure on 54 workers who resisted 'voluntary retirement', for several days encircling them on the shop-floor.

TABLE 5   WORK FORCE IN THE SHIPBUILDING INDUSTRY

	Number of Employees		Number of slashed workers (A-B)	Slash rate (%) (A-B)/(A)
	1974 (A)	1980 (B)		
Staff	63,148	43,796	19,452	30.6
Regular workers	117,605	74,470	43,135	30.7
Temporary workers	3,445	1,928	1,517	44.0
Subcontract workers	89,706	42,386	47,320	52.8
Total	273,904	162,580	111,324	40.6

Note: Based on 'Maritime Statistics Monthly Report' and 'Shipbuilding and Machinery Statistics Monthly report' by Ministry of Transport.

Source: General Federation of Shipbuilding Workers' Union (ed.), *Mitō e no chōsen* (Challenging the Unknown), Tōkyō 1981, Rōdō Jumpōsha, p. 74.

Such behaviour on the part of enterprise unions was not limited to the shipbuilding industry. In the electric machinery industry, Oki Electric Industry Company, with 13,000 employees, dismissed, for ideological (i.e. political) reasons, 93 union members affiliated to the Japan Socialist Party, the Japan Communist Party, or the 'new left'. It was the first 'Red Purge' since 1960 in the Japanese coal industry. Oki's enterprise union not only did not oppose this action, but actively supported it.

It is a fact that fixed working hours have been reduced in Japan since the period of rapid economic growth, partly as a result of the spread of the five-day working week. However, it would be wrong to see this as a result of the bargaining strength of enterprise unions.

Management sacrificed nothing by shortening working hours. A survey (see Table 6) on management's motives for shortening working hours does not show any influence of the unions' bargaining efforts. Concessions by management to labour are minimal, as can be seen in

TABLE 6   ARGUMENTS FOR THE INTRODUCTION OF A FIVE-DAY WORK WEEK

Argument Size of enterprise	For raising attendance rate	For raising production efficiency	As an effect of increased productivity	For increased safety at work	For employees' health and increase of leisure-time	To decrease commuting
TOTAL	26.9	35.3	11.8	48.5	76.6	2.1
Over 5,000 workers	13.2	40.7	20.4	41.9	86.2	3.0
1,000-4,999	19.2	42.5	13.7	42.5	85.1	4.6
500-999	22.7	40.9	13.6	42.7	76.8	3.6
300-499	32.6	41.3	14.1	44.6	77.2	5.4
Sub total over 300	20.2	41.7	14.9	42.7	82.6	4.2
1-299	30.0	32.1	10.2	51.5	73.5	1.0

Note: As the responses were given in plural, the total does not equal 100 per cent.

Source: Ministry of Labor: *Shūkyū futsuka-sei no chōsa* (Survey of Five-day Work Week), 1973.

the item of 'distribution rate of gains of increased productivity', a mere 11.8 per cent. The survey indicates that management is willing to cut working hours for the retention and effective utilisation of employees, and, as a result of this, for productivity increases. It follows that management gained more profits than before by cutting working hours.

Moreover, management has made up for the reduction in fixed working hours by freely adjusting the volume of overtime hours to suit changing circumstances. This trend is particularly apparent in the key industries that sustained Japan's rapid economic growth, shipbuilding, steel, automobile, and electrical machinery. According to Yamamoto Kiyoshi, average monthly overtime is 18 hours for the entire manufacturing industry, 12 hours, the lowest, for the chemical industry, 17 hours each for the automobile and electrical machinery industries, and 30 hours for the shipbuilding industry.[21] This reliance on overtime work is possible in Japan because the length of work in excess of 48 hours a week is entrusted to collective bargaining between the employer and the enterprise union of an individual company under Article 36 of the Labour Standards Law. Since the bargaining strength of the enterprise union is questionable in Japan, management can make employees work overtime almost indefinitely, while paying no more than an additional 25 per cent in wages.

The above findings are reinforced by an empirical study of the steel industry by Matsuzaki Tadashi.[22] At major Japanese steel corporations working hours were altered in 1970, for the first time in 50 years, from three teams working three shifts to four teams working three shifts. Labour unions advertised this as a fruit of their bargaining leverage, claiming that the change brought an additional 15 holidays a year for workers. But a closer examination of this transaction tells us that management lost nothing by changing working hours and that the bargaining strength of labour unions played virtually no part in bringing it about. A cut in working hours entailed an increase in the number of workers needed to attain a certain production volume, resulting in an increase in labour costs. Management quite naturally sought compensation for this by raising the intensity of labour, thereby increasing productivity. The policy adopted, therefore, was for companies to curb increases in the number of workers and to tighten controls during working hours.

Table 7 shows the change in the number of workers, following the 1970 change in work shifts, at the 'F' steel mill (Japan's largest, most up-to-date integrated steel mill at the time) of the 'N' Steel Pipe Company with 40,477 employees. Theoretically, the 1970 change should have increased the number of workers for one team by 1,813 or 33.3 per cent, but actually this number increased only by 246 or 4.5 per cent. When the change in work shifts occurred, the management simultaneously tried to reduce necessary personnel by reorganising the composition of each work team.

TABLE 7 CHANGE IN NUMBER OF WORKERS FOLLOWING ALTERA-
TION OF WORK SHIFTS AND SHORTENING OF WORKING
HOURS

	Old Formation (A)	New Formation (B)	(B)-(A)
Net number of workers	4,464	5,124	+660
Workers kept for lunch-time operation	201	96	−105
Additional workers not at work	608	278	(−330)
(Foremen)	(628)	(734)	(+106)
Chief workers	165	186	+21
Total	5,438	5,684	+246

Source: Matsuzaki, 1982, p. 221.

The means used by the management for slashing the work force included mechanisation of the manufacturing process; limiting the number of workers required (based on normal work volume, not peak time work volume); raising workers' technical skill standards; cutting the number of workers at workshops where work volume was decreasing; reorganising workshops; revising the frequency of operations; and slashing the number of regular workers by placing more orders outside. By thus increasing the intensity of labour, management reduced the personnel required per shift.

The management also devised another means to slash the work force: a reduction in the number of workers kept for meal (lunch) time operation. At a Japanese steel mill running a continuous operation 24 hours daily, workers were divided into six groups and by turn given 45 minutes for lunch. For this purpose, a certain number of workers were kept for lunch time operation in accordance with a set formula.[23] Management succeeded in slashing the number of 'lunch-time workers' by two methods: first it split workers who previously comprised 6 groups into 8 groups for lunch time. (An increase in the number of workers' groups eating lunch at a given time means a reduction in the number of workers held over for one lunch time operation.) Secondly, it reduced the time allowed for lunch from the previous 45 minutes to 25 minutes.

Management also tightened controls on working hours by introducing the following measures: it slashed a day's total break time from one hour to 45 minutes; it abolished the 'take-over' time of 10 minutes before commencing work and 5 minutes after leaving work (an additional wage was given to pay for take-over time since it was treated as overtime work); and it made it obligatory, instead, for workers to take-over within regular working hours. The starting and closing time, which until then had been recorded at the central office, was now recorded at the workshop level. By these means, working hours were shortened by only one hour and four minutes a week, or by 41 hours and 45 minutes a year, compared with the previous working hours. The working-hour reduction was less than half of the 98-hour a year cut the labour unions had demanded.

In addition, management drew up a yearly plan under which workers were obliged to take paid holidays on schedule. The plan was devised in order to reduce the total number of personnel required to fill vacancies occurring when workers took holidays. This meant that workers were forced to give up the legally-guaranteed right to take paid holidays freely.

Shorter working hours in the steel industry, therefore, were introduced by management at the expense of workers who had to give up rights and practices guaranteed in the previous conventional working-hour system. In other words, management employed various means to raise the intensity of labour by cutting working hours. As a result, workers at steel mills were subjected to harder labour under stricter controls.

Labour unions in the Japanese steel industry still show the same weakness. The strong competitive edge of Japanese steelmakers on the international market stems from labour-management relations such as described above.

Finally, perhaps the greatest defect of the enterprise union is that it is an 'auxiliary instrument' of personnel administration. A case study of the structure of an enterprise union under the joint labour-management consultation system and of its internal democracy at workshop level supports this claim.

The survey, conducted by the writer, throws light on the workings of the enterprise union at 'H' plant of 'H' electric company — an electric machinery giant in Japan with about 65,000 workers.[24]

Management's basic policy at the plant is to embrace the entire life-style of the employees and to integrate workers in the company as if into a 'quasi-Gemeinschaft'. To pursue this basic objective, management views the enterprise union as one component of the 'company community' and utilises it as an auxiliary organ. The institutional framework for this purpose is none other than the labour-management consultation system. Under this system, management actively propagates the whole of its business plan to the labour union, seeking its consent. For its part, the labour union intervenes only on such matters as maintenance of work load and preservation of piece wages.

Nevertheless, any measure of rationalisation taken up at the labour-management consultation is then considered to have obtained approval of the union. Thus the labour-management consultation system is, under the good name of workers' participation, an instrument which converts the union into an auxiliary instrument of management, and, as a result, employees are controlled twofold, both by management and by the union, for the increase of productivity. Under such labour-management relations, the workshop organisation of a union becomes an organisation which, under the hegemony of management, mobilises its members to increase productivity.

What follows is an outline of the results of a comparative survey of the 'H' enterprise union's two subordinate groups. One is the electrician group which is said to be the strongest in the union, the other is the casting group which is rated to be of average strength.

In the election of shop stewards for both groups, the section chief, who is not a union official, participates. After considering the production situation of the enterprise and the general political situation, the section chief recommends a certain candidate to the senior or responsible worker. Then the chairman of the shop stewards committee, himself a senior worker, nominates as a candidate for shop steward the person recommended by the section chief. Consequently, no election based on free announcements of individual candidacy has ever been held in the union at 'H' plant. A shop steward is nominated by the company's section chief. Shop stewards are chosen mainly from among the senior workers. The managerial ranking order of group chief — semi-group chief — ordinary ranks is automatically reproduced in the labour union's hierarchy: chairman of shop stewards committee — shop stewards secretary — ordinary shop stewards committee members.

Shop stewards of both groups, the electrician group and the casting group, when dealing with complaints from union members, settle matters from the standpoint of management. They are unwilling to stand up to management in order to improve working conditions but concentrate, instead, on raising productivity. The case of the electricians' section of the 'H' enterprise union (said to be 'the strongest one') is characteristic: workers there are most interested in the three 'primary' questions of overtime work, paid holidays, and standard working hours. But shop stewards make no attempt to shorten overtime work, which reaches an average of 75 hours a month per worker, despite strong demands for reductions by union members. This is because the right to conclude a contract on overtime working hours lies in the hands of the executive committee of the enterprise union which, co-operating as it does with management to raise productivity, has no interest in reducing overtime.

As for paid holidays, shop stewards proceed from the standpoint of personnel administration. At the electricians' group workshop, a break or pause is counted in minutes under a management system called the 'working rate' which oversees the workers. The 'working rate' is announced by management for each team of workers in a sum, and from it the piece wages per team are strictly calculated. Consequently, all the team members are lumped together and are obliged to strive hard to raise the 'working rate', and so are driven into competition against one another. In this situation, to take a paid holiday or even to be absent due to illness must naturally be seen as damaging the other team members' interest. The team leader, who is also shop steward, claimed that 'those who take paid holidays are the lazy ones'.

The third problem of standard working hours at this workshop is that standard working hours are inadequate to handle the actual workload which requires a high level of skills (e.g. assembly of large motors). Actual working hours often exceed the fixed standard. As a result, the piece wages of a team are reduced, and team members often call on the labour union to negotiate for a revision upwards of the standard working hours. But the shop steward, who at the same time represents the lowest echelon of the managerial ranking order, keeps an eye on team members with a stopwatch in his hand and invariably orders them to complete work according to the fixed time. In this way, the shop steward not only ignores workers' demands for extending the standard working hours but in fact acts to get an extraordinary workload fulfilled. Moreover, shop stewards assess the performance of team members in fixing their wages. This procedure, in which workers are discriminated against in terms of promotion and wages, destroys the equality principle which is fundamental to organised labour. It is a widespread practice in Japanese corporations.

The 'H' company study demonstrates clearly how a typical enterprise union is bereft of any independent functioning power at the basic level, that of the workshop, but proves instead to be an auxiliary organ of management.

Another example of an enterprise union devoid of democracy may be found in the report on a giant motor company presented by Yamamato Kiyoshi.[25]

According to this study, union officials of 'A' automaker are categorised as 'career', 'non-career A', and 'non-career B'. The 'career' official, typically a graduate of a famous university, is guaranteed a future managerial position. The 'non-career A' official is a middle or lower level clerk or technician and a graduate of a second-rank university or college or a senior high school. The 'non-career B' official is a 'senior worker' responsible for workers in a section or foreman. The ranking of these officials in the union is displayed in Figure 1.

FIGURE 1 COMPOSITION OF UNION OFFICIALS IN ENTERPRISE FEDERATION (JIDŌSHA RŌREN) AND ENTERPRISE UNION OF 'A' CORPORATION

xx Chairman of Federation of Japan Automobile Workers' Unions (Jidōsha rōren), W	x Secretary General (Head Office, Personnel Administration, W)	x Chairman of A Union (Head Office Sales Dept.)	xx Vice-Chairman of A Union (T Factory, Experiment, W)		x A Branch Chief (Computer Shop, W)
					xxx B Branch Chief (Casting Shop B)
		xxx Vice-Secretary General (Y Factory, Engine Shop, B)	xxx Vice-Chairman of A Union (Y Factory, Tools, W)		xx C branch Chief (Staff, Engineering Work, W)
			xxx Secretary (O Factory Assembly Line, B)	x Chief of Organization Dept. (Z Factory, Personnel Administr. W)	xxx D Branch Chief (Painting Shop, B)
		x Chief of Planning (Head Office, Personnel Administr. W)		xx Chief of Youth Dept. (Y Factory, Production, W)	xxx E Branch Chief (Machine Shop, B)
		xx Vice-Chief of Planning (Y Factory, Accounting, W)		xx Chief of Information (M Factory, Production, W)	xx F Branch Chief (Inspection Shop, W)
		x Information Dept. Chief (Head Office Personnel Administration, W)		x Chief of Personnel Administration (Head Office, Personnel Administration, W)	xx G Branch Chief (Body Shop, B)
					x H Branch Chief (Staff, Business Work, W)

Note: 1. x = 'Career', xx = 'Non-career type A', xxx = 'Non-career type B'.
2. (. . .) = shop of origin, town (abbreviated).
3. B = blue collar workers, W = white collar workers.

Source: Yamamoto, 1981, p. 223.

The 'career' officials occupy leading positions. Many of them become union officials after about seven years' work in the personnel and labour divisions of management. After completing their stint in the union, they return to their previous divisions and assume posts at the level of department chief. In the labour union of 'A' corporation, the 'career' officials play the major role in planning union policy and activity. The chairman of the Federation of Japan Automobile Workers' Unions is seen as representing and balancing the interests of both 'career' officials and 'non-career' officials.

As in 'A' company, the democracy prescribed by union rules is not observed in the elections of union leaders. Table 8 shows that in 'A' corporation the number of seats on the union's standing committee and the number of candidates were always equal. This is because the number of candidates chosen by the union's executive committee never exceeded the number of vacancies. Rank-and-file union members are, therefore, in reality denied the freedom to stand as candidates for election.

TABLE 8   ELECTION OF STANDING COMMITTEE OF 'A' CORPORATION'S LABOUR UNION

Month of election	Full number of positions	Candidates	Voters	Voting rate	Effective voting rate	Average polling score rate
				%	%	%
1972.8	182	182	59,908	99.72	99.08	98.58
1973.8	193	193	63,653	99.75	99.08	98.59
1974.8	198	198	65,131	99.78	99.32	98.83
1975.8	205	205	66,115	99.94	99.44	99.00
1976.8	210	210	67,719	99.97	99.74	99.48
1977.2	7	7	9,333	99.99	99.85	100.00
1978.8	218	218	71,737	99.96	99.90	99.69

Note: The election held in February 1977 was a mid-year election.

Source: Yamamoto, 1981, p. 45.

Another curious fact is that the polling score is reportedly as high as 98.58 per cent to 100 per cent in every election. The reason for this seemingly miraculous finding is that balloting is not secret: in fact, department chiefs and union officials keep watch on the voting, and sometimes votes cast in opposition are even checked to identify the voter. In short, there is no freedom to abstain from voting or to cast a vote against the executive committee.

At 'A' corporation's labour union, the persons heading the company's personnel and labour divisions occupy the union's key posts, closely supervise union members and thus co-operate with management in raising productivity. This kind of labour-management relations provides Japanese automakers with a competitive edge in international markets.

Conclusion

The enterprise unions in key industries do not play an effective role in tackling members' problems such as wages, working conditions, and shortening of working hours. Nor do they implement internal democracy. Rather they function as an auxiliary to management in the personnel sector. The positive assessment of such unions contained in the established theory is contradicted by a wealth of evidence gained in systematic, empirical investigations.

Democracy derailed: citizens' movements in historical perspective

Beverley Smith

I

Near Matsukawa, in Fukushima province, about 160 kilometres north of Tokyo, a monument has been erected to commemorate the outcome of the famous postwar trials of 19 men and one woman on a charge of criminal conspiracy. It has been alleged that these people were responsible for the derailment of a passenger train in the early hours of 17 August 1949. The Matsukawa case was before the courts for 14 years, including two hearings before the Supreme Court; and throughout this period, as the monument records, there was continuous public protest by those who believed that there had been a gross miscarriage of justice.

> The size and scope of this movement of popular solidarity has no precedent in either Japanese or world history. . . . on September 12, 1963, the people finally grasped total victory — the judgment of not guilty . . . When the people unite, their struggle is limitless. This monument commemorates the people's triumph.[1]

The public response to this case came to be known as the Matsukawa 'movement' (undō). As the first major popular movement of its kind in the postwar period it has an important place in the history of Japanese democracy.

At the outset of the Allied Occupation, the dominant concern in the minds of the Allies was to change the political structure so as to end a long history of authoritarianism and militarism. The expansionism of the 1930s was seen as no passing aberration but the outcome of policies laid down in the Meiji Restoration of 1868 and consolidated by the 1889 Constitution. The new Constitution introduced in 1947 not only banned war but also provided scope for civil liberties of a kind that had

157

never before existed in Japanese society. It was these reforms which made possible the outcry over the conduct of the Matsukawa trials.

It is sometimes said that Japanese democracy was imposed from above by General MacArthur. Such an interpretation overlooks the way in which the Japanese people, through their own actions, demonstrated both understanding and support of the spirit of the reforms. Both were necessary in the face of conservative opposition to social change.[2] It is true that accepance of the new ideas was a slow process and that the old authoritarian order was sustained by attitudes and social relationships associated with personal obligations to family, village, and state.[3] The reforms focused attention on the relationship between citizen and state, and discussion of this issue was not confined to intellectuals.[4] People long constrained by authority set about making their own decisions. In some places, workers took over factories, in what was known as production control *(seisan kanri),*[5] and farmers took charge of delivery of goods to ensure fair rationing. The official process of democratisation then went into rapid reverse. The Occupation authorities, in cooperation with the Japanese establishment, took action against what came to be seen as a threat to the restoration of conservative power.

According to Roberts, ten US intelligence agencies, with their Japanese agents, infiltrated virtually every politically significant organisation after 1945.[6] In Roberts' view:

> . . . taken as a whole, this joint operation to suppress the left wing was perhaps the most massive and certainly the most sophisticated machine for political sabotage ever set into motion, and whatever its net effect may have been, it was fervently welcomed by its beneficiaries — *zaikai* potentates and their right wing political establishment.[7]

The enemy they were mobilised against was not the right, reaction or fascism, but the left, and the struggle for grassroots democracy.

This was the background to the act of sabotage at Matsukawa. Those arrested were employees of the railways and the nearby Toshiba factory. It was alleged that they had planned the derailment as an act of reprisal against sackings. This was one of a number of similar crimes that occurred in 1949 for which the Japanese Communist Party was held responsible. After the war, Communists had been prominent in union leadership, and the Party was gaining in electoral support. These incidents, combined with the purges in the following year, reversed this trend. While many people accepted the official explanation of what happened, others had doubts. Some believed that the defendants had been framed and that the case was one of sabotage instigated by the Occupation authorities in collusion with the Japanese establishment. Criticism of the way in which the investigations and trials had been carried out was pervasive. Many feared a reversion to prewar practices of enforced confessions and collusion among police, prosecution and legal profession.

Public dissatisfaction was expressed through a number of organisations, the most prominent being the Matsukawa Case Counter Measures Council. Set up in 1958, this group included many citizens acting independently rather than as members of organisations. It was not a communist front, nor was it under the control of any single group; its purpose was confined to the Matsukawa issue. As it evolved, the organisation had 32 prefectural branches, workers' associations in every industrial city, and defence circles within numerous enterprises. A feature of the protest was the long marches which took place over hundreds of miles to attract public attention to proceedings in the courts. This citizen action took place concurrently with union protest, including assistance from Sōhyō, which backed the movement from 1956. Well-attended union picnics were held at Matsukawa for many years. The Japan Socialist Party did not support the movement until 1962, one year before the final verdict was handed down.

The influence of the Matsukawa movement carried beyond the participants to the general public through the press, films,[8] and popular literature. The writings and activities of the liberal intellectual, Hirotsu Kazuo (1891-1968) were very influential. A writer of the realist school of literature and translator of Chekhov,[9] Hirotsu became convinced of the defendants' innocence in 1953, and from then on was a prominent figure in campaigns. He wrote six books on the case as well as regular articles for the monthly journal *Sekai*. The Matsukawa case, with other crimes of the Occupation period, was a common theme in such best sellers of the period as *The Black Mist over Japan* by Matsumoto Seichō.[10] Matsumoto believed that the derailment of the train was one of a number of incidents planned by American intelligence agencies to discredit the left and prepare the way for anticommunism and the Korean War.[11] The popularity of such literature reflects the interest in politics and history that characterised the early postwar period.

Citizens acted independently, yet in an organised way, so that the response to the Matsukawa case was one of the first postwar citizens' movements. Such action reached a climax with the massive citizen protest at the renewal of the Japan-US Security Treaty in 1960, a protest both against militarism and the undemocratic way in which the treaty passed through parliament. The Prime Minister at the time was Kishi Nobusuke, a central figure in the industrial rationalisation programme of the 1930s, and a prominent member of Tōjō's wartime cabinet. The term 'citizens' movement' *(shimin undō)* was used in connection with the protest against the ratification of the Treaty and was later applied to citizen protest on environmental issues *(kōgai)*, including neighbourhood action on local problems, the campaigns of pollution victims and their supporters, and citizen opposition to developmental projects. *Kōgai* is usually translated as 'pollution' but the connotation is wider than that — *kōgai* can refer to factory noise, vibration, water shortage, obstruction of sunshine, and so on. The implication is one of 'public nuisance' or 'public wound' — a political as well as technical problem.

Political activity in the 1950s was intense. There is abundant evidence of distrust of the state, and concern over civil liberties, especially in action over changes to the education system and police powers. The restructuring of the economy and transition from coal to oil led to numerous industrial disputes and attempts to defend democracy in the workplace.[12] In his study of protest involving violence between 1952 and 1960 (numbering about 1,000 incidents), Yoshio Sugimoto found that in most cases the activists were workers, students, and Koreans.[13]

The citizens' movements which emerged in the 1960s were rather different. They have been described as 'spontaneous', meaning that the participants acted as individuals on their own initiative and not as members of organisations. Their sphere of activity was usually local, and their purpose specific.[14] These movements broke new ground in functioning as open, non-hierarchical associations in which the individual had scope to use his own initiative both in proffering ideas and taking action. A citizens' movement is different from a neighbourhood association whose activities, in the normal course of events, tends to conform to the needs and policies of the establishment. The problem of pollution and environmental destruction led to sharp conflict between citizens on the one hand and the bureaucracy and corporations on the other.

II

The high degree of centralisation and planning in the Japanese economy gives a distinctive character to environmental politics in Japan. While the 1947 Constitution provided for extensive local government autonomy, very poor provision was made for funding. This paved the way for conservative central government domination of local government for many years. Local autonomy was further diminished as the conservative forces revised the legislation in various ways between 1946 and 1955.[15] In the 1960s, the desirability of industrial development was articulated by the bureaucracy in close relationship with industry. In accordance with the All Japan General Development Plan of 1962, local government offered incentives to new industry including free land, tax incentives, and infrastructure. Control was maintained in the interest of the large corporations through the system of funding, assigned functions, and seconding of personnel.[16] Hata Hiromi described the outcome as a colonial type development.[17] In general, as local government attracted new industry, highly paid workers were introduced from outside the area, good opportunities for local people were few, and the bulk of profits flowed to Tokyo and Osaka. In addition, the localities suffered not only because of pollution but also because of the financial drain on local government in its effort to provide the infrastructure for incoming industries. As the pollution problem worsened, the bureaucracy, business and experts acted to suppress facts, evade action, and harass critics.[18] The use of riot police and company thugs *(sōkaiya)* was not uncommon.

It was as a result of public pressure that the first law concerning pollution was passed in 1967 (the Pollution Counter Measures Basic Law). It contained a qualification, insisted upon by MITI, that whatever measures were taken must be 'in harmony with the healthy development of the economy'. The lag in social development and the human suffering this entailed is well documented.[19] By 1970, environmental crisis had become the leading political issue. Fourteen more anti-pollution laws were passed and the phrase 'in harmony with the healthy development of the economy' was deleted. Apart from the pressure of public opinion, concern about the long term availability of raw materials and other factors indicated the need for change of policy, and the decision to make a major shift in the structure of the economy towards knowledge-intensive industries was announced at this time, before the oil shock. While there is no doubt that public pressure through citizen action, the media, the courts and local government had an effect on policy-making, it is not clear whether the outcome reflected any major compromise between bureaucratic and popular forces.

The impact of the citizens' movement on participating citizens and on particular institutions is obvious. Through citizen action it was established in the courts that citizens had environmental rights and corporations had a responsibility to protect life and wellbeing. The movements did much to establish the legitimacy of protest, no minor matter since ostracism and all kinds of intimidation had been common. For example, on the outbreak of *itai itai* disease, women, who were particularly susceptible, were told that they had no right to complain since it was woman's nature to suffer.[20] Women became involved through neighbourhood associations, but more significantly they also took part in political campaigns and direct action. Women young and old were prominent in the long and bitter struggle over mercury poisoning at Minamata; at Uzuki Bay women took direct action on their own initiative when health and livelihood were threatened by the construction of a large cement factory.

People began to use their own resources of knowledge and experiment. Since the experts often acted in the interests of bureaucracy and the corporations it was only by self-reliant action that they could establish the facts. Citizens' groups conducted opinion surveys, carried out environmental tests, prepared reports, developed alternative plans and undertook fact-finding journeys. The gap between layman and professional was bridged as people learned to value one another for complementary skills and insights. Ui Jun, of the Faculty of Urban Engineering at the University of Tokyo, set up *Jishu Kōza* (Citizens' Forum) at the university for the discussion of environmental problems. A progressive theory of knowledge pertaining to the study of science and society began to emerge.[21]

At the institutional level the gains were also clear. Locally based movements organised political campaigns, and by 1974 41 per cent of the population lived in prefectures or cities with progressive chief executives. In 1975 there were progressive governors in nine prefectures, including Tokyo, Kyoto, and Osaka. These governments introduced many innovatory measures in social welfare. Similarly, action through the courts in connection with pollution at Minamata, Niigata and Toyama not only secured compensation for victims but resulted in a significant body of case law relating to responsibility for pollution (1967-1969).[22]

Against these gains one must also consider the limits of the citizens' movements as a progressive force. Many of the participants in prevention-oriented movements seem to have been members of organisations of some kind. It was partly this that made political action possible. For some citizens it was their first experience of social protest, but this did not necessarily mean that they became involved in a new type of organisation. In many cases the campaigns were co-ordinated by committees whose members came from progressive organisations like the Japan Socialist Party or Japan Communist Party as well as conservative organisations like neighbourhood associations and agriculture co-operatives. It was at this level that an attempt was made to achieve a broadly participatory method of procedure in which no group would be dominant. While this encouraged people to avoid hierarchic structures, at the same time it set limits on the scope of discussion. Participants of all citizens' movements agreed that responsibility for the environmental crisis lay with the large corporations, bureaucracy and government.[23] Yet the movements provided little opportunity for deep discussion, let alone action, on social change at this level. Considering the scale of the problems and the extent of disaffection, citizens' movements may be said to have acted as a safety valve, confining popular disaffection at the level of local government and leaving central government and other institutions very largely untouched. As Ronald Acqua points out in his study of policy in medium-sized cities:

> Proponents of local reformist movements point with pride to their achievements in such areas as environmental protection and social welfare — and yet they find it difficult to relate these initiatives to the acquisition of real power in the Tokyo-based national political system.[24]

In their combined impact the citizens' movements appear to have been an effective progressive force. Yet, according to the surveys conducted by Margaret McKean, there was a significant conservative component in the prevention-oriented movements.[25] In some cases the reforms initiated by progressive governments were adopted generally. In other cases resistance in one location was obviated by co-operation elsewhere. A powerful state can take advantage of the vulnerability of a particular district, as happened in Fukui prefecture where cooperation between the central and local governments led to a proposal that nine nuclear power plants be located along Wakasa Bay in a district whose economy was suffering from overseas competition.[26] While the localised nature of the citizens' movements enhanced democratic decision-making and participation, the lack of any coordinated plan of action restricted their effectiveness. However, the very number and diversity of citizens' movements was at times an advantage since the authorities might more readily have neutralised a single organisation with a readily-identified executive.

Movements in defence of victims (of environmental pollution, etc.) had more difficulty securing official action than those in opposition to new industrial development. The latter had to confront opposition in communities divided by economic interest, as well as violence at factory gates, in offices, board rooms, and in the streets. That they were eventually successful may well be due not only to their own persistence and courage but also to the fact that there were at the time so many other actions, including the more conservative prevention-oriented movements. Where disease broke out in rural areas the victims could draw support from their own communities as farmers and fishermen, but the situation was different in the cities. The victims of pollution or adulteration in urban areas tended to be scattered and have few organisational resources. Because the cities have grown quickly, old and new residents sharply divided by political interests and loyalties may live in the same district. The arrival of a factory which carries with it a solid bloc of conservative votes may have a decisive effect on a neighbourhood. In any case, a protest of victims shows up the weakness of democracy; any resulting political successes are already too late.

Was the citizens' movement in Japan stimulated or inhibited by the Allied Occupation? Some authors refer to the provisions for local government in the 1946 Constitution as an American contribution to Japanese democracy.[27] Yet to the extent that American policy was directed at the restoration of conservative power (purged only of military influences) so it set in motion powerful forces against the 'grafting on' of the Constitution.[28] The struggles of the left and in the defence of the Constitution, linked in a spirited movement from the end of the war through to 1960, are expressions of democracy. The citizens' movement in Mishima, Shizuoka prefecture, in protest against the construction of a petrochemical complex on Enoura Bay, and a precursor of similar environmental movements which flourished in the early 1970s,[29] had its roots in the early postwar period. Among the leftists who were influential in Mishima was a group of intellectuals who had left Tokyo during the war to avoid the air raids and repression. In 1945 they set up in Mishima a Citizens' University open to all, its purpose among other things being to discuss the Constitution.[30] Similarly, Japan's first progressive local government, that of Governor Ninagawa in Kyoto, who took office in 1950 and held it until 1975, had its origins in opposition to the restored power of the corporations. Here too there was a positive attempt to encourage citizen understanding of the Constitution.[31] In Fukuoka prefecture, where the miners at Miike persisted for 300 days on strike, both local mayor and governor were socialists. The full weight of conservative American and Japanese pressure was imposed on these democratic initiatives.[32]

The citizens' movement in Mishima in 1963 was the first phase of the postwar environmental movement. Why, in view of the high level of political activity in the 1950s, was it only in Mishima that citizens perceived the implications of the new economic plans and made a stand for local interests and autonomy? In retrospect it seems that, in spite of the level of citizen interest in politics and the militancy of some unions, no dent had been made in conservative power by 1960, that union activity had never fully recovered from the setbacks of 1945-49,[33] and that the Japan Socialist Party had no comprehensive social programme or mass base. The Security Treaty was renewed in 1960 and the LDP remained in power. In response to this situation the JSP began to consider the need to pay more attention to grassroots politics. It was conviction on this matter which prompted Asukata Ichio (who became party chairman in 1977) to relinquish his Diet seat and to contest, successfully, the position of mayor of Yokohama.

Asukata's decision, and perhaps also some progressive decisions in the lower courts, provide strands of continuity between the 1950s and 1960s. Yet it is the discontinuities which are most striking. In 1960 Prime Minister Ikeda announced an income doubling scheme and, in the words of a 1963 Public Security Agency Report, 'the general expectations of rising living standards are now overwhelming and diffusing the progressive political movements'.[34] Built into economic planning were elements of social control that perpetuated the power of the state and obstructed opposition. By the 1960s, militant unionism had been contained within the structures of enterprise unionism in a dual economy where those with most cause for disaffection (temporary workers in large corporations, workers in small factories, day labourers, women workers and so on) had the least organisational resources. The rural population, on the other hand, had been the immediate beneficiaries of Occupation reforms and agricultural policy. This, coupled with gerrymander, made the countryside a secure foundation for the LDP during the turbulent period in the cities. Only after the penetration of rural areas by new industries did pollution and social diversification lead to changes of attitude and scope for political action, but by then the organised section of the working class, politically perceptive in the 1950s, was locked into company loyalties and poorly disposed to a wider view of social issues.

Just as the political activity of the 1950s became a spent force in the 1960s, with the exception of student protest, so the surge of political interest and activity in the citizens' movements also later lost its momentum. At the height of the environmental protest there was strong opposition to high economic growth rate policies (GNP-ism). Higher wages were seen as no compensation for the neglect of public amenities and health, and there was talk of 'the new poverty' *(atarashii hinkon)*. But, as in most industrialised countries, recession led to caution. Japanese people responded to officially inspired appeals to solidarity in the face of national difficulties such as energy shortage, or external problems such as the cold war and trade wars. Komiya Ryūtarō has written about the appearance of a 'siege mentality'.[35]

In the 1950s politics focused on factories, mines and schools. In the 1960s the arena shifted to the new industrial areas as entire communities were subjected to national plans for heavy industry. In the 1980s the critical issues are back in the workplace: automation and other technological change, the transfer of factories and agribusiness overseas, and the development of nuclear power. Only in the case of the nuclear power plants are these the kind of issues which would readily fall within the reach of citizens' movements. As in the 1950s those responsible for restructuring of the economy have set about coopting support in key areas. (Moves towards the unification of unions under right wing auspices are discussed in the labour section in this volume.) The rapidity of social change since the war, and the way in which it is guided by the state, has had a direct effect on the scope and effectiveness of opposition. Just as the political activism of the 1950s was checked, so the momentum of social protest generated in the late 1960s may well prove irrelevant to the new range of social problems.

While the citizens' movements opened up new concepts of citizen rights and access to power, their contribution to the growth of democracy has to be evaluated in the context of these wider interactions. There are signs that some of the apparent gains made by citizens' movements are already lost or in jeopardy. Whereas citizens' movements were able to establish rights of access to some public documents, new regulations make it a crime to release corporate secrets.[36] Reference to Minamata disease is being deleted from school textbooks.[37] In nuclear power plants, maintenance is carried out by some 100,000 day labourers in conditions grossly neglectful of health and industrial rights.[38] Whereas citizens in the early 1970s had perfected their own methods of monitoring environmental stress, much of the new technology will operate beyond the observation of most citizens. Saturated with television and other alienated forms of entertainment, the generation of the 1980s compares poorly with the politically-aware and literate generation of the 1950s. For a combination of reasons, the challenge to conservative power has been checked. At the local government level, the progressive gains have not been sustained.

III

Although there has been a decline in scale in the citizens' movements, the general political malaise has not affected them all. Those in opposition to nuclear and thermal power, the citizens' movement on Okinawa, and opposition to the airport at Narita are notable exceptions. Recent developments include the establishment of links between citizens' movements and industrial workers. While right wing trends have affected the labour movement in general, some minority labour organisations have emerged to give support to citizens' movements at Narita and elsewhere. The workers involved include metalworkers, electric power and textile workers, and railway men. These groups have ideas about citizen autonomy in relationship to the workplace and to economic and political structures in general. They offer strong resistance to the conservative appeal to national solidarity in the face of crisis.

The protest at Narita began as an attempt by farmers to defend their land against plans drawn up by the authorities without consultation with affected communities. This issue brought together activists who had been connected with the kind of conflicts characteristic of the 1950s, such as opposition to the presence of American bases, and union struggles.[39] The farmers also attracted support from citizens who had been opposed to the renewal of the Security Treaty and to Japan's indirect involvement in the Vietnam War. Though connected in the past with radical groups, especially students, it would be incorrect to regard the farmers' organisation as in any way a front. The farmers have maintained control over their movement. In 1967 they expelled members of the JCP for sectarian intervention, and in 1983 they expelled members of the Revolutionary Communist League on similar grounds.[40]

The decision to build the airport at Narita was made in 1962 after the rejection of other sites, some of which had a history of peasant struggle dating back to Meiji times.[41] The very fertile Sanrizuka district had once been imperial pasture. Some farmers had been living there for many generations, others had reclaimed land after the Pacific War. Among the activists were farmers, such as Shibuya Teisuke, who had been members of radical tenant unions before the war.[42] The Opposition League was formed at a meeting of 1,000 farmers in June 1966, within days of the official announcement of the choice of site.[43] The majority of the newcomers, some of whom were part-time farmers, accepted the government's terms of settlement, but the League launched a campaign of petitions, deputations, leafleting and action in the courts. In October 1967 the farmers clashed with 2,000 riot police who came to survey the land. From November 1967, Tokyo university students participated in the daily battles against the land survey, culminating in a violent confrontation with the authorities in September 1971. In 1973, one runway and facilities had been completed but by then the League had erected a 62 metre iron tower on the runway, and a smaller one of 31 metres. In 1977, following the announcement by the Fukuda Cabinet that the airport would be opened, a large national rally took place with support from anti-nuclear and anti-pollution movements, and minority organisations such as the *Buraku* (Japanese outcasts) Liberation League. On 6 May, in a surprise attack at dawn, riot police destroyed the towers, but in the face of continuing protest, the opening date was postponed. The League then carried out a campaign called 'the month of action connecting Sanrizuka with the rest of Japan'. During September, people from all over the country marched 700 kilometres from Osaka through Tokyo to Sanrizuka to express solidarity with the farmers. A 20 metre ferro-concrete fortress was erected by the League but dismantled by the authorities. In March 1978 the control tower was invaded and wrecked. Nevertheless, in May 1978, in the presence of 14,000 riot police, the new Tokyo International Airport was opened. In twelve years of controversy, five people had been killed, 7,000 wounded, 3,000 arrested. The fields of Sanrizuka had assumed the aspects of a civil war.

From the outset the struggle of the farmers was associated with foreign policy issues. About 50 of the farmers had actually struggled against the presence of American military bases in Japan in the 1950s.[44] It was argued that Narita might be used as a military base, or that the airport was necessary only because of the use made of Haneda (the existing Tokyo airport) by the United States in connection with the Vietnam War.[45] As Roger Bowen points out, the struggle was seen as an extension of the Vietnam War. The tactics were those of civil war.

Until his death in November 1979, the elected chairman of the Opposition League was Tomura Issaku, a Christian Socialist. In 1974, Tomura visited Thailand. On his return he spoke of the lynching by right-wing gangs of 27 peasants who were members of the Thai Farmers' Federation.[46] What was happening in Thailand was significant to the League because a precipitating factor in the overthrow of the Thai military dictatorship in 1973 was opposition to US bases. From 1973, American intelligence agencies had been giving support to Thai right-wing groups that were harassing peasant organisations.[47] When the Japanese Prime Minister, Tanaka, visited Thailand in 1974 he was confronted by large demonstrations in protest against the activities of Japanese enterprises. In Japan these developments were seen in the context of the Narita problem, and the relationship between the United States and Japan.

In the history of Japan's relationship with Southeast Asia, the Tomura visit and his discussion with Thai farmers is of historic significance. Since 1974, the Narita activists have maintained contact with Southeast Asia. In 1981 Koizumi Hidemasa, a member of the youth organisation, wrote to a correspondent in the Philippines:

> The ruling circles in Japan tell us that we live in the world's freest country. Our freedom however is purchased at the price of other people's bondage; big Japanese capital oppresses people not only at home but in the countries of the Third World. True freedom does not exist in Japan either; there are few free souls among us today. Instead of freedom we are given bare survival. So many Japanese live and toil under inhuman conditions. What kind of future lies in store for a dissolute country like ours? Only those willing to fight to preserve human values have managed to retain an independent spirit and they are not many. But they are this country's hope.[48]

The Opposition League has attracted funds and support from farmers elsewhere in Japan who are critical of the present state of Japanese agriculture. Unable to secure a livelihood from the heavily-capitalised but tiny farms, many farmers are obliged to combine seasonal work on the farm with poorly paid work in the cities. These people cannot fully enjoy the benefits of either rural or urban living, not to mention continuity of family life. On a national scale, self sufficiency in grain declined from 83 per cent to 43 per cent during the 15 years from 1960 to 1975. Fertile land lies fallow while foodstuffs are imported from the United States and Southeast Asia. In defending their own land, the Narita activists argue against the present relationship between town and country. They resist as bribery the government's offer of an irrigation project in return for cooperation over the airport. They also resist the more subtle state blandishments described by Irokawa Daikichi:

'If you want to break down the villages,' the rulers seem to say, 'just let them consume more than they produce. The way to smoke them out of their village ratholes is to send in a constant stream of cheap consumer goods — they'll have to come out and work to pay off their debts.'[49]

Margaret McKean found similar attitudes in other citizens' movements: affluence was seen as something 'forced on society by profit-seeking industrialists dependent on the perpetual expansion of markets', and it was argued that 'Japanese consumers would readily surrender this affluence if offered a choice and respite from advertising'. In this respect, McKean sees the environmental movement in Japan as further to the left than comparable groups in the United States.[50] Other writers have drawn attention to disillusionment with consumerism and industrialism as quite widely prevalent attitudes, and some argue that one reason for the high percentage of people dropping out of political parties is that no party has addressed this problem.[51]

While these attitudes may have led to apathy elsewhere, this is not the case at Narita, where citizen action has taken on a quasi-institutional character. The Worker/Farmer Unity Huts act as a head-quarters attracting visitors from other parts of Japan and Southeast Asia. Other movements, including those opposing nuclear power, have taken Sanrizuka as a model. But, in spite of attempts to create links across Japan, these movements are more isolated and vulnerable than in the early 1970s when citizen protest was nation-wide. The Narita struggle is associated in the minds of many Japanese with student violence and the Red Army, while the farmers' viewpoint and the issues involved have been obscured and played down by the media.

The issues are easily obscured. In the words of Eugene Smith, whose photographs record the tragedy of Minamata:

> When victims sue, when victims protest, when a desperate move causes public disruption of the daily status quo, it becomes terribly easy to reverse the role of the protagonists. Too often, it is somehow quite easy to believe that those who seek justice after being injured are the attackers, and those who have caused the injury are the victims.[52]

The fishing families at Minamata were victims, but the Minamata protest movement was neither passive nor conservative. Those who protested over the mercury poisoning explored fundamental questions of peace and war, and true social accord, in their desperate search for the meaning of what had happened. A speaker addressing bystanders in a Tokyo street challenged the authorities:

> . . . having destroyed mud snails, leeches, sand crabs, many wild things . . . now what are you doing to people? How can you ask people to bear such babies? . . . Rise up, rise up, this venomous world must be overturned. Fight this war, the Minamata war, the last war of the human race . . .

With the historical integrity of great artists, Maruki Iri and Toshi have chosen to convey these salient contemporary themes in their panels on atomic destruction at Hiroshima and Nagasaki, and on mercury poisoning at Minamata. The concern of Japanese citizens over 'pollution export' is the reverse of the militarist and economic expansionism of the Japanese state. But the prospects of redress through the political system seem elusive.

IV

In both ideas and practice the Sanrizuka movement has attempted to find answers to the questions posed by Kuno Osamu in his discussion of the 'citizen ethos' in 1960:

> [How] can a profound awareness be instilled in each individual in any field, that his own occupation or job is fundamentally separate from political authority, and that he is always free to decide for or against a government decision; to what extent can each individual be made strong enough to resist state controls and interference; and how can common values and standards of judgement be built up across national borders among employees and colleagues in similar fields?[53]

Unlike many of the citizens' movements which flourished in the early 1970s, the Sanrizuka action has the characteristics of class struggle which were more evident in the political disturbances of the 1950s. There are similarities also in the Okinawa movements and in the movements against nuclear power, and all of these link their critique of domestic problems with the international context.

Superficially it may seem that the farmer protest has much in common with peasant uprisings in the past. Irokawa Daikichi has compared the Chichibu uprising against the Meiji Government in 1884 with the popular resistance at Sanrizuka.[54] He disagrees with those who see the old village community as an impediment to the growth of modern democracy, and regards the villagers' susceptibility to emperor-centred fascism less as an expression of the undemocratic features of village mores and more as the result of profound changes brought about in the village by industrialisation and the global depression.[55] Emphasising not coercion but co-operation as the foundation of village life, he considers the citizens' movements as a continuation of tradition in a society where, until very recently, about half the population lived in the countryside. In his view they also point the way forward to 'a new regional community engaged in mutual [and self sufficient] enterprise on the scale of medium-sized zones'. Similarly, Hidaka Rokurō finds among the Minamata fishermen 'the birth of a new quality of personality that is both traditional and modern as well as showing revolutionary tendencies against the status quo'.[56]

Although to resist industrialism was once seen as resisting progress, the new critique does not reject modern technology but focuses on the importance of self-reliance and self-management.

Chalmers Johnson has described Japan as a developmental state in which, for the past 50 years, priority has been given to economic development. Japan's high growth system he sees as 'the product of one of the most painful passages to modernity any nation has ever had to endure'.[57] He emphasises the continuity in economic policies since the early 1930s. But Johnson is enthusiastic about the implications of the progressive refinement of bureaucratic rule in Japan, which he spells out in the following:

> This means, concretely, that the legislative and judicial branches of government must be restricted to 'safety valve' functions. These two branches of government must stand ready to intervene in the work of the bureaucracy and to restrain it when it has gone too far (which it undoubtedly will do on various occasions), but their more important overall function is to fend off the numerous interest groups in the society, which if catered to would distort the priorities of the developmental state. In the case of interests that cannot be ignored, deflected, or satisfied in symbolic ways — or upon which the perpetuation of the political system depends — the political leaders must compel the bureaucracy to serve and manipulate them.[58]

Johnson observes that one of the consequences of this type of political system is that 'groups without access to the system will on occasion take to the streets to call attention to their disaffection . . .'[59]

This of course is precisely what happened in the case of the environmental problem. Victims and their sympathisers had the conviction and organisational skill to press their case, local governments were prepared to act on their own initiative and at times in opposition to the central government, and both press and judiciary were willing to take an independent stand. Yet one can scarcely overlook the fact that so much depended on the determination of citizen protest, nor can one ignore the costs involved in loss of life, anxiety and suffering through violent clashes with riot police, struggles at factory gates, and the indignities of face-to-face confrontation in executive offices.

The need to re-establish a sense of community on a new basis is a recurring theme in Japanese sociology, stressed, among others, by Fukutake Tadashi.[60] Fukutake points out the serious effects of the housing problem on the care of the aged and the young. He sees no prospect of Japan becoming a 'welfare state'. Welfare confined to the large corporations is less satisfactory than ever as the population ages and job security declines.[61] 'Prosperity' has been measured in wages and the abundance of goods, but both of these are ephemeral when compared with social capital well spent: well-planned cities and a thriving countryside. The elements of a new society are clearly evident in the orientation of the citizens' movement, the tentative steps towards worker control in the factory and co-operation in farming. But the conservative Japanese establishment, given its second chance by the Americans in 1945, sees the tradition of the popular movement and popular struggle as a threat to be neutralised rather than a seed to be nurtured.

Seen in historical perspective, the study of citizens' movements draws attention not only to the conflicts in Japanese society but also to the integrative powers of the state as exercised through the political structure, economic planning, the co-opting of privileged groups and the mobilisation of public opinion. While the citizens' movements made advances in defining citizen rights and the legitimacy of opposition, the nature of the organisations and the issues they addressed set limits on the scope of discussion, especially in exploring the relationship between citizen and state. With the exception of the movement at Narita and a few others like it, the element of perceived class conflict is now much less than in the early postwar period. Most Japanese are said to regard themselves as members of the middle class, but the reality is social inequality.[62] To the outside world, the Japanese 'economic miracle' was made possible by social cohesion, yet in many different ways this 'stability' has been maintained by disrupting family life and neighbourhoods, and isolating people from one another. In a period of renewed appeals to national solidarity the prospects for a deepening of the democratic tradition rooted in the citizens' movement are diminished; in its stead the bureaucratic developmentalist state praised by Chalmers Johnson seems likely to become more firmly entrenched.

Women in the new Japanese state

Sandra Buckley and Vera Mackie

The character of the present-day Japanese state has been shaped by the Constitution and Civil Code created during the Occupation period and the high economic growth that has characterised much of the last thirty years. It is commonly agreed, however, that Japan has reached a turning point in the 1980s, and this is particularly true of the position of women in modern Japan.

The Constitution of 1947 granted women rights they had never before experienced — the right to vote and stand for public office, rights to property and education, and freedom of choice with respect to marriage, divorce, and procreation.[1] During the period of high economic growth which reached a peak in the early 1970s, more and more women moved into the workforce. Increased participation in economic life was accompanied by a flowering of political activity. Women have come to see the contradictions of their position in Japanese society — an advanced capitalist society — and are demanding far-reaching changes to the legal system so that they may participate fully in Japanese society and see the hollow guarantees of the Constitution translated into reality. Their demands have reached a peak during the United Nations Decade for Women, and the Japanese Government has pledged to make the legal changes necessary to ratify by 1985 the United Nations Convention on Ending All Forms of Sexual Discrimination.

Women's demands for change, however, come at a time when both external and internal pressures are pushing the Japanese state in an increasingly conservative direction. Structural changes to the Japanese economy will make women workers more vulnerable and US demands for Japan to take a more active military role in Asia will put pressure on domestic welfare and education policies. The position of Japanese women in the future will depend on how the needs of the remodelled state are reconciled with the desire of the government to show a progressive face to the world by ratifying the UN Convention.

The policies of the Nakasone government and the implications of his proposed 'administrative reform' *(gyōsei kaikaku)* have been well-documented in this volume. McCormack has noted 'a gradual shift of military/strategic questions from the periphery to the core of Japanese political life and in due course a much enhanced role for the military in the determination of state policy'.[2] Nakasone himself has been quoted elsewhere as saying that this administrative reform is 'clearing the way' for Constitutional reform and he has compared this period with the (Showa) twenties (late 1940s/early 1950s).[3] Proposals for reform are couched in spiritual terms reminiscent of the State Shinto of the prewar period, but this time are backed by the right-wing religious group *Seichō no Ie* (House of Growth). Increased expenditure on defence and economic 'aid' will be paid for by cuts to the welfare and education systems. The burden of welfare will revert to the family, a move sanctioned by a revival of the ideology of the *ie,* or household, and the so-called 'group mentality' of the Japanese. This will be supported by an increase in the ideological content of education: a recent LDP document[4] called for greater emphasis on domestic science courses in schools and the recent furore over history textbooks highlights the state's attempts to erase the memory of Japan's military activity in the 1930s and 1940s.

In the so-called 'Japanese-style welfare state' the family (in effect, women) will bear the major burden of looking after the sick, the handicapped, and the aged. Women will in this way be prevented from participating fully in economic production but may be employed as part-time workers when this does not interfere with 'reproductive' work. It happens that such a role fills the needs of Japanese capital.

Technological changes and the increased use of 'offshore' production have transformed Japanese industry. The domestic economy is undergoing a major process of restructuring — from a manufacturing base to an information and technology base. These changes affect not only the type of work being performed, but the conditions of work. Morris-Suzuki notes that 'between 1970 and 1982 the share of managerial, technical, clerical and sales personnel in the workforce rose from 35.1 per cent to 44.4 per cent'. This period has seen a decline in the percentage of workers in large firms and a trend away from patterns of lifetime employment and age-related promotions.[5] Most new jobs created have been part-time, temporary or seconded *(haken)* positions. Although 33.7 per cent of all workers in 1978 were women, 65.7 per cent of these were married women and 40 per cent of new jobs created were temporary positions.[6]

Technological change has resulted in increased fragmentation of the work process so that more and more work may be performed by semi-skilled part-time workers. Hall has described the advantages for capital in having such a work force:

> The capacity to fragment and deskill work, to casualize work, to shed labour, to meet peak demand without incurring the increased costs of penalty rates and overtime . . . and to employ cheaper and less labour in reduced and deskilled jobs are essential aspects of the rapid transformation of industry in the most profitable way. The process of fragmenting tasks into small highly formalized skills with highly centralized control of work makes it increasingly possible to run industries with largely part-time workers, while full-time workers retain management control. In this process, any prospects of worker participation and/or control of decision-making are undermined.[7]

It is most often women who perform such part-time work: firstly, because many of these jobs are created in areas already designated as 'feminine' — service, clerical and assembly[8] (in the electronics industry, for example),[9] and secondly, because part-time work allows women to take the burden of welfare from the state:

> Part-time work has the effect of compensating men and the state for the inadequacy of socially necessary services such as child care, care for the sick and elderly and social welfare services. For much of this work women are paid compliments — not cash — and pay a very high price in pay and conditions for time out of the workforce.[10]

The needs of capital affect not only Japanese women, but women in south-east Asia generally. Women in Korea, Indonesia and the Philippines provide labour for offshore production in the textile, electrical goods and electronics industries.[11] So-called 'hospitality girls' and *kisaeng* provide sexual services for Japanese tourists; the tourism industry in these countries is heavily infiltrated by Japanese capital. The boundaries of the Japanese state have, in effect, been extended to south-east Asia. Recent US pressure for a more active military role in Asia is an attempt to force Japan to back its economic influence with military power.[12]

Thus both political and economic pressures are pushing women back into the family and relegating them to a marginal role in production. Ideological structures in religion, education, the media, and language (discussed below), support this process. Women's demands for changes to the legal system — where the ideology of the family is encoded to a greater or lesser degree — must be understood in this context. Recent struggles have centred on the Nationality Law, the creation of an Equal Opportunity Act and proposed changes to the Eugenic Protection Law.

Before World War Two the Japanese people were organised into households *(ie)*. Each individual was registered in the *koseki* (family register) under the name of the father, and he had responsibility for the conduct of all members of the family and rights to all property. On the death of the father such rights and responsibilities passed to the eldest son. (Women had no rights to property. In the absence of a son a suitable male would be adopted into the family.) The family structure was explicitly patriarchal and the rule of the father over the household was said to be analogous to the rule of the Emperor over the people.[13] Under the postwar Civil Code the *ie* system was officially dismantled and wives and younger siblings could share in the family inheritance for the first time.[14] Remnants of this system may be seen, however, in the modern *koseki* system. It is still necessary for each Japanese citizen to be registered and a new *koseki* can only be created on marriage. Although it is possible for a *koseki* to be created under the wife's name, both partners must take the same surname and it is still necessary to have a nominal head of household.[15]

The logic of the *koseki* system shaped the postwar Fationality Law. Until recent amendments foreign wives of Japanese men could enter their husband's *koseki* and their children could take on Japanese nationality. A Japanese woman, however, could not create a *koseki* with a foreign husband or pass Japanese nationality on to her children.[16] In addition, it was much easier for non-Japanese wives to be naturalised than non-Japanese husbands.

Under the Draft Bill to Amend the Nationality Law, presented to the Diet on 23 February 1984 and passed on 18 May 1984, both males and females are able to pass on Japanese nationality to their children, and both husbands and wives may seek naturalisation under the same conditions.[17] These amendments came into force 1 January 1985. This is an important step forward, and bring Japan closer to ratification of the UN Convention. It is also necessary, however, to change the *koseki* system which gives the family a formal status under Japanese law and discriminates against non-Japanese.[18] Sugimoto[19] has described how the *koseki* and *jūmin tōroku* systems may be utilised for the purposes of social control. Recent LDP rhetoric is once again emphasising the family system.[20] Although it is unlikely that there will be a return to the prewar *ie* or household system, a new family is being shaped by current political, ideological and economic pressures.

A major demand of the women's movement has been the creation of an Equal Opportunity Act. The group known as *Tsukuru Kai*[21] has been most active, but has always had support from other women's groups. In addition to more conventional activities, they have staged sit-ins and hunger strikes and formed a human chain around the relevant government building.[22] The government is now working on the drafting of such an Act in preparation for ratification of the UN convention.

The Equal Opportunity Act must be considered in conjunction with the Labour Standards Law. At present the Labour Standards Law prohibits discrimination in wages and also has certain protective provisions. It must be noted that the stated aim of these provisions is to protect 'motherhood' *(bosei hogo)* and not individual women. Even menstruation leave is granted on the doubtful grounds that working when she is menstruating may affect a woman's future reproductive capacity.[23] As well as being granted maternity leave, nursing time and menstruation leave, women are prevented from working late at night or working excessive overtime. Employers argue that all provisions except those that directly concern pregnancy should be repealed when the Equal Opportunity Act is implemented. Discussion of maternity and nursing leave is academic, however, in those companies which require women to retire on marriage or childbirth. These provisions do not apply at all to small companies or to part-time and temporary workers.

For some time the women's movement was divided over whether or not these protective provisions should be retained, but recently the terms of the debate have been changed. The movement is no longer divided over 'Equality *versus* Protection'. Recent demonstrations and statements have called for 'Equality *with* Protection'. Removal of these protective provisions would expose the most vulnerable factory and part-time workers to a possible worsening of conditions. A recent article described the implications for women in the electronics industry:

> Nevertheless, the semi-conductor producing companies are attempting to have the ban on women working the night shift removed. No matter what, these companies intend to be able to use the women — the cheaper labour — on the night shifts too.[24]

The working conditions of most Japanese men make it impossible for them to share in 'reproductive' work in the home. It is thus necessary to reexamine the working conditions of both men and women. The Japan Council of Trade Unions *(Sōhyō)* takes the position that all workers should have a five-day week, reasonable working hours and a proper system of paid sick leave and annual leave.[25]

A committee composed of representatives from labour, employers and the public sector was commissioned to draft an Equal Opportunity Act, but the three groups have been unable to agree on what form the Act should take. There have been divisions over whether the scope of the Act should cover hiring only, or the whole period from hiring to retirement, including opportunities for promotion and further training within the company.

The major division is over punitive provisions. Labour representatives say that it is useless to frame an Equal Opportunity Act without penalties for non-compliance. Employers state that the Act should simply be a set of guidelines with which employers will be asked to cooperate.[26] The government is in a dilemma. It wants to ratify the UN Convention for the sake of its international reputation, but a truly effective Equal Opportunity Act would go against the interests of

Japanese capital. There is a 'dual structure' of labour whereby certain privileged men enjoy superior working conditions in large companies and routine manufacturing and service work is carried out by part-time workers.[27] Morris-Suzuki documents how technological change has widened this gap.[28] The compromise is to frame an Equal Opportunity Act just strong enough to comply with the UN guidelines but not strong enough to provide a real threat to the intersts of capital. These interests are stated succinctly by the journal *Agora*.

> The employers have cried that 'the Japanese economy will fall apart if the Equal Opportunity Act is implemented'. Could we have any further proof that Japan's high economic growth has been based on the exploitation of women?[29]

Cabinet had, in fact, recently approved a watered-down draft of the Equal Opportunity Act but as of mid-1984 this had not yet been presented to the Diet.[30]

As part of the right-wing philosophy espoused by the LDP and supported by *Seichō no Ie,* there have once again been moves to revise the Eugenic Protection Law. Under the present Eugenic Protection Law a woman may have her pregnancy terminated on the grounds of mental illness or hereditary illness, when the mother suffers leprosy, if she has been raped, or if the pregnancy will damage her health for physical or economic reasons. There have been regular moves to delete the words 'for economic reasons' from the law. Moves to change this law in the 1960s and early 1970s saw some of the earliest demonstrations by Women's Liberation groups and the creation of the group *Tatakau Onna* ('Fighting Women') by Tanaka Mitsu.[31] The most recent moves to amend the law started in 1982 and have been opposed by a well-organised coalition of women's groups.

The National Eugenic Law *(Kokumin Yūsei-hō)* of 1940 was said to be modelled on the Sterilisation Law of Nazi Germany and was promulgated during wartime in order to ensure the reproduction of healthy citizens to serve the country. Clauses concerning the welfare of the mother were only added in 1948, resulting in the present Eugenic Protection Law *(Yūseihogohō).*[32] Protective provisions, however, are once again aimed at preserving the woman's role as mother *(bosei hogo),* rather than her health as an individual. The removal of the 'economic reasons' clause would only reinforce this view of women — as primarily existing for motherhood.

The Eugenic Protection Law treats women's fertility as an instrument of the state. Women do not have the right to control their own bodies, particularly when there are no safe, reliable methods available and sex education is inadequate. It is illegal to prescribe 'the pill' for contraceptive purposes, so the most widely used method of contraception is the condom which effectively places responsibility for contraception on the male partner. Abortion thus becomes a 'back-up' for inadequate contraceptive methods, with the medical profession having control over decisions concerning a women's fertility.[33] Women are expected to reproduce or engage in productive work, depending on the needs of the state.

In 1982 it was Murakami Masakuni who instituted moves for the deletion of the 'economic reasons' clause from the Eugenic Protection Law. Murakami is a leader of the right-wing religious group *Seichō no Ie*. This group harks back to the State Shinto of the prewar period, but also has links with Buddhist groups and the Moral Majority in America.[34] The *Seichō no Ie* political alliance numbers Nakasone Yasuhiro and Fukuda Takeo among its members. It has been described as a 'cocktail religion' and the 'variety store of religions' because of its hybrid background,[35] but there is a unity in the ultra-conservative policies it promotes — revision of the Constitution, return of the 'Northern Territories', restitution of Yasukuni Shrine, and revision of the Eugenic Protection Law. In its campaign (under the slogan 'Reverence for life' — *Seimei no sonchō*) it has used propaganda from the Moral Majority and Right to Life groups in the United States. Mother Teresa was even brought to Japan as an advocate for the cause.[36]

The proposed amendment was not carried, but the law as it stands does not allow women control of their own bodies. Women oppose not only the proposed revision, but the philosophy underlying the Eugenic Protection Law. The 'Eugenic' philosophy, they say, is linked with discrimination against the handicapped and other weak members of society. Women have called for a rethinking of the Eugenic philosophy and the removal of the crime of abortion (*datai zai*) from the Civil Code.[37]

There has been a change in the strategies employed by the women's movement in the last decade. In the 1970s, for example, women were content to see the proposed amendment to the Eugenic Protection Law defeated. The 1982 campaign, however, was carried out by a coalition of over 70 groups.[38] They recognise that moves to change the law relating to abortion are part of a coherent right-wing philosophy of increased spending on military expansion and the resulting privatisation of welfare. The coherence of women's response is reflected in the fact that the 1982 coalition included anti-war, anti-pollution, and anti-nuclear groups. In June 1983 representatives of this coalition also chose to participate in a rally against what they saw to be Nakasone's policy: militarism and co-operation with the United States.[39]

Feminists have challenged public expressions of patriarchal ideology in the legal system and this debate has been carried out in the public domain. However, it is the covert expressions of these power structures in language, education and the media that are more difficult to identify and challenge because of their perceived neutrality.

Recent feminist research has concentrated on showing how language and the media construct and reinforce the dominant world-view.

Publishing houses, television, popular film, and radio and advertising agencies have constructed an ideal image of womanhood. The media addresses two age groups — the young, urban working woman and the married 'lady'. The young working woman is projected as active, outgoing, fashion-conscious and well travelled. Her primary objective in life is marriage and her whole life is spent in preparation for that goal. The married 'lady' is projected as self-deprecating, softly spoken and drawing her satisfaction and identity from her dual roles of wife and mother. These two images are not unique to Japan as a glance at any newspaper stand or television guide in New York, Sydney or London will show. What is striking in the Japanese case is the lack of any alternative to the ideal model within the mass media.

Saitō Chiyo, an editor of the feminist journal *Agora*, points out that '99 per cent of information in Japan originates from males . . . only 0.7 per cent of journalists are female'.[40] Women in television frequently complain that they are there only as decoration. Murakami Setsuko, of Nippon Television, sued her employers when she was transferred from her position as announcer. Murakami convinced the court that she had been transferred because 'I was no longer pretty and too old to be an announcer'.[41] The continued absence of women from anchor positions in news and compere teams and the dearth of women in administrative positions within the electronic and printed media point to the continuing subordination and under-representation of women in these crucial areas.[42]

Another important aspect of the construction of a popular image of womanhood has been the growth of non-fiction writing developed around the theme of 'women's education'. Two of the more popular works of this genre are Hamao Minoru's *How to Bring Up Girls — A Guide For Raising A Nice Child*[43] and Kawakami Gentarō's *I'd Like To See Their Parents' Faces*.[44] These works assert the inferiority and weakness of women, and the primacy of reproduction. The mother is identified as the role model for her children and held responsible for any deviations from the 'norm' her children may exhibit. Both Hamao and Kawakami emphasise the importance of women's education. But what they are referring to is something quite distinct from the equal education guaranteed women in the Constitution. Hamao asserts that textbooks for girls should not stress theory. A science textbook for girls, he says, should explain 'how the wash gets whiter when you use bleach and why milk curdles when you add orange juice'.[45] That both authors are also educators in women's tertiary institutions is particularly disconcerting.

In response to the prescriptions for womanhood constructed across the range of Japan's mass media (or 'masu-komi'), the women's movement has attempted to create alternative channels of communication. The term 'mini-komi' was coined in the 1970s by Tanaka Mitsu[46] to describe an alternative network of communication between women's groups across Japan, and now refers to the whole spectrum of alternative media. The publications funded and distributed through 'mini-komi' oppose the popular image of women in the mass media and offer a forum for political debate and the dissemination of information on a range of issues from international defence to consumer rights and contraception. Over the last decade these publications have included such journals as *Feminist, Agora, Onna Eros* and *Ajia to Josei Kaihō (Asian Women's Liberation)*. In addition to these established journals there are also countless handwritten and roneoed newsletters and broadsheets distributed by the diverse interest groups that constitute the women's movement. Many 'mini-komi' publications are concerned with the 'policing' of discrimination in the media and misleading advertising, and work in close alliance with consumer groups.

As in the case of 'mini-komi', Japanese feminists have shown an acute awareness of the place of language in the subordination of women. At the most obvious level some are rejecting the marked language of women's speech with its characteristic high pitch, hesitation, and implicit humbleness. This is a difficult process, however, in a language for which there is essentially no neutral form. Nothing short of a redefinition of language — both masculine and feminine — is called for. At one level women are redefining particularly significant words as a step towards such language reform. Perhaps the most well known example is the case of *baishun,* the word for prostitution. Originally written with the character to sell *(bai)* (売) and the character for spring (春 *shun*), it is now written with the character to buy (買) also read as *bai.* In this way the anti-prostitution campaigners have effectively shifted the emphasis of prostitution away from the woman to the man who buys her 'services'. The new writing of *baishun* underlines the treatment of women as commodity within a patriarchal capitalist economy.

Young feminists campaigning for better facilities and legal support for rape and incest victims have also recognised the need to define rather than be defined by language. Both the word for rape *(gōkan)* and for incest *(kinshinsōkan)* end in the same character *kan* (姦). The character is a conglomerate of three women (女) and carries the value of wicked or lewd. In rejecting the words *gōkan* and *kinshinsōkan* feminists reject the accusation of blame or responsibility implicit in the graphic representations of the words.[47]

Feminists have identified and challenged the false images of women in the media and language and are working to re-define a non-androcentric identity. They have also been active in education. The power of education to shape popular values to fit the objectives of the state is something older feminists are well aware of. Various teacher and feminist groups are now publishing materials to promote non-discriminatory textbooks and education policy. *The Equal Opportunity Education Series* is one such publication which scrutinises textbooks, classroom methodology and language, and promotes political lobbying for educational reform.

The private/public, productive/reproductive dichotomies are reinforced through the representation of women in a domestic role in textbooks across the range of subjects at all levels. The absence of women from history books, the lack of female protagonists in readers, the marginalisation of women writers in literature courses, and references to stereotypical, non-biological gender differences in textbooks all contribute to the socialisation of female and male roles in schools.[48]

The compulsory teaching of domestic science for girl students only is one of the most overt reinforcements of the division of labour within the education system. The status of domestic science courses is a direct contravention of the United Nations guidelines and yet there has been no move within the Education Department to alter the situation.

Although the Constitution calls for equal education opportunities, the majority of private high schools outside Tokyo and Osaka are segregated. Given that only 50 per cent of the students proceeding from middle school to high school can be accommodated within the public system, this predominance of segregated schools in the private system has serious implications for equal education.[49] The range of courses offered in all-girls' schools and the emphasis of timetabling away from science, mathematics and technical subjects encourage female students towards a course structured to qualify them only for the domestic role.

The lesser status attached to women's education is further evidenced in the two-stream tertiary system of two- and four-year universities. Only 12 per cent of female high school graduates enter four-year universities compared with 39 per cent of males.[50] In addition, 90 per cent of junior university students are females[51] and 40 per cent of these take majors in home economics.[52] The statement that more women than men now proceed to tertiary education is true but in no way reflects equality of educational opportunity.

Statistical data suggests that the better educated a woman is, the less likely she is to enter full-time employment.[53] One possible reading of this situation is that elite tertiary institutions are more accessible to women for whom employment is not a pressing issue. In this context a tertiary degree from an elite institution adds to a daughter's eligibility for marriage rather than prepares her for a career.

While teaching is traditionally an area in which women are well represented in Japan (50 per cent in elementary, 25 per cent in junior high),[54] the percentage of female teachers drops dramatically in senior high schools. In the context of intense competition for university entrance senior high schools are seen as the crucial stage of education. Women are apparently not trusted at this level. Only 2 per cent of principals are female[55] — a fact that reflects the transferral of the role of wise mother/educator into the elementary and junior classroom but only under the guiding hand of the pater/principal. Similarly, while it is mothers who are active in parent-teacher associations, the membership is traditionally listed under the father's name and office holders are frequently elected from among the non-active fathers rather than from the active female members.[56]

It is significant that the only two aspects of education mentioned in LDP policy on the family[57] are domestic education in schools (*kateika kyōiku*) and adult education for women. *Kateika kyōiku* will become a vehicle for the conservative values necessary for 'administrative reform'. Central to this process is perpetuation of the public/private split and the division of labour. This will be supported by adult education classes directed at wives and mothers. Education will once again serve the needs of the state rather than the individual, with the state (*kokka*) and family (*katei*) being closely aligned.

Current employment practices and the lack of an adequate welfare system make survival outside the family system difficult. Inadequate pensions mean that the family must take responsibility for the sick, the aged, and the handicapped. The difficulty of obtaining alimony and the inadequacy of supporting mother's benefits push women back into the nuclear family. (The highest monthly benefit available is Y 30,000 (A$150) plus Y 5,000 (A$25) and Y 2,000 (A$10) for the second and third children. This is reduced according to the mother's income and even the former husband's income is taken into account.)[58] The division of labour is further supported by increments and allowances available only to married male employees.[59] Early retirement for women, lower salaries for female employees, enforced retirement on marriage or pregnancy, and restriction of women to non-career positions all act to persuade women that there is little alternative to the domestic role.[60]

Recent promotion of volunteer work for women is reminiscent of the 1940s and this suggests a possible key to an understanding of the present situation. The last mobilisation of women's volunteer work was in the 'general mobilisation system' (*sōdōin taisei*) of the last war. It is no coincidence that calls for volunteer service have re-emerged at a time when matters of national security have once again come to the fore. Enloe has described the post-war era as a 'militarised peacetime':

> In these latter decades of the twentieth century militarization is proceeding at a breathtaking pace, though we are allegedly in 'peacetime'. In reality, this 'peacetime' is thought of by national security officials as an era of global threat. Consequently, 'peacetime' has come to be defined today in terms of national insecurity and an obsession with defence.[61]

In such a period, public sector spending on education and welfare will be cut in order to maintain defence spending. As welfare is relegated to the private sphere, it is necessary to resurrect the ideology of the family. In this sense the Japanese state of the 1980s has similarities to both the present-day United States and United Kingdom and wartime Japan.

McCormack[62] has described Nakasone's links with Kishi, and at times their rhetoric is frighteningly similar. Kishi remains a leading figure in Japanese politics and heads the campaign for reforming the Constitution. In 1954 Kishi lamented the dismantling of the *ie,* or household system, in the following terms:

> . . . because it is said that there is no obligation towards parents, the elderly are sent off to institutions. Is this the best way to do things in the Japanese situation? I believe that the concept of family which is so well suited to Japanese conditions, customs and traditions is essential. And the family will become the bases for the construction of the nation and in turn the basis for Japan's international progress.[63]

Such views are echoed in the LDP's vision of the 'Japanese style Welfare State', as described in the Report of the Special Commission on Administrative Reform:

> From now on it will be necessary to further develop the special character of our country's society. We will have to plan to implement a welfare [system] in which an appropriate share is met by a highly efficient government, but which is based on the solidarity of home, neighbourhood, enterprise, and local society, which is in turn founded on the spirit of self-help and independence of the individual.[64]

In his calls for 'administrative reform', Nakasone refers to the late 1940s when the last major reforms to the Constitution and Civil Code took place. He says that 'this time there is no MacArthur',[65] but in fact the reforms described domestically as 'sovereign' and 'independent' *(jishuteki)* have been instituted in response to pressure from the United States. Increased military spending and a revised Constitution serve the needs of the Japan-US-Korea alliance.[66] This link cannot be disguised by appeals to Japanese culture, tradition, or religion. Elevation of the family to a cult, with patriotic and religious overtones, is one way to defuse criticism, but many women realise that the new family will serve the needs of capital and the State rather than the individual.

Women's groups have responded to the coherent conservative programme of the Nakasone government with an equally coherent critique of militarism and conservative policies. In challenging employment and welfare practices, the *koseki* and Nationality Law and reform to the Eugenic Protection Law, women are striking at the heart of conservative policies. Women will no longer allow these issues to be marginalised under the label of 'women's issues'.

It is significant that the last few years have seen a new unity in the women's movement and a shift away from single-issue campaigns. The major campaigns on abortion, the Nationality Law, and the Equal Opportunity Act have been carried out by coalitions of concerned groups. Not only women's groups but also anti-war, anti-pollution, and anti-nuclear groups campaigned against the revision of the Eugenic Protection Act. Women's groups, in turn, have been a major force in the peace movement, in the struggles of rural women to reclaim their land from the Self-Defence Forces, and in opposition to pollution and corruption in Government.

According to Nakasone, 'the first task of the Japanese people is to bow to the *kamidana* (ancestors), or bow to the *butsudan* (Buddhist gods). Then ring the ceremonial bell and fold our hands in prayer'.[67] Japanese women are in the process of defining a radically different set of priorities: to expose the links between militarism, conservative politics, and the subordination of women and to bring discussion of these issues out of the 'mini-komi' and into the political mainstream, stripped of religious and ideological rhetoric. The state's response to this discourse will shape the Japanese state of the future.

Crime, confession, and control in contemporary Japan

Gavan McCormack

The treatment of minorities, the handicapped, radical dissenters, prisoners, the poor, the old, and all who, for whatever reason, are weak and vulnerable, must rank as a crucial measure in assessing the state of any country's democracy. Prominent among those aspects of contemporary Japanese society that have drawn admiring attention from Western commentators and scholars has been Japan's high degree of social order and apparent harmony. This paper focuses attention on some of the costs involved in achieving this appearance of harmony. The accompanying article by a Japanese lawyer, Igarashi Futaba, deals with some little known but significant aspects of contemporary Japan: the powers of the police, the rights of suspects in criminal cases, the treatment of members of radical dissenting groups, and the administration of punishment, including capital punishment.

One case alone should be enough to cause disquiet. In July 1983, Mr Menda Sakae, who had been in prison under sentence of death for murder for 33 years, was declared not guilty. Twenty-three years old when arrested, he eventually walked out of prison and the shadow of the gallows at the age of 57, an innocent man terribly wronged.[1] He had been longer under sentence of death than any other prisoner known to Amnesty International. What the Igarashi article reveals is that Menda's case cannot be regarded merely as an isolated human tragedy, but that is is part of a general pattern of abuse of human rights in the area of police and crime in Japan which, little enough understood in Japan itself, is virtually unknown outside the country.

The article is one of many which has appeared in the Japanese media since 1982, prompted by the release from prison or police detention of a number of people who had been wrongly arrested, convicted, and imprisoned. Most had actually 'confessed' to the crimes with which they were charged. A group of lawyers representing the

186

three Tokyo Bar Associations investigated the circumstances in which this occurred and the Igarashi report draws heavily on that investigation.

This study strongly suggests it still to be the case that, as Chalmers Johnson wrote in 1972, 'In dealing with criminal cases Japanese police, procurators, and judges think of the confession as the "king of evidence" *(shōko no ō)*.'[2] The constitutional provision in article 38(3) that 'no person shall be convicted or punished in cases when the only proof against him is his own confession', has yet to be realised in practice. Johnson noted in his book that, to 1972, all five of the most important criminal cases of postwar Japan involved 'a false, coerced, or contested confession', and each one required eight to fifteen years to reach settlement.[3]

In prewar Japan, 99 per cent of all criminal convictions were based on confessions.[4] That percentage has dropped only slightly, to 86 per cent, in today's Japan, and convictions result in 99.99 per cent of cases sent to trial.[5]

In prewar times, however, 'crime' included political deviance or unorthodox thought. In the 1930s a generation of Japanese intellectuals, including large numbers of Japanese communists, underwent a spiritual reorientation in which they 'confessed' to the crime of thinking dissident thoughts and were converted to the nationalist consensus. This phenomenon itself was not unique, but its scale, and the peculiarly concentrated state pressures designed to achieve conversion rather than to eliminate opposition by execution or prolonged incarceration, was unusual.

Social control and the regulation of dissidence is achieved in contemporary Japan by much more subtle and diffuse methods, as Hidaka Rokurō and others have argued,[6] and the role of police, procuracy and judiciary is slight in inducing political or spiritual reorientation. However, confession remains central to the judicial and penal process, and these organs appear still to be mobilised in the combating or neutralising of political radicalism (if not in positively converting dissenters).

Several of the great waves of dissenting political activity and mobilisation in postwar Japan have been broken in part by the impact of judicial proceedings. The Matsukawa case in 1949 is most famous, although there were several others at around the same time of almost equally great impact. In the Matsukawa case a group of railway workers was indicted for an act of apparent sabotage of the railway line at a place called Matsukawa at a time when militant workers were resisting forced 'rationalisation' policies and the conservative forces of the Japanese state were emerging from the paralysing crisis of wartime defeat and occupation to reassert their social hegemony against the challenge of the left. The attribution of an act of indiscriminate violence to the organised worker movement seriously damaged that movement and shifted it on to the strategic defensive by tying it to a prolonged process of litigation. Not until September 1963 were the convictions quashed against all twenty defendants, five of whom had initially been sentenced to death. The perpetrators of the 1949 explosion remain unknown, and one hypothesis (among several) is that some branch of the state authorities (whether American or Japanese) may have engineered the explosion deliberately. Whatever the truth of the affair, the damage it did to the Japanese left at a crucial postwar juncture is unquestioned.[7]

Nineteen years after Matsukawa, Japan was in the throes of a social and political crisis of similar dimensions, though this time the focus was narrower and concentrated particularly in the universities. Throughout 1968-69 there was unprecedented upheaval in the universities, and prolonged occupations of the major campuses and repeated confrontations between students and riot police. The broader context of the movement was that of intensifying opposition to the war in Vietnam and to Japanese complicity in it, and opposition to the impending renewal of the Japan-US Security Treaty (due to take place in 1970). At this juncture a series of violent incidents occurred: bomb attacks were launched on various installations and facilities and letter bombs were delivered to the homes of various officials. Members of left-wing organisations on various campuses were arrested for these acts and their trials, like those of the Matsukawa case in the 1950s and early 1960s, took many years to reach a conclusion. After periods of up to ten years in prison, all the defendants in the major cases were again found innocent, and the actual perpetrators of the crimes remain undetected.

The two major cases covered by the Igarashi report are the so-called 'Cigarette-tin bomb' cases and the case of the 'Chief of Police's residence'. A brief note on the major points in these cases follows.

Cigarette-tin bomb (and other, related) cases[8]
On 24 October 1969 a round-shaped 'Peace' brand cigarette tin packed with dynamite was thrown at the gate of the Riot Police barracks in Ichigaya in Tokyo. On 1 November of the same year a similar bomb was delivered to the American Cultural Center in Nagatachō in Tokyo. Neither bomb exploded.

On 18 October 1971, two women delivered a package across the counter of the underground Post Office in the Japan Petroleum Company building in Nishi Shimbashi in Tokyo. One person was seriously injured in the explosion which occurred later.

On 18 December 1971, Mrs Tsuchida Tamiko, wife of the head of the Criminal Investigation Section of the Police Department, was killed when she opened a package that had been delivered by mail to their residence.

In September 1972, Masubuchi Toshiyuki, then a student of Hōsei University in Tokyo and a member of the 'Lenin Study Group' at that university, was arrested. He was charged with the following:

i. Theft of 43 volumes of the Collected Works of Lenin from the library of Hōsei University during the student occupation of that building in late June 1969 (with three accomplices).

ii. Theft of four tyres from parked cars in the car park of a Tokyo apartment building on 9 December 1969 (with three accomplices).

iii. Together with 12 accomplices having manufactured bombs in a 10 square metre tatami sized room in Nagatachō in mid-October 1969.

iv. Being responsible, with five accomplices, for the police barracks bombing, and with three accomplices for the American Cultural Center bombing, and being responsible, with a group of accomplices including Enoshita Kazuo and Nakamura Ryūji, for the Tsuchida bombing case. A total of ten were indicted for this bombing.

In a prolonged trial, the prosecution sought the death penalty for Masubuchi and a twelve year sentence for Enoshita and Nakamura, and various sentences, including life, for the others.

In March 1982, a not guilty verdict was returned on Masubuchi and all the other defendants because of the insufficiency or inconsistency of the evidence against them.

On 25 May 1982, Makita Yoshiaki, son of one of Japan's leading industrialists, the president of Mitsubishi Heavy Industries, Makita Yoichiro, held a press conference to proclaim that he and associates of his had been responsible for the manufacture of all the bombs used in the above cases. He claimed to have stolen the dynamite in September 1969 and to have built between 50 and 100 bombs with it, which he then handed over to various groups, including the Japanese Red Army. According to Makita, none of those who had been indicted and imprisoned for nearly ten years had anything to do with the case. Makita had appeared as a witness for the defence in the last stages of the trial. Because of the period of time involved since the crime, he was no longer liable to indictment or punishment.

As of early 1984 an appeal by the procurators against the not guilty verdicts on six of the group, including Masubuchi, Enoshita, and Nakamura, was still continuing.

Chief of Police's residence attempted bombing case
In August 1971 an attempt was made to set a time bomb at the residence of the Chief of Police. The culprit escaped. A group of activists from the 'Joint Struggle Committee' of Japan University was charged with the crime. Sudō Masashi, owner of a car which was said to have been used on this occasion, was one of this group.

On 9 March 1983, all the accused in the case were held not guilty. The Chief Justice remarked: 'There is insufficient objective evidence to identify the defendants as the criminals. The credibility of the defendants' confessions is slight. They have alibis for the day of the crime. There is no evidence of crime'.[9]

While there is no doubt that some leftist groups — the Japanese Red Army prominent among them — decided in the late 1960s to resort to armed struggle in a strategy of violent confrontation with state power, and while the Makita statement indicates that some bombs at least were manufactured and some assaults launched with them, the police appear to have used the occasion of the bombings to crack down indiscriminately on the leftist movement, deliberately manufacturing a case against representative elements of the 'new left' as they appear to have done against representative elements among the railway workers in the late 1940s. The combination of choice of violence on the part of sections of the leftist movement itself and exploitation of the incidents by the police was devastating. The whole movement of political dissent and reform, apparently so broad-based in the 1960s, disintegrated and vanished almost without trace in the 1970s.

The remaining cases considered by Igarashi are of conventional crimes — murder, arson, robbery.[10] Although there is no overt political implication in these cases, they also point to serious problems in the area of criminal justice in Japan.

In the period between 1945 and 1980 a total of 569 executions were carried out in Japan.[11] It is highly probable that at least some of those executed were innocent victims of circumstances such as those described in the Igarashi report. When Amnesty International's mission visited Japan in March 1983 it found 54 prisoners under sentence of death and, such was the secrecy with which the matter was treated by the Japanese government, Amnesty could not even find out if anyone had been executed in the preceding year.[12] How many Menda Sakae's are there still on Japan's death rows?

There are two other cases, not referred to by Igarashi, in which death penalties have been handed down and appeals are continuing, which are of considerable interest and raise related problems about justice in contemporary Japan. A brief note about each of them follows.

The East Asian Anti-Japanese Armed Front[13]
In the early 1970s, as the radical movement in the universities and elsewhere suffered extreme confusion due to the failure to prevent the renewal of the US-Japan Security Treaty, 'normalisation' of the universities and bitter internal factional splits, a number of groups tried to find a way out of the impasse by adopting different tactics. The Red

Army was one. The East Asian Anti-Japanese Armed Front was another. The latter began by bombing monuments which they believed were offensive or redolent of Japanese aggression, imperialism, or militarism, whether against the Chinese or Korean peoples or against the aboriginal Japanese inhabitants, the Ainu. From a careful concentration on symbol, however, they then moved to conceive of an attack on a living symbol, the man they believed to be the physical embodiment of all the aggression and violence and brutality in Japan's past, the emperor himself. The plan to blow up the train in which the emperor was travelling went awry, however, and was aborted at the last minute. The group was left with unused bombs on its hands. In a hastily devised and disastrous change of plan they placed the bombs in the offices of Mitsubishi Heavy Industries instead, intending a further dramatic symbolic protest against the contemporary expansion of Japanese capitalism into the Third World and especially Southeast Asia. This plan too went wrong, but this time the bomb exploded (on 30 August 1974); seven people were killed and hundreds injured. On 19 May 1975, eight members of the group were arrested. One drank poison to commit suicide at once. Three others were released by the Japanese government during 1975 and 1977 in response to demands made upon it during hijack incidents in Kuala Lumpur and Dacca. Another three, who had not been arrested, committed suicide during 1975. That left four: on 12 November 1979, Daidōji Masashi and Kataoka Toshiaki were sentenced to death, Kurokawa Masayoshi to life imprisonment, and Arai Mariko to eight years imprisonment.

Unlike other cases considered here, there seems no reason to doubt that those accused and eventually found guilty and sentenced were the actual culprits. Three slightly different problems arise. First is the appropriateness of the death penalty for such a politically motivated (however misguided) crime. Although the capital sentences were handed down over the Mitsubishi bombing, whose fatal consequences appear not to have been intended and for which members of the group expressed their regret, it is hard to believe that the *plan* to assassinate the emperor could have been immaterial to the sentences. There are few parallels to such an act in Japanese history,[14] and even though this particular emperor only escaped trial and almost certain execution as a war criminal in 1945 because of a political decision by the US authorities, a good deal of the aura of magic and mystery still surrounds him in contemporary Japan, such that the ability of a Japanese court to achieve true detachment and equanimity in pronouncing upon a case involving a plot against his life can legitimately be questioned.

Second is the problem of the appropriateness of the death penalty after four principals in the same crime had actually been released by the state. Quite apart from the general problems associated with the death penalty, in this case a real doubt as to the justice of such a step is unavoidable.

Third is the question of the various ill-treatments and the pattern of consistent denial of their human rights as prisoners of which the defendants in this case complained.[15] Given the magnitude of what they were accused of having done, and in the light of evidence from the Igarashi report of how prisoners in general have been treated, such complaints cannot readily be dismissed.

The Hokkaido Government Office Bombing[16]

On 2 March 1976 a bomb attack was carried out against the Hokkaido Government Office. In August Ōmori Katsuhisa was arrested and charged with the crime. Ōmori was a former student of Gifu University who had abandoned his plans to become a teacher in order to identify himself with the most underprivileged of Japan's workers, the day labourers of Sanya in Tokyo and Kamagasaki in Osaka, by becoming a labourer himself. Ōmori has consistently denied responsibility, and the case against him has been made up of a compound of evidence of his radical sympathies and connections and circumstantial evidence of a missing fire extinguisher in his apartment (which police argued must have been used to furnish materials for the bomb). Although Ōmori denied that he was responsible, he declared his support for the principle of the action, out of solidarity with the oppressed Ainu aboriginal inhabitants of Hokkaido. On 29 March 1983 he was sentenced to death. Ōmori's refusal to confess, despite eight years of incarceration and interrogation, together with his bold statement of support of the principle of the bombing, stamp him as a man of unusual strength of character. The anger and impatience of the police and judicial authorities at such a man may be understandable, but the evidence against him is seriously flawed. Under the circumstances, the death sentence against him appears not so much the outcome of due process of law in a democratic system as the product of bitterness and the desire for vengeance on the part of a police and judiciary implacably hostile to what Ōmori represents.

The author of the report which follows, Igarashi Futaba, is a Japanese woman lawyer who has been involved for over ten years in the Tokyo Bar Association's 'Committee to Investigate Substitute Imprisonment', and who has three times been its chairperson. The Bar Association report she presents is based on first-hand accounts of their experiences by victims of the 'Substitute Imprisonment' system.

This system is so described because, although Japan's Code of Criminal Procedure prescribes that suspects in criminal cases may not be held by police for more than 72 hours following arrest without being taken before a judge, under the Prisons Law of 1908 the police cells may be regarded as 'substitute imprisonment' and suspects may under this provision be returned to police custody for an indefinite period of time. Prolonged police custody is at the root of the abuses described in the report.

The implications of what is described may be summed up in eight major propositions.

i. The 'substitute imprisonment' system is a relic of Japan's authoritarian past. The dangers of consigning suspects in criminal cases to prolonged police custody are universally recognised and the Japanese penal system should be brought into line with the convention among democratic countries in this matter.

ii. The terms of Article 38 of the constitution would appear to have become a dead letter:

(1) No person shall be compelled to testify against himself.
(2) Confessions made under compulsion, torture or threat, or after prolonged arrest or detention, shall not be admitted in evidence.
(3) No person shall be convicted or punished in cases where the only proof against him is his own confession.

iii. An 'International Covenant on Civil and Political Rights', based on the Universal Declaration of Human Rights, was adopted by the United Nations in 1966 and went into force in 1976. The Japanese government signed it in 1978; it was ratified in June 1979 and came into effect in September 1979. The circumstances documented in the Bar Association study constitute a *prima facie* case of breach of Japan's international obligations under at least the following clauses:

> Article 14(3). the right to be tried without undue delay [on which see also paragraph vi below].
> Article 14(3)(g). the right not to be compelled to testify against oneself or to confess guilt.[17]

iv. A clear *prima facie* case would also seem to exist for regarding Japan as in breach of the United Nations' 'Standard Minimum Rules for the Treatment of Prisoners' in so far as the Rules forbid all 'cruel, inhuman, or degrading punishment', although these Rules are non-enforceable and have only the status of declared moral principle. Article 36 of the constitution also forbids torture, but the Bar Association report leaves little room for doubt that it still exists in Japan.

v. The United Nations General Assembly, by its resolution 3453(XXX) of 9 December 1975 also pronounced that

> 1. No arrested or detained person shall be subjected to physical or mental compulsion, torture, violence, threats or inducements of any kind, deceit, trickery, misleading suggestions, protracted questioning, hypnosis, administration of drugs or any other means which tend to impair or weaken his freedom of action or decision, his memory or his judgement.
> 2. Any statement which he may be induced into making through any of the

above prohibited methods, as well as any evidence obtained as a result thereof, shall not be admissible in evidence against him in any proceedings. 3. No confession or admission by an arrested or detained person can be used against him in evidence unless it is made voluntarily in the presence of his counsel and before a judge or other officer authorized by law to exercise judicial power. [18]

The Bar Association study establishes clear *prima facie* grounds for believing Japan has not honoured its obligations under this resolution.

vi. Extreme prolixity of criminal trial and appeal proceedings is characteristic of Japan. It may be difficult to define precisely what would constitute a 'reasonable time' for such proceedings (as required by Article 9(3) of the International Covenant on Civil and Political Rights), or what exactly the constitutional right under Article 37 to a 'speedy' trial in criminal cases may mean, but it is hard to defend a system in which it takes *ten years* to reach a verdict (as in the cigarette-tin bomb case), during the whole of which period the accused are deprived of their liberty, and there are precedents in other countries which point to what is possible when a different priority is placed on the rights of the accused. Lord Kilbrandon, in his concluding remarks to a conference on the subject in 1975, had this to say:

> At the beginning of the eighteenth century the Scottish Parliament passed a law, which is strictly enforced to the present day, that once you have committed a man in custody to trial, his trial has to be completed within 100 days, otherwise he walks out a free man. Now if you made such a proposal in most jurisdictions today it would be said that it was impossible. But it is not impossible; it goes on in Scotland. [19]

vii. The death penalty, in Japan as elsewhere, is a peculiarly cruel and unjustifiable form of punishment. The case of Mr Menda Sakae alone, in itself an astonishing epic of human survival, is a powerful argument from specific Japanese circumstances to reinforce arguments based on general principle for abolition of the death penalty.

viii. Japan is commonly ranked among the top half dozen countries in the world in respect of political freedom and civil rights; [20] Japanese police are commonly thought to be extraordinarily efficient and their behaviour 'astonishingly good'; [21] prominent scholars have delcared that '*kensatsu fassho* (procuratorial fascism) no longer exists in Japan', [22] and that police violence in the securing of confessions is 'practically unheard of now', [23] but there is reason to doubt all of these propositions. The defendants in the cases described below have now all been restored to liberty and their complaints have been publicised. This is sufficient to show that Japan today is neither totalitarian nor fascist, but the injustices they suffered nevertheless add up to a serious indictment of the state of human rights and the quality of democracy in Japan today.

Forced to confess

Igarashi Futaba*

Translated and with explanatory notes by Gavan McCormack

1. Confessing to something one did not do

The 'year of the falsely accused' is how 1983 has been described. It is some years since the courts began opening ever so slightly their tightly closed gates and pronouncing not guilty verdicts on the many cases in which it is alleged that the charges are false. In May last year all the defendants were released in the case of the 'Chief of Police's residence' and the 'Peace' cigarette-tin bomb case (the unified trial defendants) — which thereby became the biggest ever postwar cases of false accusation. In July, for the first time ever in Japan, a verdict of innocent was handed down at the re-trial of a person under sentence of death, Menda Sakae.[24] The sequence of cases of victims of false accusation securing redress seemed to reach a new height. Various journals put together special issues on the 'false accusation' theme, and even the television and newspapers that had published savagely condemnatory reports at the time when these innocent people were arrested now adopted a friendly disposition towards them, as if to hasten their compensation.

But has the 'year of the falsely accused' really arrived? Will the gates of the courts go on being opened as wide as they need to be from now on for the many accused of crimes or serving sentences for crimes who are protesting their innocence? Unfortunately it rather seems that the situation has begun to move in the opposite direction.

After the mass 'not guilty' verdict in the 'cigarette-tin' case, the Justice Minister issued an 'exceptional directive' about 'giving careful consideration to the possibility of pursuing a re-trial in the case of an

* The Igarashi text reproduced here is entitled 'Kōshite jihaku o saserareta' (Forced to confess), *Sekai,* February 1984, pp. 220-232, and is an abridged version of a recent book: Tokyo san bengoshikai gōdō daiyō kangoku chōsa iinkai (Joint investigative committee of the three Tokyo Bar Associations into substitute imprisonment), ed., *Nureginu* (Falsely charged), Tokyo, Seihōsha, 1984. Notes to the introduction are by the translator; notes to the translation are, unless otherwise indicated, taken from *Nureginu.* Mrs Igarashi's permission to translate and publish her article is gratefully acknowledged.

innocent verdict' and calling for 'self-criticism over laxity in investigation'. This was not a criticism of innocent people being wrongly indicted because of the laxity of the investigation, but a rebuke to the
investigating authorities for having allowed there to be the verdicts of
not guilty. Even Chief Justice Ōkubo, just after issuing the 'not guilty'
verdict in the cigarette-tin bomb case, made his statement about 'grey'
indecisive innocence, lamenting that the evidence had been insufficient to establish guilt. Already by September, this 'grey' declaration
had spread to the Mito District Court, where it was repeated in the
case of the murder of an old woman.

It is clear that talk of 'grey' innocence was an expression of concern
for or sympathy with the investigating authorities in the rapidly disin-
tegrating power relationship between judiciary and police. However,
as the *Asahi* (evening edition) wrote on 19 May, 'from listening to what
was read out in the court there is no basis for seeing the outcome as
grey; all the case consisted of was the fact of confession'. In fact there
was no advance beyond the crude popular perception that 'one does
not confess to something one did not do'.

In essence, this 'common sense' merely states the obvious. Those
who were wrongly accused held the same view up until the time when
they were made to 'confess' to crimes they knew nothing about. Very
few people understand the circumstances of a Japanese police 'interrogation' — of the unhappy situation in which people suddenly one
day find themselves, or of the process by which they may be made to
'confess to crimes of which they know nothing'. In some cases the actual
circumstances seem not to have been understood even by the prosecutor who issued the indictments in the case, let alone by the judges, who
are not connected with the investigation.

Till these circumstances become known to the world, and till it becomes common knowledge that under this system one may be made to
'confess' to crimes one has not committed, the gates of the court will
never be opened wide enough to release all wrongly accused.

I propose to approach the process of 'confession' to crimes one has
not committed through various materials including replies to a survey
conducted of 30 people who had been falsely accused (from Menda
Sakae who was arrested in 1949 to 'F', a boy who was arrested in 1982)
which were collected by the Committee to Investigate Substitute Imprisonment of the three Tokyo Bar Associations, and also through the
shorthand record of the proceedings of a meeting of the falsely accused
held in May 1983.

2. Into the birdcages

The long months and years under false accusation begin suddenly and
unexpectedly one day. A number of men you do not know interrupt

your sleep, often early in the morning. But they do not mention arrest; they merely ask you to come along voluntarily 'to answer some questions about your friends'. After you have been taken by car to the police station, the tone of the conversation changes, and little by little you come to realise that you are being held on suspicion of some preposterous crime.

When you try to explain that this is all a terrible mistake your treatment worsens. When you issue a firm denial you are suddenly told 'you cannot go home today; you are under arrest', and handcuffs are snapped on. It is already night. While you are still numb with horror your photograph is taken (this photograph may even appear on television above the caption 'vicious criminal arrested'); your finger-prints are taken; you are stripped and body-searched, and then shoved through a lattice-work door behind the detectives' rooms and locked in. This is the police lockup.

It is also known as the 'birdcages' since it is an iron barred structure of birdcages in an empty room.

The 'birdcages' are divided by a wall, and each separate segment is known as a cell, accommodating either one person or several. They are either comb-shaped, with the cells side by side in a row, or fan-shaped, with the cells arranged in a semi-circle. According to a directive from the Police Ministry the fan-shape is to be preferred, since one man standing guard at the pivot of the fan can thereby observe the deepest recesses of every cell. If for some reason the construction has to be comb-shaped, then a television camera has to be installed or some other such arrangement made.

Those who are consigned here are under constant surveillance, without a moment's rest, day and night, till they leave. Anything that might interfere with the surveillance is removed. The toilet is open, with only a screen which barely covers the lower part of the body. However cold it may become, or however aggravating to have the fluorescent light on constantly, even while you are sleeping, it is forbidden to cover your face with the blanket. It is forbidden to lean on the dividing wall, the reason being that the guard might not be able to see behind you. Deprived of any shred of privacy, prisoners here become simply objects of surveillance.

Even the Nazis do not seem to have built such facilities. Although they constructed iron-barred prisons, the guards merely patrolled at regular intervals; there was no such thing as uninterrupted surveillance. And in Japan too, as elsewhere, prisoners who have not been formally convicted of a crime should be held in some kind of patrolled detention facilities, not in birdcages.

In shock at being placed under such extraordinary surveillance, at first virtually all prisoners are unable to go to the toilet and unable to sleep. (Eguchi, a defendant in the cigarette-tin bomb case could sleep no more than three hours a night for a period of a month.) They suffer loss of appetite and drastic deterioration of health. Then, as soon as the initial shock begins to wear off, their health is further undermined by the physical conditions of detention, the extremely poor food, clothing, and living conditions.

First, the food. The rations that are officially provided are astonishingly poor in terms of both quality and quantity. Breakfast as a rule is boiled rice (one to one and a half cups) with a couple of slices of pickled radish and a tasteless bean paste soup. Lunch is a bread roll with a little butter or margarine. The evening meal is the same as breakfast, with the addition of either a croquette or one or two fried fish balls. All of those who replied to the survey (with the exception of one who did not eat because of a stomach ailment) made poignant comments like 'I was so hungry I could not sleep', 'I lost 10 kilograms weight in two months', 'my skin crackled and came away in fine powder'. All agreed that 'it was impossible to remain healthy on official rations alone'.

There were also comments such as 'I was promised a bowl of braised pork cutlet on rice if I would confess'. From a separate source, not one of the 30 respondents to the survey, it appears that the phrase 'a one bowl confession' is common parlance among detectives. When we hear of confessions extracted because of hunger for a bowl of braised pork cutlet we have some idea of how miserable these people were, but their suffering does not end there. The prisoner must *pay* for his pork cutlet. In other words, confession is made to gain the privilege of being allowed to buy with one's own money food over and above the official rations. That is how wretched the food in the police station cells is.

After living on such food for a while, the prisoner weakens to the point where he or she 'cannot bear to be squatting on my heels on the floor'. Yet, in the birdcages, one is forced to squat upright like this on a mat (issued when one is first consigned to the cell) spread on the wooden slats which are laid over the concrete. Unless special permission to lie down is given in the case of severe illness, it is forbidden even to lean on the wall, let alone lie down and, except for leaving one's cell under the circumstances described in the following section, it is forbidden to stand up or move about. ('Outline of Regulations Applicable in the Treatment of Suspects', a directive of the Criminal Department of the Metropolitan Police.)

There are only four occasions on which one may leave one's cell:

1. to have a bath (five to fifteen minutes, once in five days in summer, once in seven days in winter);

2. for exercise, five minutes once a day (often this amounts to no more than five minutes standing around a bucket in a room adjacent to the cells, smoking);

3. for meetings with family or lawyers;

4. for interrogation sessions.

Forced to confess 199

Meetings in particular are extremely limited. In the case of some of those who were falsely accused, like Nasu Takashi of the Hirosaki case,[25] bathing and exercise time was lost because of interrogation and for more than 20 days from arrest till indictment it was not possible to bathe even once. Interrogation goes on uninterruptedly night and day and in the interrogation room too one is forced to sit up straight. When not summoned to interrogation one must just squat on one's heels in the cell, so either way it is a case of just squatting or sitting up straight all day every day.

The pain of just squatting on your heels on the floor like this is beyond imagining; one day of it produces complete exhaustion. Made to go on squatting like this day after day, some detainees developed scabs or inflammation on the skin of the buttocks. For some time after release it was impossible for them to walk properly.

The health of the prisoners suffers very quickly as a result of living like this in cells where humidity is high and, when it is not summer, it is cold. Menstruation nearly always ceases in the case of women prisoners. Many complain of general physical debility, severe loss of eyesight; some found they had become unable to climb stairs. It is scarcely surprising that only nine of the 30 who had been falsely charged said they had not become ill during detention, while two reached the stage of thinking they might not survive.

The birdcages undermine the spirit as well as the body of the prisoners. In cells facing outwards there is no window, and even when there is a window often it does not open. In the enclosed space there is no sunlight and no draft of fresh air; there is no glimpse of the outside world to be caught. Night and day the fluorescent light shines continuously and, as Eguchi Yoshiko (of the cigarette-tin bomb case) said, 'I was forced to live for 80 days without ever seeing the sun'. One loses all sense of night and day, and also of time, since watches are deliberately not shown to prisoners. 'All five senses become numbed' (Masubuchi of the cigarette-tin bomb case); 'When I saw other prisoners in hand-cuffs I thought they were wrist-watches and wondered "Why does everybody else but me have a watch?" ' (Masubuchi). Clearly one falls into an abnormal psychological condition.

Thus, before they are led into the interrogation room, the prisoners are already in an abnormal physical and psychological condition.

3. The interrogation room

Japanese police have many interrogation rooms. The police in Tokyo actually have 13 times as many interrogation rooms to detainees as do their counterparts in the United States, so great is the weight placed on interrogation (to extract a confession) in the overall investigation.

The interrogation rooms are small, about two metres square, like a row of match boxes within a larger, external frame. From these secret chambers, no sob or cry reaches the outside world. The 'suspect's chair' is by the back wall. It is small and hard and often has no back-rest. There is a desk in front of it, and the interrogation is carried out with this desk pressed up tight against one's chest or stomach; when the answer to a question is no, 'the desk was deliberately bashed against my chest' (Watanabe Masaya, suspect in the Chinnan Park case).[26] The desk serves as a kind of torture instrument.

The suspect is tied to the leg of the desk by a rope known as the waist cord, and often remains handcuffed during interrogation. The police officers sit on the side of the desk nearest the door. Generally two of them constitute a team, but 23 of the 30 surveyed were hemmed in by a large number of detectives; their interrogation took place with 25 people shouting abuse in their ears.

The falsely accused were made to sit uninterruptedly in the suspect's chair. For Menda, who experienced the longest interrogation, the process lasted for 21 hours from 2 a.m. to 11 p.m. broken only by about one hour of restless sleep. For Nasu of the Hirosaki case it lasted 19 hours; for Konta Saisuke of the Ōmori Industrial Bank Case,[27] 18 hours. Fourteen hours was most common.

In the case of 23 detainees, interrogation continued even when they dropped off to sleep from fatigue after many hours of questioning. For this to go on even for *one* day is enough to cause severe exhaustion, but most of the falsely accused were interrogated more or less without respite every day from the time of their arrest till they were able to make a full 'deposition of confession'. The longest continuing interrogation was that of Nakamura Ryūji (of the cigarette-tin bomb case). He was forced to occupy the interrogation chair continuously for 327 days, almost a year. In the case of 23 of the survey respondents it was the agony of prolonged interrogation which led them to 'confess' to crimes of which they were innocent. Since 25 of the respondents made confessions this accounts for nearly all of them.

The agony of the interrogation room does not end there. First, the suspect is given no water to drink. 'A', who was suspected of killing one of the victims of the so-called Katsuta case, complained, even though terrified, of the pain of being given nothing to drink no matter how thirsty he became after more than ten hours. A number of others were also deprived of food. They had no way of knowing when it was meal-time because they were unable to see a clock, but even if they knew the time they were not free to say they wanted something to eat. Interrogation continued during meals. While the Tsuchida case suspects were eating they were shown gruesome photographs of the corpse of Mrs Tsuchida, who died in an explosion, and asked 'What about this? What about this?' If they gagged on their food and could eat no more they were abused with 'You did it! That's why you cannot eat'. If they struggled to go on eating it was a case of 'You don't turn a hair. You just go on eating. You must be the criminal!'

As for going to the toilet, Sudō Tadashi of the Chief of Police's residence case was told 'You will not admit your guilt so you cannot go. If you admit it you can go any time'. He was always refused till 'I reached the point where I felt I could not contain myself a moment longer'. For those suffering from diarrhoea it was sheer agony.

Once one is brought to the interrogation room, the interrogation official may at his discretion refuse all the exercise or bathing that is part of life in the cages. The secret chamber known as the interrogation room is the place where confessions are extracted after the conditions of human survival, shaved to the barest minimum in the birdcages, are totally stripped away.

4. No torture?

The judicial authorities have a strong dislike for the word 'torture'. The word has not appeared in judgements for a long time; it is not used at all in the mass media. But has torture ceased?

The question 'did you experience physical violence' was included in the survey questionnaire merely for form's sake. However, in 20 of the 30 replies this time was circled. Take the case of 'B', the middle-aged former public servant who last year was falsely arrested, but not indicted, for murder. This case was included in the survey and details have also been published elsewhere.[28]

Three detectives took 'B' to a windowless three mat room 2.7 by 1.8 metres, stuck newspaper over the frosted glass on the door, and without interruption applied the following violence to him over the period from 9 a.m. to 10 p.m.

1. Beating him indiscriminately about the head with their fists. (Where bruises ensued they would beat him on the bruises; the pain was indescribable.)
2. Slapping him on the cheeks with an open palm.
3. Forcing his body against the wall and throttling him (pain to the throat).
4. Poking him in the midriff with their fists (affecting the solar plexus).
5. Cupping their hands around his ears, detectives would shout repeatedly in a loud voice from both sides 'Killer! Killer!' (Faintness and dizziness result, and ringing in the ears continued for some time afterwards. Several times he pleaded with the detectives 'Please break my eardrum'.)
6. Kicking him around the hips and legs.
7. Kneeing him in the thighs; pinning him down with their shins. (This becomes unbearably painful.)

8. Forcing his head down and bashing it against the floor while he was sitting down.
9. Bashing his head against the wall.
10. Twisting his fingers, using various tricks on the joints.
11. Pressing a large fountain-pen type ball-pen between his fingers and twisting. (Severe pain in the bones.)

Wiping away his perspiration with a running singlet, the detective concentrated on this torture, completely neglecting the interrogation. As a result of the torture, 'B' fainted, suffered severe headaches, received bruises all over his body, had continuous ringing in his ears for about three days and pain in the head, throat, and loins for about two weeks after his release. Where the violence lasts two days it takes about four weeks to recover.

Others of the falsely accused experienced various of these eleven kinds of assault. The 1977 case of the boy 'C', suspected of involvement in the burglary of apartment buildings, may be added to the others:[29]

> When I stumbled as they pulled me, they just dragged me about while I was still handcuffed. I was beaten by fists in the solar plexus; beaten with handcuffs; my fingers were forced backwards; a ruler was placed against the back of my hand and body weight applied to it from above; I was kicked in the buttocks by guards with their shoes on, slapped across the ears with a ruler, had underwear stained with menstrual blood stuffed in my mouth.

When you read such poignant entries, you wonder what those who nowadays refrain from using the word 'torture' would count as torture and whether one can say there is no torture in today's Japan.

Are we only to consider as torture the tortures of the Edo pre-1868 or prewar periods, such as forcing people to hold heavy stones or hanging them upside down? Or perhaps can we say that, even though some ill-treatment may occur, it is not constantly repeated to the point where we would say that the 'confession' is made as a result of physical pain?

Well, then, what about the case of Mr Funasako of the Kagoshima husband and wife murder case?[30] Though he suffered from a heart ailment, and even when his body was swollen and his temperature reached 38 degrees, he was forced to squat on his heels on the board floor for 14 hours a day from 8 a.m. till 10 p.m., or during the latter part of the period up until when he made his 'confession' for 18 hours a day till 2 a.m. Eventually he could bear it no longer and 'confessed'.

From cases like the assault on the president of Ōkawa city council in Fukuoka prefecture which occurred on 12 May 1983, it can easily be surmised that detectives use violence and cause injuries to suspects in the interrogation process, and that it is not confined to the cases of those falsely charged.

5. Control and submission

> I was dragged from my chair and forced to lie prostrate on the floor (Yoneya of the Yoneya case).[31]
>
> 'You, you swine, prostrate yourself!' they shouted at me as they forced me to squat upright and bow my head to the floor ('D' of the boy burglars case).

Interrogating officials seem to like making prisoners prostrate themselves, squat on their heels in an upright position, correct their posture, look straight ahead, pay attention. It is not a matter of observing propriety. The officials themselves slouch in their chairs, blow cigarette smoke at their suspects, and go on endlessly with intolerably obscene talk.

Unilateral insistence that the *suspect* adopt a correct posture is not just designed to provide a pretext for grabbing him by the hair and shaking his head; nor is it just to induce fatigue by having the same posture held for long periods of time. There is another, more fundamental reason. By not allowing any relaxation of posture even for an instant and by repeating 'straighten yourself up' or using violence on the occasion of any infringement, the interrogators induce a bodily appreciation of the fact that the relationship of suspect and interrogating official is one of submission and control. Its corollary is taking away the freedom to go to the toilet or to eat and practising violent behaviour of a kind that must be called torture.

Through control of posture, and through physical and psychological control, eventually a relationship is developed in which a signature can be obtained to whatever is written in the 'Deposition of Confession'.

For this reason, the narrow confines of the interrogation room must actually be a secret chamber. Even if it is not in physical terms completely a secret chamber, and even if the plaintive cries of the suspect being ill-treated may penetrate beyond its walls, it is a secret chamber in the sense that it is so organised that no one but the interrogating officials assigned to the case can interfere in it.

All other official authority yields as soon as one enters this room. For example, even the duties prescribed for heads of police stations — to allow prisoners to sleep from 8 p.m., to provide food at regular intervals, to provide medical treatment for the ill, and so on (Outline of Regulations Applicable in the Treatment of Suspects) — are set aside here.

> On the day I was arrested I vomited continually but the interrogation continued and I was just given some sheets of newspaper to stop the bed getting dirty (Iwabuchi Hideki of the Chief of Police's residence case).

> Though almost suffocating from an attack of asthma I was also treated the same way (Togari Naokazu of the same case).

Even after the suspect is returned from the interrogation room to the detention cells, it is the interrogating official, not the guards, who decides whether to call a doctor for the suspect. This resulted, in the case of Mr Sudō, in dangerously delayed treatment for appendicitis. Illness is most effective in implanting a sense of the superiority of the interrogator's authority. Many of the suspects who became ill felt that, if they did not comply with the wishes of their interrogator, they would not be able to escape with their lives. 'Illness is a weapon of the interrogator' (Togari).

It is the interrogating official who possesses real power, not the guards who are only nominally responsible. The interrogator has the power to allow meetings, to permit things to be sent in from outside, and to sanction the purchase of food and other items with one's own money. So those falsely accused who do not make 'confessions' are scarcely able to meet with their family or lawyers.

But the interrogator's power reaches beyond the police station. They may allow meetings in blatant contravention of the 'prohibition of interviews' measures of the courts, and they can influence the prosecutors to achieve various goals such as prolonging custody, prolonging custody on a different offence, and so on. A 'confession' made to a prosecutor before it has been made to the interrogator is an occasion for severe abuse — 'you should have told me first' (Enoshita Kazuo of the Tsuchida cigarette-tin bomb case). In cases where one makes a desperate resolve and, during the investigation by the prosecution, reverses a 'confession' made earlier as a result of being unable to stand up to the police any longer, that also attracts abuse from the prosecutor. Eleven of the respondents reported that 'not only were the police extremely angry with us when we were returned to them, but a new false confession was extracted from us by the interrogating official'. The case of nine respondents who were forced by a prosecuting attorney to sign a deposition drawn up precisely in line with the preliminary police report was similar.

Mr Sudō pleaded with the judge to recognise that he had been falsely charged as a result of torture. He based his argument on the provision in the code requiring 'indication of the reason for detention', which is designed as a check on the legitimacy of detention, but the court would do nothing. All that happened was that he was returned to police custody and continually threatened over the matter.

When visitors come, they are often trailed by detectives on their way home. The accused does not know how much to rely on a lawyer whom he has never met before when he is only able to meet with him or her for 15 minutes in ten days. The lawyer is in no position to put a stop to the actions of interrogating officials, much less do anything to rescue his client from illegal detention. When the client says 'It is hard to be investigated for something I know nothing about' all he can reply is

'Chin up!'. Enoshita remarked 'I felt the police were so mighty; all the lawyers of Japan were no match for them'.

Neither judge nor prosecutor nor defence attorney was any help to these falsely accused people as they were being driven day in and day out to 'confess' to crimes of which they were innocent. It is the investigating detective who acts as scourge to try to extract a false confession, who wields such almighty power over the suspect that he or she comes to wonder 'perhaps I will not survive'. Once the suspect comes to understand this, the interrogating official can exact from him the 'confession' to crimes he did not commit.

6. Sucked gradually to the middle of the whirlpool

Reports of 'confession by the criminal' appeared in the papers at one time or another about nearly all of the 30 falsely accused. Those reading these articles presumably imagined that 'one night' the accused 'really must have' committed the crime alleged and was now telling the full story of his crime.

But the reality of these confessions is vastly different. In the Menda case, for example, all that was objectively clear was that in 1949 the home of a certain faith healer was attacked, the husband and wife killed, and two daughters severely wounded. During the court proceedings the hypothesis of the investigating authorities was shown to be a fabrication. Menda Sakae supposedly entered the house to rob it, was caught in the act, killed the husband and wife with a hatchet, slashed the throat of the father with a fish knife, and escaped through the back of the house from the kitchen, washing his jacket and trousers in the Nutsugo River on the way home. It was a false charge. But the fabrication — what those who have been falsely charged refer to from their own experience as the 'story' — was not concocted by the accused. It is constructed in the following way.

(i) The interrogating official first starts with some relationship between friends which is unrelated to the crime. The first step is voluntary co-operation in the investigation, but gradually the 'confession' becomes the crux of the investigation. In the cigarette-tin bomb case, as Nakamura Ryūji said, 'You certainly cannot admit such an accusation when you are suddenly confronted with it'. The facts which are elicited at this stage play an important role in stage (v), which is discussed below.

(ii) In this stage, the investigating official makes various references to 'accomplices'. Both Masubuchi and Enoshita, mentioned in the example above, were implicated in the case in this way. Their 'involvement' leads to further 'evidence', as in stage (v). Other 'suspects' were told as a concrete 'fact' that both Masubuchi and Enoshita had confessed.

As mentioned above, visits to the accused by family and lawyers are severely circumscribed, especially in the case of those suspects who do not confess. In the detention centre to which one is transferred if one makes a 'confession', one can, to some extent, listen to the news on the radio, read newspapers and exchange letters, but all of these freedoms are withheld from suspects detained by the police. They are told nothing of what is happening in the world. They are placed in a news vacuum. Those detailed as 'accomplices' are assigned to separate detectives and are completely cut off from any contact between themselves. Even if they had wanted to find out whether Masubuchi and the others had really made such an admission, there was no way of doing so.

Furthermore, since you do not tend to think of yourself being taken as an 'accomplice', the tendency is to think,

> If others have made such an admission, well, that's up to them. As for yourself, you just want to get out of this troublesome mixup as quickly as possible. There are so many things outside that need your attention. And so admissions about others are extracted from you first of all (Nakamura).

And with this 'deposition' about 'a matter concerning someone else' as evidence, 'the investigation progresses'; more people are arrested.

(iii) At the next stage the matter ceases to be just 'a matter concerning someone else'. You are told

> A calculating fellow like Masubuchi was certainly using you; you just did not realise it. Tell us everything that you and your mates talked about,'

and you tell all. This is later made use of in stage (v). Even when you have said all there is to say, you are told:

> 'that cannot be all. They were engaging in a struggle with bombs. There must have been an organiser.'

From recollections of things you have read in weekly magazines and such like, you think 'there may have been such talk'. It is all very vague and you cannot say for sure whether there was or not, but you have a strong feeling of wanting this all to end quickly, and so you end by admitting that 'there was such talk'.

(iv) At this, the line of questioning changes to

> 'Since things were organized, then I suppose you were teaching something concrete?'

There is only your hobby of electricity. So you compromise with

> 'If anyone were to ask me I suppose I would have taught about electricity'

and when that is written up in the deposition it becomes

> 'I did actually teach.'

This amounts to a confession linking one as 'accomplice' to a crime. What had been a voluntary investigation became compulsory. Nakamura was arrested.

One segment of a 'story' which till this point had been taking shape underwater, so to speak, as a 'non-criminal fact', now suddenly stands revealed 'above the water' in the realm of crime.

In this way, one is gradually sucked in closer and closer to the centre of the whirlpool. You are not at this stage at the centre, but it is already impossible to escape the whirlpool.

7. Tragic quiz

(v) This process goes on more or less simultaneously with multiple 'accomplices'. What was extracted in the deposition at stages (i) and (iii) from Nakamura proves to be good material for showing to other 'accomplices', who are told 'the investigators have got this far'. Stage (iii) and (iv) material is used as the basis to say

> 'Since Nakamura has confessed in this way no one is going to believe it if you alone try to hold out.'

And, one by one, the 'confessions' of the 'accomplices' are obtained.

Between the fabrications of the 'accomplices' which surface above the water as 'crime', suddenly a linking beam is attached. A further fabrication is constructed upon this beam and the framework of a huge 'terror bombing incident' is erected on it. When the interrogating official says 'So-and-so says you did it', hatred towards your friend who has implicated you even though you are innocent leads you to co-operate with the investigating official who has to draw up the deposition. You almost put yourself in his position and agree that your friend must have done it. Thus, as the fabrications become taller and bigger, the dimensions of the overall affair also swell.

But, it is, after all, nothing but a fabrication, so cracks become evident at various points once the 'story' is put together.

Although the interrogating officials are in contact with each other about the 'accomplices', the 'criminals' themselves have to proceed in complete isolation with the task of 'remembering' something that never happened. Naturally inconsistencies emerge between what they have to say. Since their 'confessions' are sheer fantasy there are also bound to be discrepancies with objective truth. In some cases separate crimes also emerge later out of this. In some cases this may lead to the subsequent emergence of separate crimes.

(vi) At this point, since what has been confessed is too much in conflict with the facts, the suspect is put to the task of revising the deposition, that is to say of making up something in accordance with hints provided by the investigating official.

According to Enoshita,

> As for my saying that the bomb had been transported in relay-style, that was because the police said 'Someone has just told us that you were involved that day' and I thought I would just have to agree with them. But then they got angry with me, saying that was not the way it had been. What a mess!

Even when the 'story' has to be changed, the reason is always bound to be that 'the suspect lied'. Although the matter may be one which goes to the very heart of the 'deposition of confession', in such a case the suspect is abused, and sometimes is even beaten and made to sign a written statement of 'apology for having lied'. Desperately looking for some hint as to how one might be allowed to remember, you search the expression and the words used by the interrogating official for the correct answer. It is just like a quiz. And if you cannot give the right answer because you are not given good hints, the interrogating official gets angry. In Enoshita's words:

> Being abused again and again, I wept and said 'My memory is no good'. For a time I was terrified because I really thought this was so.

Interrogation is tragic, but at the same time objectively it is a ludicrous quiz.[32]

8. 'Giving-in'

> When this kind of thing continues for a while, it becomes difficult to distinguish what actually you yourself remembered from what you have made up . . . You lose confidence in yourself and just don't know what happened . . . Mind and body become disoriented. (Masubuchi, the 'principal criminal' of the cigarette-tin bomb case.)

> I felt as though I was standing on a precipice. ('C', of the boy burglars case.)

While being sucked rapidly into the vortex of the whirlpool, at the same time you try to hold out and say 'no', at least to that mind-boggling vortex.

(vii) But,

> not being allowed to sleep I became more and more sleepy. I got fed up with everything and felt that if I would do as the police said things might get easier. ('E', youth arrested by mistake in an arson case.)

> After long hours of questioning and sleeplessness day after day, I began to wonder why did I have to endure such hardships. (Sudō.)

Come what may, you want this wretched interrogation to end quickly. At the last moment you reach a stage where, although you have been resisting, you give up. As for confessing to that central bit, it becomes 'just a trifling step, a slight loss of balance'. You find that what you had been persisting in just crumbles away. In the case of Masubuchi, the 'main criminal' of the cigarette-tin bomb case, it was the shock of being given two false pieces of information that constituted 'the final thrust'. After the lawyer who had managed to arrange a one-hour interview had been sent away under the pretext of 'continuing interrogation', Masubuchi was told that,

> 'The lawyer was too busy and went home . . . Even your lawyer has turned his back on you'.
> When I heard this I was thunderstruck.
> Then he followed it up with 'Now you said the bomb came from your house.' (This was completely untrue.)

> I just lost all sense of what was what and with my reply 'alright' the deposition was suddenly drawn up. At that moment all the strength drained out of my body. I don't know whether I was sad or not, but at any rate tears came flooding out. I didn't know what to do and for a time was just beside myself.

In the 'Circumstances at the time of giving in' this was represented as 'the suspect made his confession in tears', and used to emphasise that the 'confession' was genuine. Cut off from all contact with the outside world, Masubuchi had no way of confirming the two false pieces of information fed to him by his interrogating official.

The process of drawing up of the confession that we have followed through stages (i) to (vii) is achieved precisely through the interrogation officials' control of information reaching the accused, who is confined to the place of detention and the interrogation room. It is in the 'final thrust' that the most powerful information control is brought to bear on the accused. There are two ways in which this is done.

(a) The threat to arrest and interrogate those most dear to the accused, such as parents, wife, children. In the case of Sudō, the interrogator drew up a request for a warrant for the arrest of his parents and showed it to him. It was this that made Sudō 'give in'. Even without going to such lengths, it is easy to see how people arrested for crimes they know nothing about might come to believe that their parents, spouses, etc., could suffer the outrage of arrest for 'harbouring a criminal'. And so one comes to think that it is better to accept the blame for a crime not committed rather than have wife, children or aged parents endure the torments of the interrogation. No less than 24 of the 30 respondents were threatened in this way.

(b) If you do not confess to the crime as spelt out by the interrogating official, you will be found guilty of a greater crime; you will suffer the death penalty, or you will spend the rest of your life in prison, and red paper will be pasted over your family register entry.

Twenty-five of the respondents were told this.

On the other hand,

> If you *do* confess, you will be let off lightly, allowed to go home, released on probation,

Twenty of the respondents were told this.

Anyone living 'outside', in conditions of liberty, would understand that it is not within the powers of the investigation officer to grant such things. But such things, threats or promises, can be the source of real terror for suspects confined within the unnatural limits of the bird-cages and the interrogation room and continually being made to understand the omnipotence of the interrogator over their lives.

Mr Watanabe, who encountered both (a) and (b) analysed this process as an 'excuse for selling one's soul'.

> You make that first confession because you want to get out quickly. You want to escape from the interrogation as quickly as possible, not spending even one second longer there.

That is to say, the 'last thrust' produces an effect eventually because the mind and body of the suspect have been worn to shreds over a long time. This is probably a well-developed technique honed by the history of police in Japan, in which interrogation is that which produces 'confession'.

9. The interrogator's essay

We have seen how a person can be made to 'confess' to a crime of which he knows nothing. But, even when the innocent person bows his head at the 'final thrust' and says 'Alright', that still does not amount to 'getting a confession' for the interrogator. In the Japanese investigation it is only when the 'deposition of confession' is drawn up that one has 'confession'.

The deposition is the document in which the examining official 'records' the contents of the suspect's testimony. In fact, however, as soon as Masubuchi said the word 'Alright' the examining official drew it up instantly. In the case of Nakamura it was written in a separate room; in the case of Enoshita one morning when he went to the inter-rogation room it was there, already written.

Other cases may not have been so blatant as this, but not one of these 'depositions of evidence' was actually a record of words spoken by the suspect.

Between the suspect placed in the interrogation room and the ex-amining official, time passes. After many hours or days, when the interrogator decides he wants to draw up the deposition, he inserts a piece of carbon paper in the deposition blank and writes until it is complete. In the course of doing this he may check things with the 'sus-pect' or call the 'suspect's' attention to various sections of it, but from beginning to end it is the interrogator who thinks it out and chooses the words. In Japan *all* 'depositions of evidence' are compositions, whether the investigating official be the procurator or a police official. Furthermore, the suspect signs a declaration that a record of the proceedings has been read to him and there is no error in it, but a suspect who, like Masubuchi, was prostrate for 30 minutes after he had been made to 'give-in' and unable even to hold a pen, could scarcely be expected to have had the strength to call for the revision of a deposition in which 'if one is to speak of errors, the whole thing is an error'. There are also cases where the very reading out to the suspect is neglected, or is done in a rapid or unintelligible fashion. The suspect does not 'countersign' the pages of the deposition. In some cases it has been alleged in court that sections of the deposition were substituted later, and nine of the thirty respondents who had been falsely charged said that they had 'no recollection of the deposition' drawn up in their cases.

Yet, once the 'deposition of confession' is drawn up in this way, every word or phrase in it, as the 'testimony' of the accused himself, becomes evidence of guilt. It may be that the accused's fate depends on a word which was chosen by the examining official, not by the accused himself. This is what 'guilty by reason of confession' means. Can there really be such barbarism?

The problem of confession in Japan is clear if one makes a comparison with foreign countries. I have been shown the actual reality of questioning in a Hamburg court and was given a copy of the proceedings. In West Germany, there is a typist present in the interrogation room and, although the typist does not type up the examining official's questions, the suspect's replies are typed up carefully on the spot. At the same time a tape recorder is used, and when the questioning is finished the suspect reads the typed deposition while listening to the tape and signs if he agrees there has been no mistake. Since the accused will not sign if there is a mistake the typists type correctly. Only in such circumstances is the name 'Record of Deposition' worth anything.

If in Japan confessions were taken in this way probably nearly all the cases we have had of people being falsely charged might have been avoided.

10. 'Substitute imprisonment' leads to false charges

Let us return to the initial scene of the arrested suspect being consigned to the birdcages. Those who are falsely charged have to go on living this birdcage life from day to day thereafter. The cigarette-tin bomb case was particularly long drawn out — 327 days in the case of Nakamura Ryūji — but Funasako also had to spend over 100 days in the birdcages on suspicion of a crime that had nothing to do with public order, as did Konta of the Ōmori Bank case.

According to the principles of the Japanese Code of Criminal Procedure such treatment should not exist. The criminal law code principle is that an arrested person may be held by the police for up to 72 hours (although many scholars do not accept that even this is permitted by the Code of Criminal Procedure). Within that interval, the suspect must be brought before a judge. If the judge grants 'detention' or formal physical confinement, the place where the accused is to be held is 'prison' (presently known as the detention centre). He should not be held by the police. The dissenting view referred to above holds that the suspect should be confined in prison right from the moment of arrest.

All Western states, or states which possess a modern criminal judicial system, have adopted legislation to this effect. The principle that the accused should not be returned to police custody after having been taken before a judge has also been confirmed frequently by international conferences in which developing countries have participated. (I was in Hamburg in 1977, after participating in a conference of the International Association of Penal Law which passed such a resolution, when I received a copy of the deposition of testimony mentioned above.)[33] This principle is regarded as important because, if the police are allowed to interrogate the accused over a long period, the kinds of things described above will occur.

Police who are entrusted with investigation try hard to solve the crime. Rather than undertake an objective investigation, which takes time, they short cut the process by having the accused himself make a confession. Investigating officials always go enthusiastically about interrogation; it is a common failing of mankind throughout the world that, carried away by enthusiasm, the investigator pressures the suspect to get a confession. If the suspect does not confess he is subjected to long interrogation, denied food and drink, refused permission to go to the toilet, and so on.

Many countries confirm from bitter historical experience that it is not enough to rely on the training of police officials and on the division of labour within the police (between investigation and guarding) to prevent too much weight being attached to a confession. Japan should have recognised this principle and, after the war, incorporated it in the code of criminal procedure.

But, as described above, the suspect in Japan is detained for long periods by the police. This occurs because in the Prisons Law (1908) there is a clause which reads 'Places of detention adjacent to police stations may be used as substitutes for prison'. As a result, the police station cells, the birdcages, are defined as 'substitute prisons', and suspects are confined there and interrogated day after day until the examining official has a 'deposition of confession' that he thinks is adequate in terms of both content and quality. The length of detention is an indication of how long the wrongly-accused has struggled to avoid 'confessing' to crimes he did not commit.

There are cases in other countries of people being falsely accused of crimes. But in Japan the outstanding characteristic of such cases, what might be called the Japanese model of false accusation, is the 'confession' by the falsely accused person himself (or 'confession' by an 'accomplice', which is viewed in the court as virtually the same thing). Substitute imprisonment leads to Japanese-style false accusations.

The recent succession of 'not guilty' verdicts on wrongly accused people has at last begun to shake the popular perception, mentioned earlier, that if one confesses one must be the real criminal. But, so long as the substitute imprisonment continues, 'anyone treated like this would confess'. Twenty-four hours enclosed in the confined spaces of the birdcages and interrogation room undermines both the health and the spirit of the suspect. Furthermore, the investigation of the crime, which is the crux of the confession, goes on for tens or hundreds of days under the overwhelming power of the examining police official unrestrained by any third party till the suspect 'confesses'. So long as this sysem lasts, anyone can be made to 'confess'. So long as substitute detention continues, falsely accused people will confess.

It is possible that the ordinary person's 'common sense' may change if 'not guilty' verdicts continue to increase. People may incline towards doubting the substitute imprisonment system and towards disallowing the exercise of unrestrained power by the police authorities in the name of crime prevention.

The 'self-criticism over the laxity of the investigation' is a recognition of this possibility. The judge's use of the expression 'grey judgement' seeks to weaken the 'undesirable effect of the not guilty verdicts' by reinforcing the conventional view that 'he who confesses must be guilty'.

Attaching undue weight in the investigation process to the confession blocks objective investigation and leads to error. In the cigarette-tin bomb case, searches were conducted and dust collected with powerful electric vacuum cleaners in more than 90 places all over the country, including the residence of Masubuchi, the supposed principal criminal. But no material evidence, such as powder relating to the bomb incident, was found.[34] If the direction of the investigation had altered in the light of this lack of evidence, there would have been no false charges and it may even have been possible to arrest the real criminal.

The substitute imprisonment system was introduced in 1908 and has remained in use since then because of the 'unavoidable circumstance' of insufficient prisons. It was originally thought that it was only a temporary measure. For many years, the Government told the Diet that at the next opportunity for revision of the Prison Act this system would be abolished. But the Criminal Facilities Law and the Police Cell Act brought forward in April 1982 (in other words, laws for the regularising of substitute detention, known jointly as the 'dual law on confinement') are designed to make the substitute imprisonment system permanent by making the detention cells a lawful place for detaining people. The law that is being drawn up openly rejects the international principle determined at Hamburg and elsewhere.

Japan is now preparing to move rapidly in the direction of a dark age. Both the dual law on confinement and the 'grey judgement' statement are signs of this trend in the field of criminal law.

Science, morality and the state*

Atuhiro Sibatani

1. Science

Bioethics is the field in which one examines and tries to solve ethical problems imposed on society by science and technology — pertaining, for example, to the genetic, developmental, reproductive, and clinical manipulations of human life. The latest, hotly-debated bioethical problem originated in Melbourne only very recently, when the team at Monash University announced that a human embryo produced by *in vitro* fertilisation, and frozen for four months, could later be successfully implanted in a uterus to produce a pregnancy. Although this achievement obviously gives benefit to a certain group of people including childless couples and gynaecologists/scientists performing the operation and associated research, it produces a host of tangled ethical problems concerning the question of how far this new technique can and should be implemented in the daily life of our society.

Since problems of bioethics are generated by the progress of science, it may be thought that suitable solutions can also be obtained by scientific enquiries. For science is in its essence a problem-solving activity. Some 'technological fix' can always be found. Or so one might suppose. However, as there are necessary limitations to our cognitive powers and our capacities to observe, so also are there necessarily always insoluble moral dilemmas. And the distance between our moral problems and our moral capacities (and related social formations and practices) is constantly being stretched by the ever-accelerating progress of scientific knowledge. We cannot, I believe, expect that any

* This is a slightly abridged version of a lecture given by Dr Sibatani under the auspices of the Melbourne Japanese Studies Centre at Monash University, Melbourne, on 8 June 1983. It was published in full under the title *Environment, Man, Science and Technology in Japan* as No. 9 in the series Papers of the Japanese Studies Centre, Melbourne, 1984.

kind of 'technological fix' will get rid of the moral problems generated by science and technology; and the prospect of some suitable 'sociological fix' seems equally unlikely, though it is in the development of new, pluralistic social formations that the greatest hope is to be found.

2. Non-scientific nature of bioethical decisions

The problems of bioethics may arise in part as an outcome of the tension between traditional moral values and the findings of modern science. If this be so, there may not be any adequate unique answer to this problem. The progress of science poses difficult problems for society, which science itself may not be able to solve. What should we do about it? Watanabe Itaru,[1] the founder figure of molecular biology in Japan, has been warning the Japanese of this problem since the mid-seventies. He suggested that the progress of science cannot and should not be arrested, and that society must hurry to reform itself to cope with the new problems brought about by the progress of science. Hence scholars and writers in the humanities and social sciences must work hard to match the progress of natural science. They should endeavour to design a society that can accommodate the new fruits of science, while ensuring the delivery of maximum benefits to those born into that society. Watanabe's first book had a strong impact on some sociologists and philosophers in Japan.[2]

But, Watanabe's ideas are strongly elitist, leading towards a 'manipulative society' run by bureaucrats and a few experts in social science and technology. His hoped-for solutions are illusory. An opposite approach, to which I subscribe, can be advanced to counter Watanabe's argument. It is, of course, not a 'complete' solution, but I believe it to be a better course to follow than that urged by Watanabe. Science, with or without other learned activities of human beings, will not be able to solve the new problems arising from the progress of science in an unequivocal way. Therefore, any attempts to solve them must be tentative, and hence, I believe, 'small-scale' and pluralistic in character. To illustrate further the nature of our present predicament, consider the following argument.

A recent radical critique of science[3] has made it clear that scientists and funding bodies for science are commonly parties with vested interests in the chosen objectives of scientific research. For example, it is known that scientific meetings on the basic science of developmental biology with special reference to *in vitro* fertilisation may sometimes be heavily subsidised by pharmaceutical companies. This is because such companies are interested in testing their products for undesirable side effects on human embryos, since the toxic effects of some of their products may be species-specific. For example, the notorious thalidomide which curtails limb development in human foetuses apparently causes no harmful effects in developing mice.[4]

Of course, science and scientists can supply information that is relevant to bioethical problems, but they cannot provide an answer that is uniquely and objectively derived from scientific analysis. Rather, it is obvious that bioethical questions are basically of a political nature in the sense that there is usually unequal and sometimes unjust distribution and delivery of the benefits and damages generated by scientific progress.

So, because bioethical problems involve the life and death of ordinary people in one way or another, the political decisions about it — and there are no purely scientific decisions as I have just explained — must be made by ordinary people,[5] desirably informed but not necessarily excluding those who are not well informed. Of course the final decision may vary from one community to another and from one historical period to another, hence adequate resolution of bioethical problems is incompatible with large centralised government. It seems reasonable to suggest that small-scale pluralist governments may offer a greater diversity of approaches for the solution of bioethical problems, with greater opportunities for flexible approaches, such as are impossible for huge administrative monoliths. A country like Australia, with a federal government and several state governments for a population of 14 million people, is, in principle, better suited to bioethical decision-making than a country like Japan with a centralised government for a population of 120 million people.

3. Management of biohazards — Japan and Australia

Let us turn from bioethics in general to the management in Japan of bioethics and other vexed social problems associated with science and technology.

I have some data which throw light on the decision-making processes — in relation to the social effects of science and technology — used in Japan and some other science-intensive countries, particularly English-speaking nations including Australia.

Experience of public participation in matters of science and technology, and interest in such problems, is rather limited in Japan, as compared with anglophone countries. Partly this is because democracy in Japan has not been entrenched long enough. Hence public participation has not been firmly institutionalised and all sorts of immature arguments are advanced that assert that efforts to ensure the public participation in social decision-making are inappropriate.

The Constitution of Japan[6] does not allow for the holding of referenda, other than for its own revision, and Japan has not held a referendum since the promulgation of the Constitution in 1947. Japan leans heavily towards formal representative democracy and it is generally not interested in direct or participatory democracy. Although the need to involve lay representatives in social decision-making has been pointed out repeatedly, I have never seen any initiative, other than token gestures, taken by the establishment to institutionalise such a procedure.

My own experience is a case in point. In mid-1982 I thought that there was an unexplored aspect of genetic engineering that pointed to the absence of sufficient experimental evidence to be sure of the safety of recombinant DNA work, as revealed by the recent progress in molecular biology — conspicuously assisted by the recombinant DNA work itself. At the time, the Japanese government was inviting submissions from all and sundry on the then-current proposal to relax the guidelines for recombinant DNA work. So I made one.[7] I also wrote to the Australian Recombinant DNA Monitoring Committee of my concern over this newly-revealed safety problem. The Australian Committee wrote back in due course and since then there has been an ongoing exchange of opinions and information on this point. On one occasion my colleague, Dr Ditta Bartels of the University of Sydney, and I attended the Monitoring Committee's Scientific Sub-committee and a suggestion was even made that I join the Sub-committee, though I did not accept this for personal reasons.[8] There were some tangible positive effects and the Monitoring Committee in Australia made some changes in procedure and advice in response to our action.[9] Dr Bartels, Dr Hiroto Naora of the Australian National University and I wrote a joint article on the same subject, which was published in an international journal *Trends in Biochemical Sciences (TIBS)*[10] in March 1983. Dr Bartels wrote another article for a wider audience which was published in *Search*[11] in April 1983.

The course of events in Japan was by no means so reassuring.[12] There was not even an official acknowledgement of my submission, so that I had no way of judging whether the Committee, which was set up in the Ministry of Education, was functioning properly. Further, there has been no direct official or personal contact with me in written or spoken form on the substantive problems raised in my submission.[13] Moreover, there has been some ridicule levelled at me, for my alleged ignorance, by one of the Committee members, and I understand that this person has actively suppressed reporting by the mass media on the problems that I have raised. Then an erroneous negative comment, given by the Committee Chairman, was reported. He later apparently withdrew this[14] but there has been no public or personally addressed statement or apology made by him. I translated both the *TIBS* and *Search* papers into Japanese, but so far neither has been published by established scientific professional journals comparable to the status of *TIBS* or *Search*, despite some effort towards their promotion on my side.

(They have, however, eventually been printed in a book of my own[15] and in a radical magazine for the critique of science and technology.)[16] I conclude from this episode that the machinery for external participation in bioethical issues appears to be decidedly underdeveloped in Japan. And it is practically non-existent for the lay public.

Another example in this connection is the construction of a high-security maximum-containment facility (P4 laboratory) for recombinant DNA work at the Institute for Physical and Chemical Research in Tsukuba Science City,[17] a plan strongly promoted by the Japanese Government's Science and Technology Agency. In 1981-82 the local government of Tsukuba area was opposed to the construction, chiefly because of the laboratory's location in a residential area. Members of the local government and community groups had a few workshop-type meetings with scientists and administrative people of the Institute. However, the objective of the research facilities was never defined consistently. Rather, it became clear that the workshop had been planned as a trap to get the critics to voice their opinions and then have them attacked one-sidedly in their absence by the scientists in favour of the scheme so that the criticism could be dealt with and contained easily. By means of this stratagem a green light would be given for the construction. In the spring of 1982, a group of some 350 scientists from Tsukuba Science City, largely working in fields not related to biotechnology, issued a statement requesting the construction of the P4 laboratory, apparently under pressure from the Government, the main funding body for their research. Finally, in May 1982, some of the members of the local government changed camp and passed a motion approving the construction. (This appears to be a situation similar to that which occurred in the Northern Territory in 1978, when the Aboriginal people made a final decision to agree on uranium mining.)[18] No independent officially appointed third party assessed the problem, and against local protests, construction of the facilities was begun in late 1982 behind high walls (not a metaphor) to conceal what was going on from outsiders.

A similar maximum-containment biological laboratory has been built at Geelong, Victoria, for the CSIRO Division of Animal Health in which work with imported foot-and-mouth disease virus strains has been planned. However, opposition from Australian farmers,[19] who organised an International Conference on its feasibility in late 1982, sparked scepticism about the wisdom of that plan, and finally both the Australian Science and Technology Council and the Australian Academy of Science voiced their reservations, making it likely that the very expensive laboratory (costing $150 million) would become a white elephant.[20]

Occurrences such as these are not exceptional in Japan's recent history of public/government confrontations in relation to problems at the interface of science/technology and society. One recalls, for example, the events associated with the construction of Narita Airport near Tokyo and of a number of nuclear power stations. The usual course of events has been that the government first proposed to construct the new facilities. It then gave a superficial (and sometimes flippant) explanation to the local community about national needs, public interests, and possible compensations. Such explanations were often subsequently shown to contain false statements, including an underestimation of possible harmful effects. Almost invariably, such confrontations developed into head-on clash between the government and the local communities, sometimes involving violence.[21] As a result it would probably be difficult for the government to opt for a more conciliatory course now in new ventures like the P4 laboratory or relaxation of the guidelines for recombinant DNA work. Any concession on the government side would lead to questioning of the propriety of earlier decisions.

4. Nuclear power stations

In the case of the nuclear power stations, at an early period of confrontation in 1975, the proponents planned to divide the format of public hearing into two separate meetings: one discussing local problems and the other discussing, at a national centre, safety problems of nuclear power stations in general.[22] The former was to be open to the local community, whereas the latter was to be restricted to professionals only. Moreover, the former also imposed various restrictions on the number of attendants, the duration of the hearings (one or two days only), the agenda, the manner in which the questions and discussions were to be conducted, and the venue (often inconveniently sited). Naturally, the critics of nuclear energy were violently opposed to the format of the public hearing. Hence a farcical situation arose. Opponents and critics of nuclear power stations boycotted the government-sponsored 'public hearing' while the proponents, backed up by the police force, could hold the hearings and then declare that these meetings had approved the safety of the construction of the nuclear power stations in question, thus rendering the whole matter a *fait accompli*. This pattern lasted until May 1983, when, for a public hearing on a new power station at Shimane, local groups decided to participate, though without the support of many other opponent groups from other areas. In the event, the group at Shimane apparently succeeded, at least partially, in disclosing weak points in the evidence and arguments provided by the proponents.[23]

Protagonists of nuclear power in Japan have often said that the events at Three Mile Island were not relevant to the Japanese scene, because as was well known in many sectors of modern industry, the US labour force was inferior in quality to its Japanese counterparts, and the various mishandlings seen in the US power stations were unlikely to occur in Japan where the quality control of the work was extremely high.[24] Indeed, some proponents of nuclear power went so far as to declare that in Japan public debate was not relevant: the essential thing was to establish a national consensus, which, once obtained, would direct the excellent Japanese work force to accomplish whatever was required technically and safety-wise. All problems would eventually be solved with quite satisfying results.[25]

5. Propensity to human experimentation

Another important aspect in contemporary Japan is the preparedness (for historical reasons outlined below) of the medical profession to be involved in human experimentation. As has been revealed by the novelist Morimura Seiichi and the journalist Takasugi Shingo[26] and others,[27] the Japanese army had a highly organised, large establishment for lethal human experimentation in medical research and chemical and biological warfare in northeast China (Manchuria) during the Sino-Japanese War and actually waged biological war in the mainland of China (south of Beijing). An estimated three thousand victims, comprising largely Chinese and Soviet prisoners of war and anti-Japanese activists, as well as some others picked up arbitrarily without any criminal or military charges, are believed to have been murdered in a number of inhuman ways, including vivisections.

The most alarming part of this horrifying story is the fact that the army corps that was engaged in this clandestine activity (Unit 731) was exempted from the war-criminal charges after the war, presumably in exchange for supplying relevant data to the US Occupation Forces. Doubtless this information later found its way to Fort Detrick. Most of the army and the recruited medical and paramedical professionals who were engaged in this operation successfully covered up their connections with this chemical and biological warfare establishment and their involvement in human experimentation. But, quite a few of them proceeded to use their acquired expertise in peace time for preventive medicine (e.g. production of vaccines) and other medical activities, and some of them rose to key positions in the medical community in postwar Japan. Only a small number of them committed suicide in remorse, or were charged by the Soviet Union War Criminal Court in Khabarovsk.

Upon reading Takasugi's book on the postwar follow-up of the personnel involved, I realised that as one of the young leaders of molecular biology after the war I had had contact with those who had allegedly been involved in the criminal operation of the above establishment, and that the initial rise of molecular biology in Japan was in fact made possible by the actions of a number of those key medical figures. They had assisted young would-be molecular biologists against the general opposition of biologists, who were hostile to the emerging new discipline of molecular biology. Thus the medical community in Japan at least partially relied for its prowess on results obtained through human experimentation during the war. Needless to say, it failed to state that fact openly. It is perhaps significant, therefore, that at the moment, when experimentation with human embryos is being debated world-wide, the Japanese medical community, if not the general public, seems to be largely insensitive to the issue. In fact, in April 1983 one of the triennial General Assemblies of All Medical Societies in Japan was held in Osaka with the title of 'Medicine: science and human beings'.[28] There the delegates talked of the techniques of *in vitro* fertilisation as they should have, but only from the *practitioners'* point of view. Indeed, there was apparently no attempt to resolve the ethical dilemma through the involvement of the general public in decision-making.

6. Scientists' reticence

Early in 1983 there was an active campaign among conservative members of parliament in Japan to repeal the clause in the Eugenic Protection Law which permits abortion for economic reasons. Generally speaking, the argument was based on the assumption (not unknown in the West) that human life starts at the moment of fertilisation.[29] Quite a few opposition movements were organised, mainly by women, and I was asked by one of them to publish an open letter to the government stating that biology does not support such a view and that it cannot specify any definite time-point as the beginning of human life.[30] The campaign against abortion came to a halt when the proposal was shelved, albeit temporarily, probably because of the strong protests made.[31] I now realise that no other biologists in Japan involved themselves in the protest movement. This reluctance on the part of Japanese scientists to speak up in public is conspicuous in scientific communities and meetings all round the world.

I suspect that this reticence is not unrelated to a subtle control of funding for research workers. In Japan, with the rise of an ample national economy, research grants are becoming quite generous. But to remain active as a research scientist it is essential to secure a suitable research grant because the maintenance funds for universities are fairly limited. Now, unlike grant systems in Australia or the USA, the peer review system for grant applications is carried out rather haphazardly in Japan. Unsuccessful applicants do not receive referees' comments on their reasons for failure. Moreover, the allocation of grants is in the hands of a very limited number of powerful academic 'bosses', and rank and file scientists are afraid of antagonising them even slightly. Hence, unlike the time when Japan was much less affluent, Japanese scientists have become quite wary of speaking up over matters not directly related to their research projects. In fact, there is a remarkable lack of open discussion in Japan on any controversial scientific matter, even if it is purely scientific.[32]

It may be said that all the fuss about more democratic procedures, seen in the English-speaking countries, is just window-dressing, eventually leading to the same results that Japan is overtly seeking, be it in genetic engineering, uranium mining, *in vitro* fertilisation or construction of dams and airports. Giving full opportunity for the expression of democracy may be a much more expensive and slow business, which ends in nothing but inefficiency — an ideal prey for the highly competitive Japanese predator.

The argument against this view is that even if the net results appear to be the same in the short run, experiences accumulated on both sides by the parties involved in the confrontation, through the course of democratic debate, could, in the long run, suddenly generate a salutary change in society. Whereas the Japanese way will make people apathetic, more passive and obedient, and not interested in seeing the true causes of the problem, the other way, by means of active participation and struggle, will motivate people to see the problems more clearly.

7. Universal versus non-universal

Let us now turn to some of the more general implications of these various facts.

As is well known, the economic performance of Japan after the war has largely been a great success. Even in the midst of the current grave economic recession, the Japanese performance is believed to be better than that of most other industrial nations in the free world. Japan's success in the world economy was not anticipated by any of the major economic theories of European origin. Therefore, Japan has good reason to assume that the social science and political philosophy of modern Europe was insufficient and/or inadequate. Two conclusions have been drawn in Japan:

(1) Now that conventional European models and guidelines have become obsolete, Japan has to devise an alternative theory about how and whither to proceed.

(2) The Japanese feel confident about themselves, and they tend to assume that they are superior to most other nations.[33] This refers not only to their intelligence or their way of organising work and employment, but also to their life-style, for the Japanese now have the longest life expectancy in the world (76 years).

Above all, however, Japan realises that its current rise is due to its successful use of technology. Spokesmen for Japan chant in unison that they won the battle in cars and in robots.[34] Moreover, it seems very likely that they will also win in artificial intelligence, new industrial materials, and biotechnology.[35] These are ostensibly all peaceful industries, and the prospect seems flattering to most Japanese. Consequently, at the moment, any criticism of technology in Japan may be construed as a kind of 'defection' in a country whose people believe that, lacking resources, they are vulnerable and cannot survive without powerful science and technology to support their exports.

That atmosphere of triumph, combined with the suspicion that western science may, after all, not have been as infallible as was once thought, is driving the Japanese to pursue values which may be peculiar or uniquely suited to them but which need not be readily applicable to other nations.

In postwar Japan — in the traumatic soul-searching period — we initially strove for firm principles with international validity. The Constitution of Japan,[36] promulgated in 1947, declared, especially in its Preamble, universal values which were believed to apply to all human beings and societies. It reads, in part:

> Government is a sacred trust of the people, the authority for which is derived from the people, the powers of which are exercised by the representatives of the people, and the benefits of which are enjoyed by the people. This is a *universal principle of mankind* upon which the Constitution is founded (my italics).
> We the Japanese people desire to occupy an honored place in an international society striving for the preservation of peace, and the banishment of tyranny and slavery, oppression and intolerance for all time from the earth. We recognise that *all the peoples of the world* have the right to live in peace, free from fear and want (my italics).

But, the present-day Japan no longer seems to seek similar universal values. Today, many Japanese people are apparently not particularly impressed by their Constitution. They would not be worried if their preferred value system did not apply to others, because theirs has proved to be superior. And if this peculiar value fails to apply to others, it is due to the inadequacies of others and is not the fault of the Japanese.

This mentality has been evident for quite some time in Japan. The remarkable popularity of 'Nihonjin-ron' (or 'debate on the Japanese') may have a root here, especially because the hypothesis or paradigm of the 'unique Japanese' is widely subscribed to, although a number of scholars, including the Australian group led by Yoshio Sugimoto and Ross Mouer, have been attacking it.[37] Back in 1972, the Japanese government issued its 'Unified View' on the relationship between the right of collective defence on the one hand and the Constitution, which has abandoned war fought by the nation as a means of resolving international conflicts, on the other.[38] This Unified View was as follows:

> all the peoples of the world have the right to live in peace, and the people's right to life, liberty and pursuit of happiness shall be the supreme consideration in governmental affairs (Article 13).

The Unified View argued that Japan need not abandon its pursuit of existence and its people's survival in peace; and self-defence was a legitimate means to those ends. Yet the words of Article 13 are preceded by an opening sentence 'All of the people shall be respected as individuals', which binds the government to act for the benefit of the people rather than its own ends. The government's interpretation of the Constitution downgraded the statement of a universal value in the Preamble and bent it to mean a particular pursuit by the Japanese people, rather than of the people of the world. Also, the context of Article 13 is altered in the Unified View so that the government can act in a paternalistic manner to defend the people, rather than recognising them as independent individuals — ultimate units of existence and action, including self-defence.[39]

Now there is a danger that this nationalism of Japan may come into conflict with the growing recognition in the West of the significance of diverse values for different human beings. Eurocentrism is currently breaking down even among some Europeans.[40] The danger is that a westernised Japan will ride on the crest of the philosophy of 'multi-value' systems, dismissing the need for universal human values. In my opinion, what is required is the universal recognition of the non-universality of values. By comprehending this seeming paradox one may hope for the tolerance and understanding needed to relieve the human condition. But in Japan, which has never properly (or only reluctantly) acknowledged any universality of human rights and values, there can be a failure to appreciate unique value systems of individual nation-states or ethnic groups, let alone of individuals as opposed to a community tied together with 'harmony'. Needless to say, the value systems in Australia and some other nations are obviously heading in the opposite direction.

8. Originality in a manipulative society

But, to sustain its good performance in a technology-based economy, Japan needs originality. The social system, which seeks to generate 'harmony' among its own people, while working marvellously well for adapting known technologies and for producing minor innovations which assist the economy, may not encourage originality in science or philosophy at large. This does not necessarily mean that all Japanese are conformists and uncreative. It means only that Japan, while continuously innovating in technology, has learnt how to 'contain' non-conformists. But this system may no longer work if Japan wants to develop an originality of a higher order, which will be essential if it wishes to surpass the West in any trade war. If a policy is now implemented in Japan to encourage originality above the present level, it will surely unleash all sorts of criticisms which will go to the very core of the present methods of management and social manipulation (which effectively limit almost all demand for public participation in decision-making). The emergence of public participation is, however, likely to slow down economic growth, as it does in many western countries. Too much originality may prove to be a self-destroying proposition in Japan.[41] How will it escape this dilemma?

The Japanese academic market-place has recently, for the first time since the war, been opened to overseas people.[42] Whether the same will apply to large companies relying on modern technology is still uncertain. There is, however, already a trend in this direction in that Japanese companies are starting to run their research institutes overseas rather than in Japan, thereby defending their social values back home against an invasion of international research workers in science and technology. For instance, Ōtsuka Pharmaceutical Co. is presently opening new research laboratories in Bethesda, Maryland, USA, to recruit non-Japanese scientists for research in biotechnology.[43] If we extrapolate this trend, and also the overall success of the Japanese economy into the future, the Japanese may proceed to 'buy', with their surplus money, Harvard, Stanford, Cambridge, or even the British Museum, not relocating them, but letting them thrive on or in their own cultural soils. The traditional originality of Europe and USA will be encouraged there as usual, but its 'cream' may be utilised most profitably by the Japanese to maintain their high economic and technological performance. The resulting manipulation could be quite subtle. The Japanese like to say that they have a distinctive tradition of bureaucracy that has lasted more than a millennium without any significant break. The wisdom accumulated during that time will not (they think) easily be matched by (say) that of the Americans, whose system has, after all, existed for a mere two centuries.

In Japan, the Mercantile Law has recently been changed, and as a result the commercial publication of liberal and leftist highbrow magazines has become difficult.[44] Increasingly, industrial companies have been contributing towards cultural activities, generously subsidising the publication of the quality periodicals.[45] And intellectuals are being rewarded handsomely for their semi-academic contributions. They are guaranteed freedom of speech for the expression of their liberal, progressive, or even radical causes. But if and when the bulk of the cultural market is taken over by industry, and if the intellectuals have failed to maintain, or rather, build up their own independent media (as they are doing more successfully in the West than in Japan),[46] eventually only conformists may be allowed to practise. In addition, if the takeover of western centres of intellectual excellence occurs as described above, then such conformity may be enforced even at the international level. For if world centres of learning are governed by subtle Japanese international manipulation, then the specifically Japanese value system may ultimately come to replace traditional western values and so gain a new universality. Thereby the participation of the general public in technological decision-making may be largely phased out, suppressing all the then non-universal value sources.

The problem faced not only by the Japanese but also by the world population at large is, therefore, I suggest, a choice between two alternatives. One is that the world will be satisfied (or pacified) with the economic and efficient 'Japanese' way of utilising the world's limited resources (think of Japanese cars) and (somehow) finding the space for waste disposal, trusting the Japanese with hegemony over the global economy and allowing them to manipulate human aspirations throughout the world. Such an economy will necessarily tend to serve the interests of only a minority of the world's population (hence the need for very skilful manipulation). The other alternative is to realise that such a trust, if given to the Japanese by the rest of the world, will pose a threat, through the exercise of an ultra-efficient control of technology, to the existence of autonomous and diverse human values. According to this line of thinking, the new ways of living in Europe, as exemplified by the Greens of Germany[47] or the Socialists in Spain, may unite with the public (but probably not the leaders) of the Third World to struggle against the super-efficiency of the Japanese and their characteristic ways of handling moral and social problems.

I am indebted to Yoshio Sugimoto for giving me the chance of writing this paper, Gavan McCormack and Alan Mackay for calling my attention to Takasugi Shingo's book and other references on Unit 731 (notes 26 and 27), Hiroto Naora for useful information and David R. Oldroyd for critically reading the manuscript and offering many useful suggestions.

Personal retrospective

Hidaka Rokurō*

Part One
The crisis of postwar democracy

I

The question of change in postwar Japanese democracy greatly interests political scientists, sociologists, historians, cultural anthropologists, and psychologists. My approach is primarily from a political science perspective. The history of Japanese democracy since the Meiji Restoration of 1868 may be divided into six phases:

First phase. The Meiji Restoration, when the country was opened to western influence, was a period of Japanese enlightenment with a movement for liberty and people's rights that contained a partial internationalist, democratic trend.

Second phase. With the defeat of the movement for liberty and people's rights, the age of 'Nation's Rights' and nationalism commenced. The Constitution of the Great Japanese Empire (1889) and the Imperial Rescript on Education (1890) determined the character of the modern Japanese state. The Sino-Japanese War (1894-95), the Russo-Japanese War (1904-05), and World War One (1914-18) followed. Japanese capitalism and imperialism, though backward in comparison with the advanced powers, emerged. The goal of the Japanese people became 'Catch-up with the west'. Modern Japan began to move forward along the line of 'Cast off from Asia and join Europe'.

Third phase. During this period, known as Taisho Democracy, the world-wide trend towards peace and international cooperation

* Professor Hidaka's paper is an abridged and edited version of the lectures given by him in Melbourne during his Australian visit in September 1983.

influenced Japan. Various social movements during this period included the Rice Riots of 1918, the labour movement, the peasant movement, the 'buraku' liberation movement, the women's rights movement, and the socialist movement. The *tennōsei* ('emperor system') state began to experience certain constraints.

Fourth phase. In 1931 the Japanese army commenced military operations in northeast China beginning the Japanese invasion of China. Militarism and ultra-nationalism came to dominate Japan.

Fifth phase. Japan's defeat in 1945, the greatest turning-point in modern Japan, marked entry into a period when peace, democracy and basic human rights became the measure of value. However, the Americans occupied Japan for the first seven years of this period. Furthermore, confusion and difficulties beset the political parties and labour unions at the centre of the movement for democratisation.

Sixth phase. Following the opposition (1959-60) to the Japan-US Security Treaty, which generated the largest mass movement of the postwar period, the conservative administration devoted its attention to economic rather than political problems. The period of high economic growth began under the income-doubling policies of the Ikeda cabinet. Japan became the second greatest economic power in the free world. This accomplishment may be seen as the realisation of the 'Catch-up with Europe and America' goal which Japan pursued in the Meiji period. But, both in Japan and abroad, some people caution that the achievement of economic great power status may foreshadow Japan's becoming a military great power.

Looking back in this way one notices that relatively 'democratic' periods have alternated with militaristic or nationalistic periods. I do not believe that history repeats itself, but I cannot help noting that nationalist forces defeated the liberty and people's rights movement of the first phase and the Taisho Democracy of the third phase. Should this misfortune be repeated a third time, then postwar Japanese democracy will face an acute crisis. If we consider the reasons for the failures of the liberty and people's rights movement and of Taisho Democracy, we may learn important lessons. And now that Japan has become a great economic power, it becomes very important to analyse as accurately as possible the special characteristics of Japanese society, the roots of postwar democracy, and the special societal characteristics of economic superpower Japan.

II

To get a concrete grasp of the problem consider the history of postwar parliamentary elections. Since the end of the war, with the exception of very brief periods during the occupation (the Katayama cabinet of

June 1947 to February 1948 and the Ashida cabinet of March to October 1948), Japan has had an unbroken succession of conservative governments. Of the advanced liberal countries only Japan has had no change of government.

In the June 1983 elections to the Upper House, the Liberal-Democratic Party again won a great victory. The Chairman of the defeated Japan Socialist Party resigned. The decline of the JSP, Japan's major opposition party, indicates that conservative government (or at least governments of conservative and centrist forces) may continue for a long time.

The absence of the possibility of a change in government creates quite serious problems in a parliamentary democracy. The repeated cases of actual corruption and bribery hardly influence elections. Political, financial and bureaucratic collusion deepens while the political indifference of the masses increases.

Could a change of government have occurred in the past? In the general elections of 1958, for example, the Japan Socialist Party won 166 seats (35.5. per cent of the seats). Although this was well below the Liberal-Democrats' 287 seats (61.5 per cent), the JSP gave the impression then of being a young party which would continue to grow.

The year 1955, three years before these elections, has special significance in postwar Japanese political history. First, the Japan Communist Party engaged in self-criticism; it decided to end its adventurism and to adopt a mass line. The left and right factions of the Japan Socialist Party united and the Liberal Party and Democratic Party also united to form the Liberal-Democratic Party (LDP). Anticipating the fluctuation of government, conservative and progressive political parties entered a period in which two major parties confronted each other. Political scientists later described this as the '1955 system'.

When this two party period began, the influential and perceptive LDP Diet member Ishida Hirohide published an article arguing that the Japan Socialist Party would certainly gain power in the relatively near future. His reasons, consistent with trends evident in postwar public opinion surveys, were that

1.   youth was more progressive,
2.   townspeople were more progressive than villagers,
3.   those living on wages and salaries were more progressive, and
4.   those with high educational qualifications were more progressive.

If these trends continued, the JSP would inevitably form a government.

In 1963 Matsushita Keiichi, Fukushima Shingo, and I were responsible for a survey of political consciousness in the Tokyo and Chiba areas. We discovered an extremely interesting trend, which, while not exactly reversing the accepted wisdom of opinion survey people up to that time, exhibited the beginnings of a substantial change. When I met JSP Secretary Narita Tomomi, I warned that if the trend continued, the JSP would weaken, a forecast that proved correct.

Take, for example, the trends among youth and students. According to various opinion surveys, in the immediate postwar period about ten per cent of university students supported the conservative parties while the Socialist and Communist parties together attracted the support of more than sixty per cent. In the late 1960s, however, university student support for the LDP approximated that of the so-called 'reformist' parties, while by the 1970s a majority of university students supported the LDP.

The common expectation that the Japan Socialist Party would be strong in the cities and weak in the villages also changed. In the 1983 Upper House elections, the JSP suffered defeat in the ten prefectures of the heavily industrialised Pacific coastal region between Saitama and Hyōgo. The loss of this region, which includes Tokyo, Kyoto and Osaka, greatly shocked the JSP.

Why did this happen? The postwar period can be divided into two phases: the phase of postwar democracy and the phase of high economic growth. Qualitative differences distinguish these two periods: the JSP could cope during the first, but not during the second. In other words, the JSP could not keep pace with the changes in the consciousness and in the livelihood of the people that resulted from high economic growth. Furthermore, contradictions among socialist states on an international level helped to weaken the position of the JSP, which advocated socialism.

III

I wish to consider now the significance of Japanese neo-nationalism. The various streams within the Liberal-Democratic party can be divided into two general groups: the conservative mainstream emphasising economic objectives and a right-wing group demanding the revision of the Constitution and the expansion of armaments.

A January 1982 article in the official organ of the Liberal-Democratic Party made several suggestions about the education of party personnel. These suggestions may be referred to as the '1985 system', because the article proposed the views be implemented from 1985. These amazing suggestions, which reflected the viewpoint of the right-wing group, contrasted markedly with the '1955 system', which still anticipated a shift of political power between the two largest parties.

What then is the '1985 system'? First, the article recommends that government be formed through a broad coalition of all parties except the Communists and perhaps the left-wing of the Socialist Party. Such coalitions already operate at the prefectural level, where all parties, including even the JCP, often recommend the election of governors. The authors cite as another example the Imperial Rule Assistance Association *(Taisei yokusankai)*, the sole legal wartime political organisation which was formed to support the imperial rule. The article's authors comment that the wartime system worked well.

Secondly, the article recommends that trade union organisation be based on cooperation between labour and management. The article claims that most trade unions already favour this principle and notes the wartime Association for Service to the State through Industry *(sangyō hōkokukai)* was not necessarily bad. This recommendation essentially proposes the dissolution of trade unions.

Thirdly, the article claims that although residents' movements and citizens' movements at present defy the government, they will eventually compromise with government policies.

The realisation of the '1985 system' would be nothing other than neo-fascism. Perhaps the platform represents an extremist viewpoint. Considering, however, that the article was published in the official bulletin of the Liberal-Democratic Party, many observers feel their fears that Japan will return to its prewar political system are justified.

I do not believe the '1985 system' will be implemented, but the article clearly reveals a movement towards a new type of nationalism, a new pattern of statism. What form will this new neo-nationalism or statism take?

In the prewar period, the state unified the Japanese people by fostering loyalty to the Emperor. Today, the state co-opts the people by elaborately redistributing profits to meet the people's expectations. This is the very secret of the conservative political power which, except for one short period, has maintained its ruling position ever since the war. The high-growth economy made this ability to redistribute profits possible.

Prewar Japanese society had a pyramid shape. The ruling class included very few people and even the middle class was not large. Poor farmers and factory workers comprised the overwhelming majority. Today Japan has an egg-shaped society in which 80 per cent of the people believe they belong to the middle class. Let me explain figuratively. Imagine that one-third of the population profits through the ruling power's redistribution. Another third somehow gets along just well enough to maintain their humble lives. They fear, should their lives deteriorate a little, they will fall into the lower class. Thus, the middle class means, in effect, the class that fears falling into the lower class. They hope no substantial change will occur and they concentrate on keeping their present job or status.

The satisfied class and the uneasy class clinging to the present society combine to provide enough votes for the conservative party to win a majority of the Diet seats. Although this 'control state' *(kanri kokka)* returns profits to the people, it cannot diminish the social gaps between the classes. In particular, it gives very little consideration to minority rights. Above all, the Japanese high-growth economy can, in fact, exist only at the expense of the Third World, especially the East and Southeast Asian countries.

This new nationalism or statism, manifested in the phenomenon of the 'control state', is not only characteristic of Japanese society. A similar development can occur in any advanced industrial country which can guarantee a certain standard of living in response to popular demand or other factors. The form of control may be different, but the same phenomenon also occurs in socialist countries.

IV

After the war, many people believed ultranationalism to be the main obstacle to the democratisation of Japan. They saw the traditional community *(kyōdōtai)* and community consciousness as the basis of ultranationalism. Such communities included the family, the village, the neighbourhood, the company, and the state which, of course, was the highest form of community.

Today, 40 years after the war, many argue that it is this community and community consciousness, which used to be criticised, which has produced the present day economic success. For me this interpretation is too simplistic, as there can be no doubt that the postwar processes of urbanisation and industrialisation have greatly weakened community and community consciousness.

During the immediate postwar period, as already mentioned, the Socialist Party polled poorly in the rural areas, but grew stronger in the cities. Today it performs poorly in both rural and urban electorates. On the other hand, the Liberal-Democratic Party campaigns successfully in rural areas, where community consciousness remains strong. For instance, in the Noto electorate in Ishikawa prefecture, the only electorate where the Socialists have never taken a seat, the Liberal-Democratic Party has consistently won all three seats. But in the large cities, particularly in Tokyo and Osaka, the LDP has considerable competition from the other political parties. But compared to the LDP, the Democratic-Socialist Party, the Kōmeitō, the Communists, and the Socialists are relatively weak. Generalising about the large cities we find the relatively affluent classes enjoying economic security support the LDP, the small and medium businessmen and their employees support the Democratic-Socialist Party, the lower class dropouts support the Kōmeitō, organised labour and a section of the intellectuals support the Socialist Party, while the unorganised workers and a different section of the intellectuals support the Communist Party.

Why was the postwar expectation, that liberation from the yoke of community would bring a liberation from conservatism and statism, incorrect?

The rapid economic growth of the 1960s undeniably increased the standard of living throughout Japanese society, thereby weakening the community and increasing 'individualisation'. Two processes of individualisation may be distinguished. In the first process, for example when some Japanese women liberated themselves from the family system, people achieved individuality and independence. In this process, people acquired a high degree of political consciousness and became actively involved in social issues. In contrast, individualisation for many has come to mean fulfilment in one's private life and attainment of a pleasant and comfortable lifestyle. Some, using Japanese English, have called this 'my-homeism' (maihōmushugi). The children of 'my homeism' developed what we can call 'me-ism', i.e. complete egocentrism, which did not result in political activism, but in political indifference.

Differentiating clearly between the two types of individualism is sometimes difficult. The difference between individualism and egoism is ambiguous. One seeks individuality as well as pleasure, human rights as well as a comfortable life, liberty as well as licence. These two processes frequently coexist within one individual, but people with a strong 'my-homeist' inclination form a clear majority in present-day Japan.

In this way individuals, though liberated from their communities, become conservatives in their life-style and in their politics. They fear any change in their present life and do not wish to notice the underprivileged minorities of their own country or those facing starvation in the Third World.

Nevertheless, most of these people support democracy and dislike totalitarianism. They support the Japanese Constitution and oppose attempts to revise it. Yet, they vote for the LDP which calls for constitutional revision in its party programme. They believe the LDP, with its greater experience in economic matters, to be more trustworthy than the other parties. Of course, they expect profits, both direct and indirect, from the government and from the LDP — and they receive them.

V

In the nuclear age, an age with scientific and technological development in a wide variety of areas such as space sciences and genetic engineering, we are inevitably led towards the 'control state'. Nobody approves of nuclear war. The power of nuclear weapons is widely discussed, yet the horror of nuclear war still has not received adequate attention. Countries which possess nuclear weapons inevitably threaten the right to know and the freedom of the human spirit.

Examples of this process can be found in Japan. In Japan, the Ministry of Education removes from school textbooks topics such as the horror of nuclear arms and the anti-nuclear movement. This is the reality of politics in Japan, the country which experienced the bombings of Hiroshima and Nagasaki.

In 1955, I wrote a social studies textbook for junior high schools in collaboration with Nagasu Kazuji, a man well-known later as governor of Kanagawa prefecture. The book did not obtain the Ministry of Education's approval. The Ministry Inspector required the rewriting of nearly one hundred passages including my description of Hiroshima immediately after the bombing. In his words, my text 'exaggerated the suffering'.

This policy still continues today. Textbooks could not include the series of pictures drawn by Maruki Iri and Toshiko about the Hiroshima tragedy, which were 'too cruel'. In addition, the Inspector gave the following specific advice concerning the anti-nuclear movement:

> When writing about the anti-nuclear movement, the following information should be included: There is no possibility of realising nuclear arms reduction except through negotiations presently conducted by the US and Soviet Union. However, even through such negotiations, the reduction is virtually impossible.

This direction clearly attempts to persuade Japanese children that the worldwide anti-nuclear movement, which is spreading everywhere at grass-root level, is futile.

War is aggressive and cruel, and yet the seeds of war may be sown in people's everyday life. This point has special relevance for the Japanese people, but the materials needed to understand the point are gradually being excluded from education in Japan. This is a matter of great urgency.

Elsewhere I have written:

> There is a history of large circumstances, and within that there is a history of small individuals, like grains of rice. These two histories cross somewhere. They have points of contact. Though the individual may think the greater circumstance is irrelevant to himself, actually the individual is

never unrelated to the greater circumstance. But how is that relationship made up?

When one considers the relationship between the greater circumstance and the individual in wartime, one thinks, for example, of how individual life and livelihood are destroyed by war. While this certainly cannot be overlooked, there is another consideration. The daily life of the individual, and within that his attitude and posture towards life, is in fact a remote cause of war itself, and it constitutes part of the forces that commence and sustain war. For example, how did each individual Japanese who crossed over to China before or during the war relate to the Chinese, and how did he treat the Chinese employed in his household? This sort of thing was certainly not unrelated to war. Of course, it was the imperial Japanese government which started the war. And the military, bureaucrats, financiers, industrialists, and rightists were the moving forces behind it. Yet it must be admitted that the ordinary people too, in their everyday life, preserved the seeds of war, and fertilized them. War is not to be thought of only as that which destroys the everyday quality of the individual's life, since there is something in the everyday quality of people's lives that fertilizes the seeds of war.

Although there were good people among the Japanese living in China at that time, in the eyes of the Chinese they were Japanese who had come to China as rulers, against the background of force exerted by the Greater Japanese Empire. Their individual goodness coexisted with the aggression of the state. Within that coexistence, individual goodness sustains state aggression . . .[1]

VI

Can Japan's movement towards nationalism or statism and its development as a militarist superpower be prevented? Can the collapse of Japan's 'postwar democracy' be avoided?

Japan's largest opposition party, the Socialist Party, is very weak. The trade unions are losing their power. Although active on particular issues, the citizens' and residents' movements are dispersed all over the country like grains of sand. Joining these three forces together is not an easy task.

Nevertheless, mapping the consciousness of the Japanese people reveals one real possibility. On the map we can observe three particular groups. First, those fairly strongly or even categorically opposed to the development of Japan as a military power also oppose war and nuclear arms in particular, but they do not always speak up on the issues and they often vote conservative at elections. But, they do oppose war and may be called the 'non-militarisation group'. Second,

1 Rokurō Hidaka, *The Price of Affluence: Dilemmas of Contemporary Japan*, Tokyo and New York, Kodansha International, Ringwood Australia, Penguin, 1985, pp. 39-40.

some people actively oppose Japan's remilitarisation and speak clearly on the issue. I call them the 'anti-militarisation group'.

Finally, some Japanese are designing an overall blueprint for the future of Japan and striving to implement it. Since they can see a future beyond the age of militarism, I call them the 'beyond-militarisation group'. The blueprint they are preparing must of course, contain new alternatives which will remove the danger of the 'control state' and the 'control society'.

If these three groups establish a close relationship and work together, it may be possible to stop Japan's development as a military superpower and avoid the crisis of democracy in Japan. But, as the crisis proceeds, the first group may also seek a strong state and strong political leadership. In that case a new form of nationalism or statism could emerge; this danger is far from negligible.

Part Two
Youth and the Japanese state

The experience of Japanese youth, especially students, during the half century from around 1930 to the present may be divided into two different periods. During the first period, from 1931 to 1945, Japan invaded China and the countries of Southeast Asia and fought the Allies including the United States, England, and Australia. This first period coincides with the years of my youth and adulthood as I was born in 1917. The present comprises the second period.

How did Japanese young people perceive the Japanese state or nation during these two periods? In the first period Japanese youth experienced 'tragedy' and today they experience 'confusion'.

To some extent the record of the militarist and ultranationalist Japan of 50 years ago is well known, and it casts a dark shadow over the present and future perception of the Japanese state. Asian and Australian peoples might suspect that Japan, having made herself a super economic power, will again develop great military power and become a threat in the area. In fact, many feel Japan already poses an actual threat. This suspicion, which exists among Asian countries especially, cannot be totally dismissed.

On 25 July 1983, the Australian Minister for Foreign Affairs, Mr Bill Hayden, met Prime Minister Nakasone during a visit to Japan. After their meeting, a spokesman for the Japanese Foreign Ministry read an announcement to the press that quoted Foreign Minister Hayden as saying, 'I appreciate the political and diplomatic efforts of the Japanese government, and understand its gradual increase of military strength'. The major Japanese newspapers printed this announcement. On 26 July Mr Hayden held a press conference to correct the announcement. Firmly denying the statement of the Japanese government spokesman, Mr Hayden said, 'I didn't say such things', and emphasised, 'Australia would be concerned if, either as a result of external pressure or internal decision, there were a shift in Japan's basic defence posture, or a dramatic acceleration of defence spending'. He disclosed that, just before he went to Japan, the United States had asked Australia to approve an expansion of Japanese military strength and that Prime Minister Hawke had replied the Australian government would delay its answer until it could hear the Japanese government's views. Mr Hayden added, 'I am concerned that the Japanese defence policy will change qualitatively and structurally'. He pointed to three concrete aspects: (1) a large-scale increase in warships and other vessels capable of operation in the Pacific Ocean, (2) the introduction of strategic bombers, and (3) qualitative and structural changes in strategy and tactics.

The Japanese newspapers wrote that Mr Hayden's rather unusual press conference forced the Japanese Foreign Ministry to admit that their spokesman's announcement had been incorrect and to send a high ministry official on a special visit to Mr Hayden to apologise and correct the error. Foreign Minister Hayden's decisive step, which made the Japanese government correct its spokesman's statement, deserves high praise. I believe the qualitative and structural changes in Japanese defence policy, which Mr Hayden mentioned, are already underway. Against this background the significance of the tragedy of Japanese youth in the past and their confusion at present may be readily appreciated.

The first period, the 15 years of war between 1931 and 1945, was the darkest time of tragedy for Japan's young people. War, needless to say, always brings tragedy, especially to youth. For Japan's youth, however, the war situation was tragic in a very complicated manner.

In 1931 the Japanese army invaded Northeast China and made Manchuria a Japanese puppet state. The next 15 years until the defeat of Japan in 1945 were years of continuous wartime for both the Japanese and Chinese peoples. The war, which began between China and Japan, extended to Southeast Asia and then to the Pacific. Therefore, some leading Japanese historians and intellectuals name this period the Fifteen Year War. In this Fifteen Year War, Japanese youth, especially the students, experienced two tragedies. In the first tragedy, evident in the early stages of the war, the state authority forced youth, who knew this was a war of aggressive invasion, to the battlefields. The second tragedy occurred in the late stages of the Fifteen Year War, when students went to the battlefields blindly trusting their national leaders in the government and military who declared the war sacred.

The first tragedy resulted from the fairly substantial voice of dissent or heresy which arose among youth even in those ultranationalist and militarist days. I myself belonged to the heretical minority. When the Japanese army began to invade Northeast China, I was fifteen years old and in the third year of junior high school. That year I was baptised into heretical thought.

I was born and grew up in China, the son of a Japanese businessman. My eldest brother, a university student in Tokyo, greatly influenced me. In the late 1920s Japan suffered a severe depression with harsh poverty, especially in the countryside. In the economic crisis of the world depression that followed, Marxism attracted many Japanese youths, especially university students. After reading several textbooks and papers on Marxism, I felt as if the blinkers had fallen from my eyes. From a patriotic boy who had believed the Emperor to be God and Japan the land of the gods, I now came to believe my own country aggressive and imperialist. Having lived in China where masses of poor people existed, I felt Marxism could explain what I had seen and heard there.

Wartime Japan is sometimes thought of as an all-black totalitarian state where no freedom of speech, expression, or academic pursuit existed. Certainly, worship of the Emperor infiltrated deep into people's minds to an extent which might now be beyond imagination. Yet, in its aim to become a modern state, Japan needed to import European technologies. This required modern higher education. While preparing for modernisation, how could we possibly repress our curiosity about the world as a whole? And how could we repress the critical spirit that this curiosity created? The political leaders of the totalitarian state here fell into a dilemma.

During the period of international cooperation after the First World War, a democratic trend developed to some extent in Japan. It was called Taisho Democracy after the reign title of the emperor on the throne from 1912 to 1926. During this Taisho era, when I was born, the labour movement, farmers' movement, women's emancipation movement and socialist movement developed rapidly and Marxism caught the minds of Japanese youth.

Marxism is often thought of as the extreme opposite of liberalism. However, in a pre-modern feudal or semi-feudal totalitarian state, both Marxism and liberalism develop to criticise the regime. For many in Japan then, Marxism provided a kind of pacifist opposition to militarism and a critical ideology opposed to the Emperor system. Context naturally affects how people perceive various streams of thought and where they locate them in the map of ideas.

After studying Marxism, I became a pacifist in 1931, but more than Marxism influenced me. In those days many Japanese people enthusiastically read the works of Tolstoy and he too affected me. The philosophies of Marx and Tolstoy differ; indeed, they are antithetical. Nevertheless, a fifteen-year-old Japanese boy, far from Europe and knowing little about the history of European social philosophies, not unnaturally combined these two different thoughts.

Since then, for over half a century, I have both been and acted as a pacifist. Although I later became a non-Marxist who still respected Marx, I continued to be a pacifist. I believe I became a pacifist in a deeper way.

Looking at Japanese youth in the beginning stages of the Fifteen Year War on one hand and in the last stages of the war on the other, I find a surprising difference in their way of thinking. In the early period, many young people, especially students, saw Japan's activities as an imperialist invasion. Toward the end of the war, however, youth became totally ensnared by chauvinist enthusiasm. Roughly speaking, their philosophy changed three times, i.e. they changed their minds three times during the 15 years. First, they endorsed Marxism. With the suppression of Marxism, many students took liberalism and humanism as the foundation of their thought. Finally they accepted nationalism. Some then left this for existentialism. During those 15 years the alternation of thought accompanied the alternation of the generations.

Such a drastic change of thought could occur even within the same individual. This process is called 'conversion' (*tenkō* in Japanese). Following arrest and torture, or persuasion by family or friends, an individual holding anti-war or socialist ideas changes his views. He begins to have doubts about the movement and organisation in which he has worked. He begins to feel his own ideas to be too idealistic and too far removed from the national tradition. Conversion, thus, begins to take place, in a process full of pain, guilt, and shame, a psychological or deep-psychological drama. Conversion during the war gave birth to a new genre, 'conversion' literature.

Toward the last stages of the war, particularly from the beginning of the Pacific War, the number of young people who willingly endorsed the war increased sharply. Amid those youth, I found myself a heretic, intensely lonely and afraid.

Then came the day of defeat, crushing and fatally injuring those chauvinist, *kamikaze* youth. On that day they learned the falseness of their beliefs. The deep humiliation which the youth of that time experienced may now be hard to imagine.

Why did young people experience these two tragedies, the tragedy of defeat after resistance and the tragedy of betrayal after conforming to the times? This leads to another question: why was Japanese youth unable to brake the militarist course of Japan? The fact is that state power in a totalitarian state can brainwash almost all young people if given enough time, say ten years. This capacity of state power is not to be taken lightly.

On 15 August 1945 the war ended with Japan's surrender. For the Japanese people war has one unavoidable aspect: the strong win and the weak lose. So Japan lost the war to China and, of course, to the United States. But defeat taught the Japanese people not only that their nation was weak but also that its moral cause was unjust.

In addition to suffering physical damage and the loss of people's lives, Japan also suffered the defeat of its wartime value system. In the victorious nations, the wartime causes of 'freedom' or 'democracy' may have become more brilliant with victory. In contrast, the Japanese people experienced a double defeat. They lost both the war of strength and the war of morality.

Japan, however, did not suffer a total loss. With the defeat, the Japanese people learned the new values of peace, democracy and fundamental human rights. Among these values, the Japanese people particularly emphasised the ideal of peace. Without hesitation they welcomed Article 9 of the new Constitution which renounced war and armaments. But this attitude was later to change substantially.

The people starved and lived in poverty. Shortly after arriving in Japan, General MacArthur stated that he would not allow the Japanese living standard to exceed that of East and Southeast Asian peoples. How could one oppose his statement? Many Japanese youth including myself thought we must build an equal society, irrespective of how poor the economy might be, as well as a politically free and democratic society.

Many Japanese youth made positive efforts to rebuild Japan after the war. I recall with approbation that many students, despite their own suffering from malnutrition, joined the labour, farmers', and other political movements. In these pathetic circumstances, however, a tragedy occurred. The Japan Communist Party adopted an adventurist line and young people, believing revolution would take place in a few months, devoted themselves to direct revolutionary activities. The party later criticised its own erroneous policy, yet this policy hurt many young workers and students both physically and mentally. Once asked to sacrifice themselves for the nation in wartime, Japanese youth were now asked to do the same after the war for the sake of their political organisation.

The Korean War began in 1950. Japanese capitalism, exploiting the sufferings of the Korean people, used the war as an opportunity to restore its strength. The high-growth economy of Japan which began in the 1960s created a new state completely different in quality from the Japanese state during or immediately after the war. The defeat in 1945 certainly constituted a major turning point for Japan, but the high-growth economy in the 1960s also brought about a qualitatively different Japan.

We can begin to understand the great effects of this high-growth economy by considering some astounding figures. In 1950 the Japanese auto industry's annual output recovered to the prewar level of about fifty thousand cars. Today, Japan annually produces about ten million cars. In other words, Japan now produces about two hundred times more cars than it did both before the war and in 1950. The United States, which produced over four million cars by 1950, now manufactures around ten million automobiles, about the same number as Japan. While the United States' production increased two and a half times in the past 30 years, Japan's output expanded 200 times. With an amazing rate of growth Japan has become the second largest economic power in the free world.

What has this rapid expansion brought to the Japanese populace? What impact will this economic growth have on the future of the Japanese nation?

Contemporary Japanese youth live remote from the two different types of wartime tragedy. They live, however, in a kind of confusion which I would describe as purposelessness. This situation exists almost everywhere today, whether in the developed free world or developed capitalist states, and in the United States as well as in Japan.

At the small university in Kyoto where I teach, the students as a whole enjoy student life. Passing university entrance examinations in Japan requires hard work, and those desiring to attend a so-called 'top ranking' university face an even narrower entrance gate. As 'top ranking' university graduates have a great advantage in the future race for jobs, many high school students desperately prepare for the university entrance examinations. But, once they successfully pass the examination, the gate to the employment world is opened wide for them and their enthusiasm for study collapses. Japanese youth have a rather low unemployment rate today, though I believe this cannot continue in the future. But as long as they do not set their goals too high, they will get a job even if it is not their first preference.

Today's university students belong to the generation born after the Japanese economy began its high growth. They have grown up among abundant consumer goods. Some, of course, come from poor families, but most were born to middle-class families. With their life experience limited to home and school, they tend to see high marks at school as their only goal in life. They have an extremely narrow range of experience and imagination. Having grown accustomed to a fairly abundant consumer life, they fear poverty or life without comfort. Desire for a modern living standard overwhelmingly governs their thoughts and acts.

During and immediately after the war, students showed concern for the nation or society as an entity and sought to fulfil their societal duty even though this led to various tragedies. Today, students will only be puzzled if asked, for example, what they think about loyalty to the Emperor or to the nation. In contrast to the immediate postwar period, very few students now aspire to social revolution.

Young people today care for themselves above all else including their parents, families, friends, community or nation. In their care for themselves, individualism is difficult to distinguish from egoism. They seek individuality as well as pleasure, human rights as well as a comfortable life, liberty as well as licence. But, are there any explicit criteria with which to criticise their moral ambiguity?

One day in class I talked in detail about the wartime Japanese limitations on freedom of assembly, speech, and political activity. Afterwards, an intelligent, though somewhat cynical student came up to me and asked, 'Professor, do you know what is freedom for students today?'

'What is it?' I inquired.

'Freedom means one has money to buy things', he replied.

I recall two aspects of his statement: his making fun of an old man's idealism and his general criticism of the values of young students. Today's youth do not care about the Japanese state, but the state cares about them. The Ministry of Education deplores the indifference of youth to the nation, repeatedly insisting that education must instill a spirit of 'patriotism'. Of course, the prewar Ministry of Education most eagerly pursued precisely this same inculcation of patriotism. So, some people, both within Japan and overseas, fear an appalling brainwashing of youth will occur and Japan will again step toward ultranationalism or militarism.

I believe Japan is moving toward nationalism, but do not completely agree that Japan is on the same path as the prewar militarist state. A new type of nationalism is emerging which subtly lures youth, who think that freedom means having money to buy things, into the state's embrace.

In the prewar period, the state unified the Japanese people by fostering loyalty to the Emperor. Today, the state coopts them by elaborately redistributing profits to meet the people's expectations. This has enabled the conservative political power to maintain its ruling position, except for a very short period, ever since the war. The high-growth economy provided the basis for this redistribution.

In today's egg-shaped society only a minority is excluded from receiving profit. Although the 'control state' returns profits to the people, it cannot reduce the social gaps between the classes. After the war, people who sought democratisation showed concern 'for the sake of 95 per cent of the population' in the pyramid-shaped society. Today such people insist democracy must protect minority rights, because Japanese society has changed into an egg-shaped society. This minority includes the 'untouchable' *(buraku)* people, Korean residents, Ainu or aboriginal people, the physically handicapped, victims of pollution, women, and elderly people.

Students want to climb into the upper one-third of the society. With the rails already laid for them in the economic society, their life planning simply consists of getting onto these rails. Once on these rails, they believe, they will have a happy marriage, a comfortable home, lovely children, an adequate career, and a happy consumer's status. I call this state system, built on the foundation of a mass production and mass consumption society, a 'control state' *(kanri-kokka)* or 'control society' *(kanri-shakai)*.

Very conscious of the rails available to them, youth go to university primarily to get onto these rails. Yet, somewhere deep within their hearts they feel that always perceiving their lives only in the future perfect tense is too passive and unhappy a fate. They say, 'It certainly is not so enjoyable, but what else can I do?' They are in a state of confusion or stupefaction. They seem to have lost the true sense of their purpose in life.

Some young people, not content with this chronic confusion, however, voluntarily commit themselves to various social activities which differ in style from those of the immediate postwar period. These young people today participate in the anti-nuclear movement, the anti-nuclear power movement, the anti-pollution movement, the anti-discrimination movement and the consumers' movement, collectively known in Japan as residents' movements or citizens' movements.

I would like to mention briefly some young people involved in the movement concerning Minamata Disease, a well-known case of mercury poisoning. I cannot present a complete picture of Minamata disease, which has a history of over 30 years. Briefly, a chemical plant in Minamata City, Kyūshū, daily discharged mercury into the sea. The local people, who ate polluted fish and shellfish, became ill with mercury poisoning. Hundreds died of acute symptoms, while many others suffered chronic symptoms. Babies suffered congenital poisoning. The company initially denied the factory's discharge caused this dreadful disease. Fishing villagers with many victims among them came into confrontation with most of the citizens of Minamata, who depended on the company. Both the city and prefectural administrations remained unresponsive while the national government emphasised high economic growth and ignored industrial pollution. The government only started to take action well over 10 years after the outbreak of the problem. Only 17 years after the outbreak did the court trial end with a favourable settlement for the victims and even today over 10,000 people await official acknowledgement that they suffer from Minamata disease and are eligible for compensation. Since Minamata City has a population of fewer than 40,000, the severity of the situation is clear. Minamata lies in the shadow of contemporary Japan.

Some dozens of young people have settled in Minamata to support the ill, their labour and their court struggle. These young people do not receive any financial help from anyone and they work to support themselves. Many are university graduates. Some work as taxi drivers. Some work in the *amanatsu* orange orchards and help distribute the products all over Japan. Some work in organic farming and bring their vegetables to the market. They have a central base, the Minamata Disease Centre, built about 10 years ago with funds raised from all over Japan, where over 20 young people, live, work, and help the sick. Some couples, who met in the Centre, have married.

Mr Yanagida is one representative of this Centre. Thirty years old, he dropped out of an agricultural university in Tokyo just before graduation and joined the movement to support Minamata victims. He devoted himself to establishing the financial independence of the Minamata Disease Centre. Gradually he developed his own philosophy of society and of education. He asks, 'What is Japan's fundamental deficiency as a mass production and mass consumption society? How should we change Japan as an economic superpower which is aggressive to the Third World? What ideal values should we, as young people, have in this age?'

The intricate meshes of control, which constitute the primary characteristic of contemporary Japanese society, have not caught Mr Yanagida. Many of us, including myself, find it very difficult to live independent of the existing rails of society. Yet, he and his friends in Minamata provide us with an inspiring example. In our manner of living, our style of studying, our leisure, our obtaining information, our choosing jobs, and our ways of relating to others, can we not be a little more independent of the existing system?

Japan is moving in the direction of a new nationalism, which I have termed the 'control state'. Great military force will, of course, accompany this neo-fascism in the guise of democracy. This must gravely concern both neighbouring countries and the Japanese people. The process must be restrained, but the prospects are not particularly bright. Japan faces two serious problems. The major opposition party, the Japan Socialist Party, is extremely weak and even in decline. Among the parliamentary democracies, only Japan has experienced no real change of government in the postwar period. Secondly, the trade unions are becoming perceptibly weaker.

But can the force of the citizens' movements and the residents' movements arrest Japan's trend toward becoming a great military power and a 'control state'? At present the movements, limited to specific objectives and scattered all over the country, do not have such power, but at least those involved in these movements, including Mr Yanagida's group, are constructing new values. This is important. Japan's future depends on whether its political parties and labour unions, or rather each and every member of its political parties and trade unions, and its students, youth, women, intellectuals, unorganised workers, farmers, and so on can create new values. The new values will, of course, be different from those of the prewar era, different from those of the postwar period, and different from the existing rails within today's controlled society. A portion of Japanese youth earnestly seek these new values. In that sense, they look for an exit from today's confusion. If that proves impossible, a second defeat, probably in a political and economic form, will likely be imposed upon Japan *from the outside.*

Endnotes

Introduction: Democracy and Japan   Gavan McCormack and Yoshio Sugimoto

1   Joshua Cohen and Joel Rogers, *On Democracy*. Penguin, Harmondsworth, 1983, p.167.
2   Simon Holberton, 'Mental Homes like POW Camps', *The Age*, 19 September 1984; 'The Mentally Ill in Japan', *ICJ Review*, no.32, June 1984, pp.15-18; Totsuka Etsurō *et al.*, 'Mental Health and Human Rights: Illegal Detention and the Breach of the International Covenant on Civil and Political Rights', Paper presented to the International Congress on Psychiatry, Law and Ethics, Haifa, 22 February 1983; Takabatake Michitoshi and Kurihara Akira, 'Nihon-kei kanri shakai no kōzō' (The structure of Japanese-style Control Society), *Sekai*, January 1985, at p.51.
3   Chung Kyungmo, 'Zainichi Chōsenjin nisei sansei e no teigen' (Proposals for Second and Third Generation Koreans in Japan), *Shiarehimu*, August 1984, no.7, pp.35-136.
4   *Ibid.*
5   Ronald Dore, *'Senshinkoku to wa nanika'* (What is an advanced country?) *Asahi jānaru*, 6 April 1984, pp.108-111.
6   Chalmers Johnson, *M.I.T.I. and the Japanese Miracle: the Growth of Industrial Policy.* Stanford, 1982.
7   See Yoshio Sugimoto, *Chō-kanri rettō Nippon* (The Ultra-controlled Japanese Archipelago). Kōbunsha, Tokyo, 1983.
8   See discussion in Gavan McCormack, 'Nineteen-Thirties Japan: Fascism? *Bulletin of Concerned Asian Scholars,* vol.14, no.2, April-June 1982, at p.26.
9   Bertram Gross, *Friendly Fascism: the New Face of Power in America.* M. Evans, New York, 1980.
10   See, for example, Hidaka Rokurō, ' *"Demokurashii fashizumu" ni tsuite'* (On 'Democratic Fascism') *Shisō no Kagaku,* May 1981.
11   McCormack, as in note 8 above, at p.32.

Combining democracy with growth: the search for a formula   Doug McEachern

1   As seen in the different responses to unemployment by the 1974-1979 Labour Government and the present Conservative Government in Britain.
2   J. S. Mill, *Three Essays: On Liberty; Representative Government; The Subjugation of Women.* Oxford University Press, London, 1975.

247

3   Ralph Miliband, *Capitalist Democracy in Britain*. Oxford University Press, Oxford, 1982.
4   For the patterns of government response, see K. E. Born, 'Government Action Against the Great Depression in H. Van Der Wee (ed.), *The Great Depression Revisited: Essays on the Economics of the Thirties*. Martinus Nijhoff, The Hague, 1972; R. A. Brady, *Business as a System of Power*. Columbia University Press, New York, 1953.
5   A. A. Rogow, *The Labour Government and British Industry, 1945-1951*. Basil & Blackwell, Oxford, 1955.
6   The Bank of England over its advocacy of the return to the gold standard, the coal owners over their role in the 1926 General Strike and the steel owners over their rationalisation efforts at times of high unemployment.
7   K. Schriftgiesser, *Business Comes of Age: The Story of the Committee for Economic Development and its Impact upon the Economic Policies of the United States, 1942-1960*. Harper, New York, 1960; J. K. Galbraith, *American Capitalism: The Concept of Countervailing Power*. Penguin Books, Harmondsworth, 1956; M. Aglietta, *A Theory of Capitalist Regulation*. New Left Books, London, 1979.
8   R. N. Gardner, *Sterling-Dollar Diplomacy: Anglo American Collaboration in the Reconstruction of Multilateral Trade*. Clarendon Press, Oxford, 1956.
9   Otto Kirchheimer, 'West German Trade Unions', *World Politics*, vol.viii, no.4, July 1956; E. C. M. Cullingford, *Trade Unions in West Germany*. Witton House, London, 1976.
10   For a representative statement of his views see L. Erhard, *Prosperity Through Competition*. Thames and Hudson, London, 3rd edn, 1960.
11   Hans-Joachim Arndt, *West Germany: The Politics of Non-Planning*. Syracuse University Press, Sycracuse, 1966.
12   H. C. Wallich, *Mainsprings of the German Revival*. Yale University Press, New Haven, 1955; M. E. Streit, 'Government and Business: the Case of West Germany', in R. T. Griffiths (ed.), *Government Business and Labour in European Capitalism*. Europotentials Press, London, 1977; Eric Owen-Smith, 'Government Intervention in the Economy of the Federal Republic of Germany' in Peter Maunder (ed.), *Government Intervention in the Developed Economy*. Croom Helm, London, 1979.
13   M. Einaudi, M. Bye & E. Rossi, *Nationalization in France and Italy*. Cornell University Press, New York, 1955; J. Sheahan, *Promotion and Control of Industry in Postwar France*. Harvard University Press, Cambridge Mass., 1963; Richard F. Kuisel, *Capitalism and the State in Modern France: Renovation and Economic Management in the Twentieth Century*. Cambridge University Press, Cambridge, 1981.
14   For contrasting views see Stephen S. Cohen, *Modern Capitalist Planning: The French Model*. University of California Press, Berkeley, 1977, updated edition, and Pierre Bauchet, *Economic Planning: The French Experience*. Heinemann, London, 1964.
15   Warren C. Baum, *The French Economy and the State*. Princeton University Press, Princeton, 1958; Francis Caron, *An Economic History of Modern France*. Methuen, London, 1979; J. H. McArthur and B. R. Scott, *Industrial Planning in France*. Graduate School of Business Administration, Harvard University, Boston, 1969.
16   S. Cohen, *Modern Capitalist Planning*; J. E. S. Hayward, *Private Interests and Public Policy: The Experience of the French Economic and Social Council*. Longmans, London, 1966; R. F. Kuisel, *Capitalism and the State in Modern France*, p.259.
17   See the US Department of State, 'Basic Initial Post-Surrender Directive' and 'Dissolution of Excessive Concentrations of Economic Power in Japan (Zaibatsu Program)' in Jon Livingston, Joe Moore & Felicia Oldfather (eds), *The Japan Reader, Vol.2: Postwar Japan: 1945 to the Present*. Pantheon Books, New York, 1973; Jon Halliday, *A Political History of Japanese Capitalism*. Pantheon Books, New York, 1975, ch.7. For an account of the way in which business and state objectives are coordinated see Chalmers A. Johnson, *M.I.T.I. and the Japanese Miracle: The Growth of Industrial Policy, 1925-1975*. Stanford University Press, Stanford, 1982, and his *Japan's Public*

Policy Companies, Hoover Institute on War, Revolution and Peace Studies, no.60, Stanford, 1978.

18 Yoshio Sugimoto, *Popular Disturbance in Postwar Japan.* Asian Research Service, Hong Kong, 1981, p.121-2; Halliday, *Political History of Japan,* pp.220-3.

19 R. P. Dore, *British Factory-Japanese Factory: The Origins of National Diversity in Industrial Relations.* Allen & Unwin, London, 1973.

20 Jon Halliday & G. McCormack, *Japanese Imperialism Today: Co-Prosperity in Greater East Asia.* Penguin Books, Harmondsworth, 1973.

21 G. McCormack, 'The Student Left in Japan' in Livingston, Moore & Oldfather, *The Japan Reader, Vol.2;* see also the piece by Smith in this volume.

22 A. Shonfield, *Modern Capitalism: The Changing Balance of Public and Private Power.* Oxford University Press, London, 1965; C. A. R. Crosland, *The Future of Socialism.* Jonathon Cape, London, 1956.

23 J-J. Servan Schreiber, *The American Challenge* (Penguin Books, Harmondsworth, 1968, in French, 1967).

24 J. K. Galbraith, *The Affluent Society.* Penguin Books, Harmondsworth, 1962.

25 Baran & Sweezy, *Monopoly Capitalism..*

26 Herbert Marcuse, *One Dimensional Man.* Routledge & Kegan Paul, London, 1964.

27 P. Jacobs & S. Landau, *The New Radicals: A Report With Documents.* Penguin Books, Harmondsworth, 1967. Alain Schnapp, *The French Student Uprising, November 1967-June 1968: An Analytical Record.* Beacon Press, Boston, 1971. G. & D. Cohn Bendit, *Obsolete Communism: The Left Wing Alternative.* Penguin Books, Harmondsworth, 1969.

28 For an interesting article on the response by the US business community see David Vogel, 'The Power of Business in America: A Re-appraisal', *British Journal of Political Science,* vol.13, no.1, pp.19-43.

29 Importantly, organised business strongly supported this planning initiative and sought this closer, more cooperative policy as a deliberate response to the strengthened position of trade unions as a result of full employment in the context of slow and uncertain growth. See Stephen Blank, *Industry and Government in Britain: The Federation of British Industries in Politics, 1945-65.* Saxon House/Lexington Books, Westmead Hants & Lexington, 1973, chs 5 and 6, esp. pp.151-4.

30 Alan Budd, *The Politics of Economic Planning.* Fontana/Collins, London, 1978, ch.6; George Brown, *In My Way: The Political Memoirs of Lord George-Brown.* Penguin Books, Harmondsworth, 1971, chs 5 and 6.

31 L. Pannich, *Social Democracy and Industrial Militancy.* Cambridge University Press, Cambridge, 1976; Gerald Dorfmann, *Wage Politics in Britain, 1945-67.* Iowa University Press, Iowa, 1973, and *Government versus Trade Unions in British Politics Since 1968.* Macmillan, London, 1979; Dermont Glynn, 'The Last 14 years of Incomes Policy — A CBI Perspective', *National Westminster Bank Quarterly Review,* Nov. 1978, pp.23-24.

32 Colin Crouch identifies just this problem for trade unions in his perceptive article 'Varieties of Trade Union Weakness: Organized Labour and Capital Formation in Britain, Federal Germany and Sweden', in J. Hayward (ed.), *Trade Unions and Politics in Western Europe.* Frank Cass, London, 1980.

33 J. R. Hough, *The French Economy.* Croom Helm, London, 1982, pp.145-6.

34 Sima Lieberman, *The Growth of European Mixed Economies: 1945-1970: A Concise Study of the Economic Evolution of Six Countries.* Schenkman, Cambridge, Mass., 1977, chs 2 and 8.

35 Jon Clark, 'Concerted Action in the Federal Republic of Germany', *British Journal of Industrial Relations,* xvii (2), 1979, pp.242-58.

36 Some even thought that these circumstances made it possible for a peaceful and parliamentary transition to socialism using the state's initiatives to promote economic growth as the vehicle. See Michael Barratt Brown, *From Labourism to Socialism: The Political Economy of Labour in the 1970s.* Spokesman Books, Nottingham, 1972; Stuart Holland, *The Socialist Challenge.* Quartet Books, London, 1975.

37   David Coates, *Labour in Power?* Longmans, London, 1980; Harold Wilson, *Final Term: The Labour Government 1974-1976.* Weidenfeld and Nicolson, London 1979.

38   For a version of this position see Stuart Holland, *State as Entrepreneur: New Dimensions for Public Enterprise: The IRI State Shareholding Formula.* Weidenfeld and Nicolson, London, 1972, pp.5-44.

39   Hough, *French Economy;* OECD, *Economic Surveys: France,* 1974, 1975 and 1976.

40   Hough, *French Economy,* p.135 ff.

41   Gordon Smith, *Democracy in Western Germany: Parties and Politics in the Federal Republic.* Heinemann, London, 1979, pp.197-8.

42   G. Kolko, *Main Currents in Modern American History.* Harper & Row, New York, 1976.

43   Vogel, 'The Power of Business'.

44   The seminal essay was Phillipe C. Schmitter's 'Still the Century of Corporatism' in P.C. Schmitter & Gerhard Lehmbruch (eds), *Trends Towards Corporatist Intermediation.* Sage, Beverly Hills & London, 1979. R. E. Pahl & J. T. Winkler, 'The Coming Corporatism', *New Society,* vol.30, no.627, 10 October 1974; Bob Jessop, 'Capitalism and Democracy: The Best Possible Political Shell', in G. Little, B. Smart, *et al.,* (eds), *Power and the State.* Croom Helm, London, 1978; L. Pannich, 'Recent Theorisation of Corporatism: reflections on a growth industry', *British Journal of Sociology,* 1980; Ross Martin, 'Pluralism and the New Corporatism', *Political Studies,* vol.xxxi, no.1, March 1983.

45   Schmitter & Lehmbruch, *Corporatist Intermediation;* Suzanne Berger, Albert Hirschman & Charles Maier (eds), *Organizing Interests in Western Europe: pluralism, corporatism and the transformation of politics.* Cambridge University Press, Cambridge, 1981; R. J. Harrison, *Pluralism and Corporatism: The Political Evolution of Modern Democracies.* Allen & Unwin, London, 1980; T. Smith, *The Politics of the Corporate Economy;* L. Panitch, 'The Development of Corporatism in Liberal Democracies', *Comparative Political Studies,* 10, 1977.

46   For an account of the 'second oil shock' and the accompanying policy package, see the OECD, *Economic Outlook,* July and December, 1980-83. It should be noted that the OECD seems to have been a late and reluctant convert to the new orthodoxy, and frequently points out the social and economic difficulties that go with it.

47   There are all kinds of accounts of these policies and their revival. For examples, see, Milton and Rose Friedman, *Free to Choose: A Personal Statement.* Secker & Warburg, London, 1980; George Gilder, *Wealth and Poverty.* Basic Books, New York, 1981; Committee for Economic Development, *Redefining Government's Role in the Market System* and *Fighting Inflation and Rebuilding a Sound Economy.* USA, 1982; Arthur Seldon (ed.), *The Emerging Consensus . . .? Essays on the interplay between ideas, interests and circumstances in the first 25 years of the IEA.* Hobart Paperback, Institute for Economic Affairs, London, 1981; Ralph Harris, *The End of Government . . .?* IEA, Occasional Paper 58, London, 1980; R. Skidelsky, (ed.) *The End of the Keynesean Era.* Macmillan, London, 1977; F. Hirsch and J. R. Goldthorpe (eds), *The Political Economy of Inflation.* Martin Robertson, London, 1978. For other views see, OECD, *The Search for Consensus: The Role of Institutional Dialogue between Government, Labour and Employers.* OECD, Paris, 1982; Andrew Gamble, 'The Free Economy and the Strong State: The Rise of the Social Market Economy', *Socialist Register,* 1979, pp.1-25.

48   It is interesting, however, to note that the National Economic Development Organisation continues to function: the most obvious 'corporatist/tripartite' body to survive.

49   OECD, *Economic Survey, United Kingdom, 1982-3.* OECD, Paris, 1983, p.43.

50   For the earlier experience of France, 1976-1979, see OECD, Paris, *Economic Survey, France 1980.*

51   T. J. Pempel & Keiichi Tsunekawa, 'Corporatism Without Labor? The Japanese Anomaly' in Phillipe C. Schmitter & G. Lehmbruch, *Trends Towards Corporatist Intermediation.* Sage Publications, Beverly Hills, 1979.

52   For an account of Japan's response to the economic challenge of the recession, see
     OECD, *Economic Surveys: Japan.* 1973-1983

Beyond economism   Gavan McCormack

1   See, for example, Nagai Yōnosuke, 'Defense for a Moratorium State', *Japan Echo,*
     vol.viii, no.2, 1981, pp.71-89.
2   Sakamoto Yoshikazu has referred to the goal of 'nuclear-free, pollution-free,
     resource-saving and open society.' 'Japan's Role in World Politics', *Japan Quarterly*
     1980, p.173.
3   According to Momoi Makoto, former official of the Defense Staff College, quoted
     in J. W. Chapman, 'The Far East in German Peacetime Planning for Crisis 1925-
     1939' in J. W. Chapman (ed.), *Proceedings of the British Association of Japanese Studies*
     1981, p.52.
4   A draft proposal to this effect was tabled in the US Congress on 28 October 1981.
     Sekai, May 1982, p.112.
5   US Commerce Secretary Baldridge. *Ibid.,* p.117.
6   Quoted by Yasuhara Kazuo, 'Suzuki seiken no keizai unei' (The Suzuki Adminis-
     tration's Economic Management), *Sekai,* April 1982, p.100.
7   'Soviet Threat Exaggerated: Institute', *Japan Times,* 15 September 1981.
8   'The Security Heterodoxy', *Japan Times,* 4 September 1981.
9   Quoted in 'Hakusho-Gunjikasareru Nihon' (White Paper on Becoming-
     Militarized Japan), *Sekai,* December 1983, p.40.
10   Quoted by Derek Davies, *Far Eastern Economic Review,* (hereafter *FEER*) 16 January
     1981, pp.24-6.
11   *The Age,* reproducing *Washington Post* report, 3 April 1984.
12   Already well over 1 per cent according to NATO standards which include expendi-
     ture on pensions, etc. Estimates according to NATO standards give Japan a figure
     of 1.3 or 1.4 per cent (Mike Tharp, *FEER,* 6 August 1982) or 1.54 per cent (*Sekai,*
     May 1982, p.82).
13   Sung-Joo Han, 'Memories of Conflicts Past', *FEER,* 26 November 1982, p.35.
14   Figures quoted from *The Military Balance 1981-1982* in *Sekai,* December 1982, p.43.
15   'Nichibei anpo, *Asahi shinbun,* 7 April 1981. A commonly accepted figure now in
     Japan is about 2.5 per cent, the recommendation of Kanamaru Shin, former head
     of the Defence Agency and now head of the Japan Strategic Studies Centre.
16   Ishibashi Masashi, 'The Path to Unarmed Neutrality', *Japan Quarterly,* vol xxxi,
     no.2, April-June 1984, p.143.
17   Quoted in Mike Tharp, 'To revise or not . . .?' *FEER,* 24 December 1982, p.13.
18   *The Age,* 3 April 1984.
19   For a detailed recent study of Japan's 'aid', see Tsuchiya Takeo, 'Japan's Overseas
     "Aid" Paves the Way for a new "Greater East Asian Co-Prosperity Sphere"', *Ampo,*
     vol.15, nos 3-4, 1983.
20   *Ibid.,* p.40.
21   *Ibid.*
22   T. Kogawa, 'Japan as a Manipulated Society', *Telos* No.49, Autumn 1981, p.139.
23   For one account of this: Komiya Ryūtarō, 'Japan's Alarming Turn to the Right',
     Japanese Economic Studies Summer, 1980, pp.3-41.
24   See Wada Haruki, *Sekai,* April 1982, pp.204-14.
25   *Asahi Shinbun,* 26 September 1981.
26   Shimizu Ikutarō, 'Nihon yo, kokka tare' (Japan, Be a State), *Shokun,* July 1980,
     English translation in *Japan Echo,* vol.7, no.3, 1980.
27   For a general critical comparative study of Japan's administrative reform plan-
     ning, see Shima Yasuhiko, *et al.,* (eds), *Gyōsei kaikaku* Tokyo, Aoki shoten, 1982
     (hereafter cited as Shima *et al.*).
28   See, for example, the special issue of *Japan Echo,* vol.viii, no.3, 1981.

29   From the First Report of the Second Phase of the Special Administrative Reform Council, Shima *et al.,* p.8.
30   Quoted in Shima *et al.,* p.42.
31   From an April 1981 conference on Administrative Reform sponsored by Dōmei, the right-wing labour federation, *ibid.,* p.47.
32   *Ibid.,* p.7 and *passim.*
33   *Ibid.,* p.31.
34   Ushio Jirō, quoted in *ibid.,* p.35.
35   Quoted in Takano Hajime, *Ampo,* vol.14, no.4, 1982, p.4.
36   *Ibid.,* p.2.
37   Nakasone in 1978, quoted in Uchiyama Hideo, *Genjō daha no seiji ron* (The politics of status quo smashing), *Sekai,* March 1983, p.54.
38   Kumon Shumpei, 'Administrative Reform', *Journal of Japanese Studies,* vol.10, no. 1, Winter 1984, p.165.
39   See Shima *et al.'s* schematic representation of the 'Crisis Control System' at p.58.
40   *Nihon keizai shinbun.* 1 January 1982.
41   Yamakawa Akio, 'Militarization and Integrated Control', *New Asia News* nos. 34-35, July-August 1981. On the implications of 'Administrative Reform' plans for organized labour, see Shima *et al.,* pp.36-8.
42   Quoted in Shima *et al.,* p.55.
43   In the words of Kamei Masao, president of Sumitomo Metals, this might be seen as adopting the Japanese style of labour relations, now part of 'Gesellschaft' as the 'gemeinschaft' of society (Shima *et al.,* p.39).
44   Quoted in Ishibashi Masashi, 'The Road to Unarmed Neutrality', *Japan Quarterly,* vol.xxxi, no.2, April-June 1984, p.143.
45   Eto Jun, 'The commitments of the 1946 Constitution', *Japan Echo,* vol. viii, no.1, 1981, pp.44-59.
46   The Dietmen's League has over 300 members, or three quarters of the LDP parliamentarians. (Fujishima Udai, 'Jimintō o osaeru gunkō seiryoku', *Sekai,* December 1982, p.181.)
47   Fujishima, *cit.,* p.187.
48   *Ibid., passim.*
49   *Ibid.,* p.187.
50   Maruyama Hirotaka, ' "Sengo sō-seisan" to wa nani ka?', *Sekai,* March 1983, p.128.
51   Yamaguchi Yasushi, 'Nakasone seiken no iji to honshitsu', *Sekai,* March 1983, p.45.
52   *Ibid.,* p.40
53   Hagiwara Michihiko, 'Naimu kanryō no fukken', *Sekai,* March 1983, p.114, especially at p.129 for details of their records.
54   Tahara Sōichirō, *'Jinshin sōjū ni taketa shin naimu kanryō no taitō'* (The rise of new Home Ministry bureaucrats skilled in managing people's minds), *Asahi jānaru* 8 June 1984, p.13.
55   *Ibid.*
56   The latter amounts to $4.4 billion. (Dae Sook Suh, 'South Korea in 1981', *Asian Survey,* xxii, vol.1, January 1982, p.112.)
57   'My own view of defense is that the whole Japanese archipelago or the Japanese islands should be like an unsinkable aircraft carrier putting up a tremendous bulwark of defense against the infiltration of the Soviet backfire bomber . . . The second target objective should be to have full control of the four straits that go through the Japanese islands so that there should be no passage of Soviet submarines and other naval activities.' (*Washington Post,* 19 January 1983.)
58   Quoted in Kurt W. Radtke, 'Global Strategy and Northeast Asia', *Journal of Northeast Asian Studies* vol.2, no.1, March 1983, p.68.
59   In an *Asahi* poll in February 1983, 61 per cent of respondents said they were disturbed by Nakasone's Washington statements; 69 per cent said they opposed the export of military technology from Japan to the United States; 63 per cent said they were opposed to any increase in military spending; 49 per cent were opposed

to any revision of the constitution. (Yagisawa Mitsuo, 'Maintaining Japanese Security', *Japan Quarterly,* vol.xxx, no.4, October-December 1983, p.357.)

60 See, for example, account in Japan Information Service, Sydney, *Japan Reports,* vol.17, no.2, May 1983.

The manipulative bases of 'consensus' in Japan   Yoshio Sugimoto

1   See, for example, Ezra F. Vogel, *Japan as Number One.* Harvard University Press, 1979; Richard Tanner Pascale and Anthony G. Athos, *The Arts of Japanese Management.* Simon and Shuster, 1981; William G. Ouchi, *Theory Z.* Avon Books, 1981; Albert Low, *Zen and Creative Management.* Playboy Paperbacks, 1982.

2   For the convergence debate, see John W. Meyer *et al.,* 'Convergence and divergence in development,' in Alex Inkeles *et al.,* (eds), *Annual Review of Sociology.* Annual Reviews Inc., 1975, pp.223-246; I. Weinberg, 'The problem of convergence in industrial societies: a critical look at the state of a theory,' *Comparative Studies in Society and History,* vol.ii, no.1, January, 1969, pp.1-15.

3   This is the theme of R. P. Dore, *British Factory-Japanese Factory.* University of California Press, 1973.

4   Sengoku, Tamotsu (ed.), *Nigon no sarariiman* (Salaried men in Japan). NHK Books, 1982, pp.99-106.

5   The figures for the United States, Sweden, Switzerland, and Britain were 60, 55, 52, and 46 per cent respectively. See *Mainichi Shinbun,* 12 February 1984, morning edition, p.3; and 13 February, 1984, morning edition, editorial, p.2.

6   C. Wright Mills, *The Sociological Imagination.* Penguin, 1970, p.13.

7   Yoshio Sugimoto and Ross E. Mouer, *Nihonjin wa 'Nihon-teki' ka* (Japanology Reconsidered). Tōyō Keizai Shinpōsha, 1982, p.178.

8   Richard Sennett and Jonathan Cobb, *The Hidden Injuries of Class.* Vintage Books, 1973, p.97.

9   *Ibid.,* p.79.

10   David H. Bayley, *Forces of Order: Police Behaviour in Japan and the United States.* University of California Press, 1976.

11   For Gramsci's notion of hegemony, see Carl Boggs, *Gramsci's Marxism.* Pluto Press, 1980, p.39.

12   Hosaka Nobuto, *Kōji-machi chūgaku ni shi no hanataba o* (Send a Bouquet of Death to Kōji-machi Middle School). Taiho-sha, 1978.

13   Sennett and Cobb, *op. cit.,* p.92.

14   *Ibid.,* p.89.

15   Compare (a) Koike Kazuo and Watanabe Yukio, *Gakureki shakai no kyozō* (A Myth of Social Mobility Based on Academic Career). − Tōyō keizai shinpōsha, 1979 and (b) Takeuchi Hiroshi and Asō Makoto (eds), *Nihon no gakureki shakai wa kawaru* (Changing Japanese Meritocratic Society). Yūhikaku, 1981.

16   See Yamazumi's chapter of this volume.

17   *Mainchi Daily News,* 25 December 1982, p.12; *Asahi shinbun,* 2 November 1982, evening edition, p.5; and *Mainichi shinbun,* 29 February 1984, evening edition, p.4.

18   *Asahi shinbun,* 3 October 1982, morning edition, p.3.

19   *Asahi Journal,* 14 May 1982, p.15.

20   Shinozuka Eiko, *Nippon no joshi rōdō* (Female Labour in Japan). Tōyō keizai shinpōsha, 1982.

21   Yoshio Sugimoto, *Chō-kanri rettō nippon* (The Ultra-controlled Japanese Archipelago). Kōbunsha, 1983, pp.157-161.

22   Michael White and Malcolm Trevor, *Under Japanese Management: The Experience of British Workers.* Heinemann Educational Books, 1984.

23   Frank Parkin, *Class Inequality and Political Order.* Granada Publishing, 1971, p.86.

24   Kobayashi, Tadatsugu, *QC sākuru seikō no jōken* (Conditions for Success of QC Circles). Nihon jitsugyō shuppansha, 1982, p.84.

25   Boggs, *op. cit.,* p.89.

26   Mills, *op. cit.*, p.189.
27   *Mainichi shinbun,* 7 March 1984, morning edition, p.1.
28   Boggs, *op. cit.*, p.47.
29   *Ibid.*, p.47.
30   Parkin, *op. cit.*, pp.81-82.
31   Mills, *op. cit.*, p.191.
32   Dore has recently argued that Japan should lead other countries as a *kanri shakai* (controlled society). See Dore, *'Senshin-koku to wa nani ka?'* (What is an advanced country?)'. *Asahi Journal,* 6 April 1984, pp.108-111

Sources of conflict in the 'information society'
Tessa Morris-Suzuki

1   See for example N. Bjorn-Anderson *et al.,* (eds), *Information Society: For Richer, For Poorer.* North Holland Publishing Co. Amsterdam, 1982.
2   R. Dahrendorf, *Class and Class Conflict in Industrial Society.* Routledge and Kegan Paul, London, 1959, p.183.
3   Keizai shingikai jōhō kenkyū linkai, *Nihon no jōhō shakai — sono bijion to kadai,* 1969.
4   Nihon keiei jōhō kaihatsu kyōkai, *Jōhō shakaika keikaku,* 1972.
5   Social Policy Bureau, Economic Planning Agency *The Information Society and Human Life,* 1983.
6   *Ibid.*, p.1.
7   *Ibid.*, pp.36-37.
8   Nagatomi Yuichiro, 'The Softening of the Economy' Japan Quarterly, vol.30, 1983, pp.256-60.
9   Kimizuka Yoshirō, 'Dēta ni miru Nihon no genryō keiei', *Ekonomisuto,* 21 November 1983, p.64.
10   See D. Bell, *The Coming of Post-Industrial Society.* Heinemann, London, 1974, pp.114-15; Social Policy Bureau, *op. cit.*
11   G. Ciccoti *et al.,* 'The Production of Science in Advanced Capitalist Society', in H. Rose & S. Rose (eds), *The Political Economy of Science,* Macmillan, London, 1976. See also H. Braverman *Labour and Monopoly Capital,* Monthly Review Press, New York, 1974, pp.166-67.
12   Bell, *op. cit.*, p.127.
13   Social Policy Bureau. *op. cit.*, p.52.
14   G. Gregory, 'Hard Facts about Japanese Software', *Far Eastern Economic Review,* 3-9 December, 1982, p.50.
15   See for example M. Cooley, 'The Taylorisation of Intellectual Work' and M. Duncan, 'Microelectronics: Five Areas of Subordination', both in L. Levidow and B. Young (eds), *Science, Technology and the Labour Process,* CSE Books, London 1981.
16   Nakamura Hiroshi, 'Sofutouea — Shintō suru shisutemuka no naka de' in Keizai hyōron bessatsu, *ME kakumei to rōdō kumiai,* Nihon hyōronsha, Tokyo, June 1983, p.152-53.
17   *Ibid.*, p.154.
18   *Ibid.*, p.153.
19   'Zentai ga mieru shigoto o shite mitai,' *Ekonomisuto,* 21 November 1983, p.72.
20   Tokita Yoshihisa, *Gendai shihonshugi to rōdōsha kaikyū,* Iwanami shoten, Tokyo, 1982, pp.180-181.
21   *Ibid.*, p.259.
22   Takamine Tomoko, 'Konpyūtā rōdōsha no rōdō mondai' in *ME kakumei to rōdō kumiai,* p.189.
23   Kenmochi Kazumi, 'Gijutsu kakushin to josei rōdō' in Konpyūtā to josei rōdōsha o kangaeru kai (ed.), *ME kakumei to josei rōdōsha,* Gendai shokan, Tokyo, 1983, p.144.
24   Higuchi Keiko, 'Japanese Women in Transition', *Japan Quarterly,* vol.29, 1982, p.314.

25 Keizai kikakuchō chōsa kyoku, *Kigyō no ishiki to kōdō,* 1983.
26 Kenmochi, *op. cit.,* p.143.
27 Shibayama Emiko, 'ME kakumei to josei fuantei koyō no genjō' in *ME kakumei to rōdō kumiai,* p.168.
28 Tokita, *op. cit.,* p.352.
29 Takeuchi Hiroshi, 'Working Women in Business Corporations — The Management Viewpoint,' *Japan Quarterly,* vol.29, 1982, p.322.
30 Andre Gorz, *Farewell to the Working Class: An Essay on Post-Industrial Socialism.* Pluto Press, London, 1982, pp.69-70.

Educational democracy versus state control Yamazumi Masami

1 Suzuki Eiichi, *Nihon no senryō to kyōiku kaikaku* (The Occupation of Japan and Educational Réform), Keisō shobō, Tokyo, 1983.
2 A private discusssion group organised by Mr. Matsushita Konosuke, the founder of the National Panasonic Corporation.
3 Published in Japanese as *Taiheiyō sensō* in 1968. The English translation by Frank Baldwin was published in the United States under the title *The Pacific War.* New York, Pantheon, 1978 and in Australia under the title *Japan's Last War.* Canberra, ANU Press, 1979.

Class struggle in postwar Japan Mutō Ichiyō

1 Takagi Ikurō, 'Nihon rōdō kumiai undō ni uha no keifu' (Rightwing tendencies in the Japanese labour movement), Shimizu Shinzō, ed., *Sengo rōdō kumiai undōshi ron* (On the history of the postwar labour union movement) Nippon hyōronsha, 1983, p.392.
2 Watanabe Eiki, *et. al., Rōdōsha no sabaku* (The desert of the working class), Tsuge shobō, Tokyo, 1982.
3 Kumazawa Makoto, *Nihon no rōdōshazō* (A look at Japanese workers), Chikuma shobō, Tokyo, 1982.
4 Saitō Shigeru, *Kōzui yo waga ato ni kitare* (Apres moi le deluge), Gendaishi shuppan, Tokyo, 1974.
5 Tsuda Masumi, *Nihon no rōmu kanri* (Labour Management in Japan), University of Tokyo Press, Tokyo, 1970, p.151
6 Mukogasa Ryōichi, *et al., Kyodai kōjō to rōdōsha kaikyū* (Big factories and the working class), Shin-Nihon shuppansha, Tokyo, 1980, p.205.

The reality of enterprise unionism Kawanishi Hirosuke

1 Tokyo daigaku shakai-kagaku-kenkyūjo, *Sengo rōdō kumiai no jittai* (A study of the Postwar labour unions), Nihon hyōronsha, Tokyo, 1950.
2 Ōkōchi Kazuo, *Rōshi-kankei-ron no shiteki hatten* (Historical development of labour-management relations theory), Yūhikaku, Tokyo, 1972.
3 Shirai Taishirō, *Rōshi-kankei-ron* (Labour-management relations theory), Nihon rōdō kyōkai, Tokyo, 1980.
4 Kōshirō Kazuyoshi, *Tenkanki no chingin kōshō* (Turning point in wage participation), Tōyō keizai shinpōsha, Tokyo, 1978.
5 Koike Kazuo, *Shokuba no rōdō kumiai to sanka* (Shop floor labour union and participation), Tōyō keizai shinpōsha, Tokyo, 1977.
6 Taira Kōji, 'Nihongata kigyōbetsu rōdō kumiai sambi ron' (In praise of Japanese-style enterprise unions), *Chūō Kōron,* March, 1977.
7 Shirai, 1980, *op cit.*
8 For further details see Kawanishi Hirosuke, *Kigyōbetsu kumiai no jittai* (A study of enterprise unions), Nihon hyōronsha, Tokyo, 1981.
9 Kawanishi, H., *Shōsūha rōdō kumiai undō ron* (Movement of minority labour unions), Kaien shobō, Tokyo, 1977.

10   Sources used hereafter are taken from Kawanishi, 1981, p.8.
11   *Ibid.*, p.7.
12   Kawanishi, 1977, p.78.
13   *Ibid.*, p.8.
14   Yamamoto Kiyoshi, *Jidōsha sangyō no rōshi kankei* (Labour-management relations in automobile industry), Tokyo daigaku shuppankai, Tokyo, 1981.
15   Matsuzaki Tadashi, *Nihon tekkō sangyō bunseki* (An analysis of Japanese steel industry), Nihon hyōronsha, Tokyo, 1982.
16   Inagami Takeshi, *Rōshi kankei no shakaigaku* (Sociology of labour-management relations), Tokyo daigaku shuppankai, Tokyo, 1981.
17   Kawanishi, 1981, *op cit.*
18   Yamamoto defines the 'labour income rate' as the approximate value of the ratio of surplus value.

$$\text{Rate of surplus value} = \frac{\text{Sum profits}}{\text{Total cash wages}}$$

$$\begin{array}{l}\text{Labour income rate} =\\ \text{(Labour sharing rate)}\end{array} \quad \frac{\text{Total cash wages}}{\text{Value-added amount (total cash wages plus sum profits)}}$$

cf. Yamamoto K., *Nihon no chingin to rōdō jikan* (Wages and working hours in Japan), Tokyo daigaku shuppankai, Tokyo, 1982, p.57.

19   Yamamoto, 1981, *op. cit.*.
20   Kamata Satoshi, *Rōdō genba* (Workshop in shipbuilding industry), Iwanami Shoten, Tokyo, 1980, p.202. Original data are to be found in the yearbooks 'Kaisha shiki hō, of Tōyō keizai shinpōsha.
21   Yamamoto, 1982, p.240.
22   Matsuzaki, 1982, *op. cit.*
23   The number of workers kept for lunch-time operation (A) is determined by the following formula:
A = (Number of workers taking lunch) x (Lunch turnover rate) x Number of teams

$$\text{Lunch turnover rate} = \frac{1}{\text{(Lunch turnover times} - 1)}$$

According to this formula, the number of workers kept for lunch-time operation is almost in inverse proportion to the number of lunch turnover times. Therefore, the greater the increase in lunch turnover times, the smaller the number of workers kept for lunch-time operation. That is the reason why management increased turnover times from the previous six times to eight times.
24   Kawanishi, 1981, *op. cit.*
25   Yamamoto, 1981, *op. cit.*

Democracy derailed   Beverley Smith

1   Quoted in Chalmers Johnson, *Conspiracy at Matsukawa* California, 1972, p.297. The following account of what happened is based on this book.
2   John Dower, *Empire and Aftermath, Yoshida Shigeru and the Japanese Empire, 1878-1954.* Harvard, 1979, and by the same author, 'Occupied Japan as History and Occupation History as Politics', *Journal of Asian Sudies*, February, 1975, pp.486-7.
3   See Tadashi Fukatake, *The Japanese Social Structure, Its Evolution in the Modern Century*, Tokyo, 1982, ch.1.
4   J. V. Koschmann ed., *Authority and the Individual in Japan, Citizen Protest in Historical Perspective.* Tokyo, 1978.
5   Joe Moore, *Japanese Workers and the Struggle for Power 1945-47.* Wisconsin, 1983.

6   John Roberts, *Mitsui: Three Centuries of Japanese Business.* New York, 1973, p.458.
7   *Ibid.,* p.459.
8   The film *The Matsukawa Case* was seen by over three million people in ninety days. Johnson, p.327.
9   *Ibid.,* pp.229, 341.
10 *Ibid.,* pp.35lff.
11 *Ibid.,* pp.352,358,361.
12 Roberts, pp.446-453; Mutō Ichiyō, 'Class Struggle in Postwar Japan', *Ampo,* vol.13, no.4, 1981.
13 Yoshio Sugimoto, *Popular Disturbance in Postwar Japan.* Hong Kong, 1981.
14 Koschmann, *passim;* Margaret McKean's operational definition in *Environmental Protest and Citizen Politics in Japan,* California, 1981, pp.8-10, specifies lack of concern with foreign policy issues as characteristic, but the exceptions are important for reasons set out below.
15 Dower, *Empire and Aftermath,* pp.357-361. Also Kurt Steiner, 'Local Government in Japan, Reform and Reaction', *Far Eastern Survey.* July 1954.
16 R. Acqua, 'Political Choice and Political Change in Medium Sized Japanese Cities, 1962-1974', Kurt Steiner *et al.,* Political Opposition and Local Politics in Japan. Princeton, 1980.
17 Hiromi Hata, 'The Development of the Residents' Movements in Japan in the 1970's', unpublished paper, Asian Studies Association of Australia Conference, Melbourne, 1976.
18 E. and A. M. Smith, *Minamata* New York, 1975; Norie Huddle, Michael Reich and Nahum Stiskin, *Island of Dreams, Environmental Crisis in Japan.* Tokyo, 1975; Donald R. Kelley, Kenneth R. Stunkel and Richard R. Wescott, *The Economic Superpowers and the Environment, the United States, the Soviet Union and Japan.* San Francisco, 1976.
19 Of total public investment 1960-1969, 55 per cent went into industrial infrastructure, 26 per cent on social necessities. Ken'ichi Miyamoto, 'Japanese Capitalism at a Turning Point', *Monthly Review,* December 1974, p.21; on the social consequences, John Bennett and Solomon B. Levine, 'Industrial and Social Deprivation, Welfare, Environment and the Post-Industrial Society in Japan' in Hugh Patrick, *Japanese Industrialisation and its Social Consequences.* California, 1976.
20 McKean, pp.119-120.
21 'Citizen Investigation of Air and Water Pollution in Shimizu City', *Kogai, Newsletter from Polluted Japan,* vol.7, no.1, outlines cases of citizen research. See also Ui Jun, 'Basic Theory of Kogai', *Ampo,* no.9-10 (1971?), pp.17-21; issues of *Kogai, Newsletter from Polluted Japan.* Tokyo, 1972; 'Japan as an Advanced Polluting Nation', *Japan Quarterly,* July-September 1980.
22 McKean, p.45.
23 McKean, pp.131-2.
24 Acqua, p.353.
25 McKean, p.208.
26 *Far Eastern Economic Review,* 23 June, 1978.
27 McKean, p.224; Steiner, in Steiner *et al.,* pp.4-5.
28 Dower points out that not only did the United States abandon *zaibatsu* dissolution but also set about actively encouraging concentration, dualism, and gross disparities of wealth. Dower, 'Occupied Japan as History', p.487.
29 McKean, p.28.
30 Huddle, Reich and Stiskin, p.260.
31 Ellis S. Krausss, 'Opposition in Power, the Development and Maintenance of Leftist Government in Kyoto Prefecture', in Steiner, *et al.,* pp.394,420.
32 Roberts, pp.447-453.
33 Johnson, *Conspiracy at Matsukawa,* p.24. The percentage of workers in unions in 1948 was 56 per cent; in 1980, 31 per cent.
34 Cited by Mutō, p.32.

35   Komiya Ryūtarō, 'Japan's Alarming Turn to the Right, the Political, Economic and Social Situation', *Japanese Economic Studies,* Summer 1980.
36   Mutō, pp.22-3.
37   *Ibid.*
38   Kondō Kazuko, 'Voices from the Darkness', *Ampo,* vol.12, no.1, 1980.
39   Roger Wilson Bowen, 'The Narita Conflict', *Asian Survey,* July 1975, p.602.
40   Okada Osamu, 'Returning to the Origins', *Ampo,* vol.15, no.1, 1983, pp.22-27.
41   Kitazawa Yōko, 'Vietnam in Japan, Sanrizuka and its Links with Asia', *Ampo,* October/December 1975.
42   Mikiso Hane, *Peasants, Rebels and Outcasts, The Underside of Modern Japan.* New York, 1982, pp.36-37.
43   Fukushima Kikujirō, 'Sanrizuka, a Photohistory', *Ampo,* vol.9, no.4, upon which the following account is based.
44   Bowen, p.602.
45   *Ibid.,* p.599.
46   Tomura, 'Ten Years of Struggle. Sanrizuka and its links with Asia', *Ampo,* October/December 1975.
47   Thomas Lobe, *United States National Security Policy and its Aid to the Thailand Police,* Denver, 1977, *passim.*
48   Koizumi Hidemasa, 'Sanrizuka's Reply to a Filipino Activist', *Ampo,* vol.13, no.1, 1981. Also Amado Bernadino, 'Birth of a Dialogue, A Filipino Activist's Visit to Sanrizuka', *Ampo,* vol.12, no.1, 1980.
49   Irokawa Daikichi, 'The Survival Struggle of the Japanese Community', in J.V. Koschmann, (ed.), *Authority and the Individual in Japan, Citizen Protest in Historical Perspective.* Tokyo, 1978, p.259.
50   McKean, p.133.
51   Bennett and Levine, p.484; Murakami Yasusuke, 'The Age of New Middle Mass Politics, The Case of Japan', *Journal of Japanese Studies,* vol.8, no.1, 1982.
52   Smith, *Minamata.*
53   Kuno Osamu, quoted by J. Victor Koschmann, 'The Debate on Subjectivity in Post War Japan,' *Pacific Affairs,* Winter 1981-2, p.627.
54   Irokawa, *op. cit.*
55   *Ibid.* See also Irokawa's, 'The Subject Mentality', *Japan Quarterly,* January-March 1983.
56   Hidaka Rokurō, 'Adults are Losing Self-Confidence', *Japan Quarterly,* January-March 1983.
57   Johnson, *M.I.T.I. and the Japanese Miracle: The Growth of Industrial Policy, 1925-1975.* Stanford, 1982, pp.36-7.
58   *Ibid.,* pp.315-6.
59   *Ibid.,* p.316.
60   Fukatake, *passim.*
61   *Ibid.,* p.30.
62   Fukutake points out that 70 per cent of the population say they are working class when asked where they belong among the categories of working class, middle property owning class, or capitalist (pp.155-6).

Women in the new Japanese state
Sandra Buckley and Vera Mackie

1   These changes are described in full in Naftulin L., 'Women's Status Under Japanese Laws', *Feminist International* no.2, Tokyo 1980, pp.13-16.
2   McCormack, 'Beyond Economism', this volume, p.45.
3   Speech to *Seichō no ie,* 4 May 1982, quoted in Fujishima Udai, 'Kaiken seiryoku to Seichō no ie', *Agora,* no.28, June 1983, Tokyo, BOC shuppan, pp.305-6.
4   Jiyū minshutō seimu chōsa kai (1979) *Katei kiban no jūjitsu ni kansuru taisakuyōkō,* quoted in *Shinchihei,* no.106, August 1983, pp.67-72.

5   Morris-Suzuki, Tessa, 'Sources of Conflict in the Information Society' this volume, p.79.
6   Ohashi Terue, 'The Reality of Female Labour', *Feminist International*, no.2, Tokyo, 1980, p.17.
7   Hall, Phillippa, 'Part Time Work and Women', *Scarlet Woman*, no.18, Autumn 1984, Melbourne, p.21.
8   Hall (1984), p.25.
9   Committee for the Protection of Women in the Computer World, 'Computerization and Women in Japan', *Ampo*, vol.15, no.2, 1982, p.18.
10 Hall, 1984, p.24.
11 Kitazawa Yōko, 'Keizai shinryaku to josei' ('Economic aggression and women'), *Ajia to josei kaihō*, no.3, Tokyo, 1978, p.21.
12 Winnaker, Martha, 'Keeping the Pacific Safe for Capitalism', *South East Asia Chronicle*, no.88, February 1983, South East Asia Resource Centre, California, pp.2-6.
13 Aoki Yayoi, 'Seisabetsu no konkyo o saguru' ('In search of the roots of sexual discrimination') in Yamamoto Tetsuji (ed.), *Keizai sekkusu to jendaa*. Shinhyōron, Tokyo, 1983, p.190.
14 Naftulin, 1980, p.14.
15 Aoki Yayoi, *Josei: sono sei no shinwa* (The myth of femaleness). Origin shuppan sentā, Tokyo, 1982, p.211.
16 'Nihon no mado o hirakū shin kokusekihō', ('New Nationality Law opens the Windows of Japan'). *Mainichi shinbun*, 23 March 1984, p.2.
17 18 May 1984, *Mainichi shinbun*. 'Kokuseki hō ga seiritsu' (Nationality Law enacted), Tokyo, evening edition, p.1. 'Kokuseki hō kaisei an ni yorokobi nakaba' ('Pleased about draft for a new nationality law, but . . . '), *Asahi shinbun*, 26 February 1984, Tokyo, p.13.
18 Non-Japanese have no *koseki*, but must carry an Alien Registration Card which bears a photograph and fingerprints. A non-Japanese who is naturalised must adopt a Japanese name.
19 Sugimoto, Y., 'The manipulative bases of "consensus" in Japan', this volume, pp.69-70.
20 See note 4, pp.67-72.
21 'Watashitachi no koyōbyōdōhō o tsukuru onnatachi no kai' ('Women's group to frame an Equal Opportunity Act') formed in 1978.
22 Agora henshūbu, 'Onna no kusari — rōdōshō o hōi', *Gekkan Agora*, no.86, 10 May 1984, BOC shuppan, Tokyo.
23 Feminist Forum, 'Seirikyūka: an Interview with Alice Dan', *Feminist Forum*, vol.5, no.3, March 1983, Tokyo, p.1.
24 See note 9, p.23.
25 Sōhyō fujin kyoku, *Danjo koyō byōdō hōseika o chūshin to shita '84 shuntō ni okeru fujin rōdōsha no tatakai* (Women's struggle in the 1984 Shuntō — with particular reference to the creation of an Equal Opportunity Act), pp.12-14.
26 Agora henshūbu, *Gekkan Agora*, no.83, BOC shuppan, Tokyo, 10 February 1984, p.27.
27 Inobe Michiyo, 'Hontō ni yakudatsu danjo byōdōhō o yōkyū shiyō', *Gekkan Agora* no.81, 20 December 1983, BOC shuppan, Tokyo, p.151.
28 Morris-Suzuki, this volume, p.85-7.
29 Agora henshūbu, 1984, p.27.
30 *The Age*, Melbourne, 22 May 1984, p.7.
31 Aoki, 1982, p.219.
32 '82 Yūsei hogohō kaiaku soshi renrakukai (hen) (1982 Coalition opposing changes to Eugenic Protection Law), *Yūsei hogo hō to tatakau tame ni*. Tokyo, 1982, p.6.
33 Michele Delage, 'Contraception in Japan; from Abortion to Withdrawal', *Feminist Forum*, vol.4, no.12, December 1982, pp.1-2.
34 Fujishima Udai, 'Kaiken seiryoku to Seichō no Ie', *Agora*, no.28, BOC shuppan, Tokyo, 1983, p.303.

35 Sensō e no michi o yurusanai onna tachi no Saitama shūkai (hen), *Onna ni wa umenai toki mo aru* (There are times when a woman can't give birth), Tokyo, 1982, p.48.
36 Fujishima, 1983, pp.306-7.
37 '82 Yūseihogohō kaiakusoshi renrakukai, 1982, pp.21-22.
38 Kusano Izumi and Kawasaki Keiko, 'Japanese Women Challenge Anti-abortion Law', *Ampo*, vol., 15, no.1, 1983, p.11.
39 Kusano and Kawasaki, 1983, p.11.
39 Kusano and Kawasaki, 1983, p.15.
40 Freiberg, F. and Mackie, V., 'The Sun also Rises on Feminism in Japan', unpublished article, 1983, p.1.
41 Robins-Mowry, D., *The Hidden Sun: Women of Modern Japan*, Westview Press, Boulder, Colorado, 1983, p.177
42 The issue of *Agora*, (no.25) 'Onna to jōhō' (Women and information) examines women and the media in detail. See also the journal *Feminist*, particularly no.7, 1978.
43 Hamao Minoru, *Onna no ko no shitsukekata — yasashii kodomo ni sodateru hon*, Kōbunsha, Tokyo, 1972.
44 Kawakami Gentarō, *Oya no kao ga mitai*, Goma Shobō, Tokyo, 1975.
45 Both Hamao and Kawakami's books are discussed in detail by Mack Horton in his article 'Reactionaries on the Shelf' published in *Feminist International*, no.2, pp.28-31.
46 Robins-Mowry, 1983, p.134.
47 Feminists are now choosing to write these words either in the *hiragana* or *katakan* syllabary or opting for the Japanised version of the English equivalents — *insesuto* and *reepu*.
48 Komano Yōko, '*Kyoiku no ba de mirareru seisabetsu*' ('Sexual discrimination in education'), Shisō no kagaku, no.127, Tokyo, 1981, pp.32-38.
49 Komano Yōko, 1981, pp.35-36.
50 Robins-Mowry, 1983, p.133.
51 Lebra, Joyce *et al.*, (eds), *Women in Changing Japan*, Westview Press, Boulder, Colorado, 1976, p.21.
52 Robins-Mowry, 1903, p.140.
53 For details see the work of Mouer, Elizabeth, 'The Role of Parents In Occupational Choice Among University Educated Japanese Women', unpublished paper, 1984.
54 Robins-Mowry, 1983, p.175.
55 Robins-Mowry, 1983, p.176.
56 Komano Yōko, 1981, p.37.
57 See note 4.
58 Agora henshūbu (1984), *Gekkan Agora*, no.84, p.31.
59 Aoki, 1983, p.192-3.
60 See note 4.
61 Enloe, Cynthia, *Does Khaki Become You — The Militarization of Women's Lives*, Pluto Press, London, 1983, p.123.
62 McCormack, 'Beyond Economism', this volume, p.50, 58-9.
63 Interview with *Fujin Kōron*, published in Yuzawa (ed.), *Nihon fujin mondai shiryō shūsei*, Domesu Shuppan, Tokyo, 1983, p.550.
64 Quoted in McCormack, above, p.53. Compare LDP policy with the following quote from Margaret Thatcher, quoted in Finch, J. and Groves, D. (1983), *A Labour of Love: Women, Work and Caring*. Routledge & Kegan Paul:

     But it all really starts in the family, because not only is the family the most important means through which we can show our care for others. It's the place where each generation learns its responsibility towards the rest of society . . . I think the statutory services can only play their part successfully if we don't expect them to do for us things that we could be doing for ourselves.

65 See note 3.
66 cf. Fujii Haruo, 'A New Phase of Military Alliance between Japan, U.S. and South Korea', *Ampo*, vol.15, no.2, 1983, pp.5-10.
67 Fujishima, 1983, pp.305-6.

Crime, confession, and control   Futaba Igarashi

1   For details of the Menda case, see note 24 below.
2   Chalmers Johnson, *Conspiracy at Matsukawa*, University of California Press, Berkeley, Los Angeles and London, 1972, p.149.
3   *Ibid.*, p.403.
4   Masaki Hiroshi, quoted in *ibid.*, p.150.
5   Robert Whymant, 'Police in Japan readily use force say lawyers', *Age*, 7 March 1984. See also Johnson, p.410. The 99.99 per cent figure is from *Hanzai hakusho* (White Paper on Crime), 1982, p.155.
6   See, for example, *The Price of Affluence*, Kodansha, Tokyo, 1984.
7   On all of this, see Johnson, *passim.*.
8   Tokyo san bengoshikai gōdō daiyō kangoku chōsa iinkai (Joint Investigative Committee of the three Tokyo Bar Associations into substitute imprisonment), ed. *Nureginu* (Falsely charged), Tokyo, Seihōsha, 1984, pp.19-24. (This source is cited hereafter simply as *Nureginu.*) Also, various Japanese newspaper and periodical reports, including *Asahi shinbun*, 19 and 20 May 1982, *Shūkan shinchō*, 28 May 1982, *Mainichi shinbun*, 29 May 1982.
9   *Nureginu*, pp.18-19; also *Mainichi shinbun*, 10 March 1983.
10 For details of these cases, see notes 24-31, to the translated text below.
11 Shikei haishi no kai (Society for the abolition of capital punishment), *Shikei haishi ni mukete* (Towards abolition of capital punishment), Tokyo, 1981(?).
12 Amnesty International, *The Death Penalty in Japan: Report of an Amnesty International Mission to Japan, 21 February-3 March 1983*, London, October 1983, p.13. Also *Amnesty International 1983 Report*, p.204.
13 See my article 'Taigyakuzai to bakuha hannin' (Treason and bombers), *Nihon dokusho shinbun*, 19 October 1981.
14 The parallel which comes most immediately to mind is the infamous case of the so-called 'Treason Plot' (*taigyakuzai*) of 1910. A group of anarchists was tried and quickly executed for a supposed plot against the life of the emperor which was revealed after 1945 to have been an official frame-up.
15 See my article cited in note 13 above; also 'Prison Violence: Arai Mariko', *Namazu* Osaka, Japan, no.1, April 1978, pp.3-5.
16 In general see *Yatte inai ore o mokugeki dekiru ka* (Can you just stand by and watch what happens to me who is innocent?), by special editorial committee, San-ichi shobō, Tokyo, 1981. Also recent press reports.
17 United Nations Action in the Field of Human Rights, United Nations, New York, 1980, p.167.
18 *Ibid.*, p.160.
19 The British Institute of Human Rights, *Minimum Standards of Treatment*. Barry Rose, Chichester and London, 1975, p.xv.
20 According to Freedom House, the US-based rights monitoring organisation. See Whymant, *op. cit.*
21 David H. Bayley, *Forces of Order: Police Behaviour in Japan and the United States*, University of California Press, Berkeley, Los Angeles and London, 1976, p.4.
22 Johnson, p.165.
23 Walter L. Ames, *Police and Community in Japan*, University of California Press, Berkeley, Los Angeles and London, 1981, p.136.
24 *The Menda Sakae Case:* Menda Sakae, born on 4 November 1925, was convicted of a murder committed on 29 September 1948 in Hitoyoshi, Kumamoto prefecture, and sentenced to death by the Kumamoto District Court on 22 March 1950. The

conviction was based on a confession and other evidence. Menda later retracted his confession and asserted his innocence. Other evidence presented in the trial was questioned and an alibi produced for the time of the murder.

Menda Sakae's sentence was upheld by the Fukuoka High Court on 19 March 1951 and by the Supreme Court on 25 December 1951. Two applications for retrial were rejected; a third was accepted by the Yatsushiro branch of the District Court on 10 August 1965, but this was opposed by the Public Prosecutor's office and over-turned by the High Court.

On 27 September 1979 the Fukuoka High Court decided to grant Menda's sixth application for retrial after hearings concerning the evidence on which his conviction was based found that it was not conclusive. Rejecting an appeal from the Public Prosecutor's office, the Supreme Court upheld the decision and ordered a retrial in December 1980.

The retrial began on 15 May 1981. At the retrial, the Public Prosecutor said that Menda had not shown any sign of repentence for his alleged crime and that he deserved to be sentenced to death, even though he had already spent a lifetime in prison.

On 15 July 1983, the Yatsuhiro Branch of the Kumamoto District court found Menda Sakae not guilty. This decision became final when the Public Prosecutor's office decided not to appeal against it. Until his release in 1983, Menda Sakae had been under sentence of death for more than 33 years — longer than any other prisoner in the world known to Amnesty International. (Amnesty International, *The Death Penalty in Japan: Report of an Amnesty International Mission to Japan, 21 February-3 March 1983*, p.14.) *Nureginu*, p.14.

While this chapter was being finalized for publication, a second and then a third 'Menda affair' was reported.

The Taniguchi Shigeyoshi Case

On 28 February 1950, a 62 year-old black market rice dealer was murdered at a place called Saitamura on Shikoku Island. Taniguchi Shigeyoshi, then 19 years old, was arrested in April 1950 and on 20 February 1952 was sentenced to death for the murder by Takamatsu District Court. Appeals to the Takamatsu High Court and to the Supreme Court were rejected in 1956 and 1957. Calls for a retrial were also rejected in 1957-8 and in 1969-72 but ultimately a retrial was ordered in 1979 and opened in September 1981. On 12 March 1984 Taniguchi was pronounced not guilty.

The Saitō Yoshio Case

On 18 October 1955, the battered and burned bodies of four members of a poor farming family were found at a place called Kashimadai in Northeast Japan. Saitō Yoshio, then 24 years old, was arrested on 3 December 1955 in connection with a totally unrelated matter, but was charged, made a confession and was sentenced to death for the killings by a Sendai District Court on 29 December 1957. Appeals to the Sendai High Court and the Supreme Court were rejected in 1959 and 1960, and a further request for a retrial rejected by the Sendai High Court in 1963. An investigation into the case was reopened in 1979 by the Sendai High Court; a retrial ordered in January 1983, and Saito, having spent 29 years under sentence of death, was pronounced not guilty on 11 July 1984.

In the cases of both Taniguchi and Saitō, the evidence consisted of the confession (eventually dismissed) and circumstantial evidence of blood stains. In Taniguchi's case, the prosecution produced no evidence to connect the blood stains with the murder victim, and in Saitō's case the police refused to release negatives of crucial photographic evidence.

During his 32 years on 'Death Row' Taniguchi saw twenty-nine others, who had become his 'friends', sent to the gallows. Upon his release it was estimated that he, like Menda (and presumably later Saitō too) would receive the maximum possible compensation, probably a sum of about $300,000.

(On Taniguchi, see *Mainichi shinbun*, 12 and 13 March 1984; on Saitō, and on the problem in general, see the special issue of *Bungei Shunjū*, September 1984, on 'Shihō no hanzai' (Judicial Crimes).)

25 *The Hirosaki Case: Nasu Takashi:* On the night of 6 August 1949, a woman in Hirosaki City, near Aomori in northern Japan, was murdered. 26 year-old Nasu Takashi came under suspicion because of the evidence of various observers and, when he was unable to account for his movements at the time of the crime, was indicted on 24 August. He denied all knowledge of the crime and a district court found him not guilty in January 1951. The procurator's office appealed against the innocent verdict, however, and at a second trial Nasu was found guilty and in January 1952 sentenced to 15 years. The application by Nasu's lawyers for an investigation of the transcript of the trial of a certain T as relevant to Nasu's case was rejected, although Nasu's lawyers argued that the timing and modus of the Hirosaki case and the crimes for which T was on trial suggested a single person had been responsible. Nasu's appeal to the Supreme Court was rejected in February 1953. Ten years later, in January 1963, he completed his sentence and was released. He continued to press for a reopening of his case and the court at an eventual retrial at Sendai on 15 February 1977 declared him not guilty, declaring that there was not a shred of evidence against him. (*Nureginu*, pp.14-15.)

26 *The Chinnan Park Case: Watanabe Masaya:* Early in the morning of 16 October 1977, a group of about forty 15 to 18 year-old youths gathered at this park in suburban Tokyo and threw bottles, sticks and stones at passing motorcycles, causing injury to several motor-cyclists. Two months later, police arrested 20 year-old Watanabe Masaya and two others noticed on motor-cycles in the vicinity as putative 'ring-leaders'. At first, the three 'confessed', but later they insisted their confessions were false. In May 1978 they were found guilty and sentenced to one year hard labour and three years suspended sentence. In December 1979 the Tokyo High Court ordered a retrial and in April 1981 the District Court reached a not guilty verdict. (*Nureginu*, pp.17-19.)

27 *The Omori Bank Case: Konta Saisuke.* Before dawn on 18 October 1970, an employee of the Japan Industrial Bank in Ōmori, suburban Tokyo, was found strangled. Twenty-one-year-old Konta Saisuke was questioned first on an unrelated robbery charge and then investigated for the murder. He 'confessed', but at his trial resolutely insisted on his innocence. A Tokyo district court found him guilty in March 1973, but in October 1978 the Tokyo High Court reversed the decision, saying that the 'confession' was 'improbable, illogical, and in parts inconsistent with the objective evidence'. An appeal by the procurator's office against the acquittal was rejected by the Supreme Court in March 1982. Konta spent over seven-and-a-half years in detention (*Nureginu*, 1984: 17-19).

28 Yoshioka Yoshiharu, 'On an investigation into a "murder" suspect case', *Minshū hōritsu*, no. 176, pp.27-8.

29 *The Boy Burglars Case:* In February 1977, 'C', then 15 years old, and another youth, were arrested for a string of burglaries which had occurred since the autumn of 1976 in the Higashi Chōfu area of suburban Tokyo. They were alleged to be leaders of a gang of boys responsible for 30 burglaries in all. During interrogation, 'C' confessed to robbery and rape and the other boy to murder. On 28 May, after months of being passed between police cells, family court, and youth prison, both were held to have committed no offense. A completely different person was indicted for murder in the case to which the second boy had confessed. (*Nureginu*, pp.21-2.)

30 *The Kagoshima Murder Case: Funasako Kiyoshi:* On 18 January 1969, a husband and wife were found murdered in their small room at Kagoshima in south-west Japan. There were no clues, so the police postulated madness or revenge as the motive. Funasako Kiyoshi, a former classmate and associate of the couple, was arrested on an unrelated charge in April and, after he 'confessed' to the murder, was indicted on 25 July. Though in court he rejected the 'confession' as the product of ceaseless

interrogation, he was found guilty in March 1976 and sentenced to 12 years. His appeal was rejected in March 1980, but in January 1982 the Supreme Court ordered a retrial, saying 'the contents of the deposition of confession are at odds with the facts, there are many dubious points'. As of early 1984 the retrial was continuing in the High Court in Fukuoka. (*Nureginu*, pp.16-17.)

31   *The Yoneya Case:* In March 1952, 30 year-old Yoneya Shirō was arrested for the rape-murder of a 56 year-old woman the previous month in Aomori in northern Japan. He 'confessed', and although he later withdrew the confession was indicted, found guilty, and sentenced to 10 years (in December 1952). The sentence was confirmed in August 1953 and eventually he was paroled in February 1958, having served his sentence. In February 1967, a nephew of the murdered woman was indicted for the same murder, after having made a confession. He too, however, changed his mind and was found not guilty in a district court hearing. A retrial was ordered, however, and during the retrial, in May 1970, he committed suicide. In August 1967, Yoneya began efforts to secure a retrial. His efforts were rewarded; the retrial commenced in October 1976 and in July 1979, after 26 years, he won a not guilty verdict. (*Nureginu*, pp.15-16.)

32   The meaning of interrogation is starkly revealed in Enoshita Kazuo's *Boku wa hannin ja nai* (I am not a criminal), Chikuma Books, Tokyo.

33   Twelfth International Congress of Penal Law, Hamburg, 16-22 September 1979.

34   *Asahi shinbun,* 20 May 1983.

Science, morality and the state   Atuhiro Sibatani

1   Watanabe, I. *Ningen no shūen* (The end of human beings). Asahi shuppansha, 1976. Watanabe, I. and Noma H. (Dialogue), *Ningen no yukue* (Whither the human being?) Shinsensha, Tokyo, 1979.

2   Tamanoi, Y., *Ekonomii to ekorojii* (Economy and ecology). Misuzu shobō, Tokyo, 1978, pp.2-3. Nakamura, Y., *Patosu no chi* (Knowing by pathos). Chikuma shobō, Tokyo, 1982, pp.50-51.

3   Sibatani, A., *Hankagaku ron* (An essay on antiscience/an antiessay on science). Misuzu shobō, Tokyo, 1973. Sibatani, A., *Anata ni totte kagaku towa nani ka?* (What is science for you?). Misuzu shobō, Tokyo, 1973. Ravetz, J., *Knowledge and Its Social Problems.* Oxford University Press, Oxford, 1971. Rose, H. and Rose, S., *The Radicalisation of Science/The Political Economy of Science.* Macmillan Press, London, 1976. Takagi, J., *Kagaku wa kawaru* (Science is changing). Tôyô keizai shinpôsha, Tokyo, 1979.

4   Bartels, D., 'The production of embryos by *in vitro* fertilisation: can the public participate in decision-making?' *Search*, Sydney, in press. Anon., 'The Xth Congress of ISDB (International Society of Developmental Biologists): early plans,' *ISBD Newsletter, Southampton,* 11 November 1982, announcing a tentative theme 'Developmental Biology: Impacts upon Modern Society' for its meeting in Los Angeles, 1985.

5   Bartels, D., *ibid.*

6   For the Constitution of Japan, see *Facts about Japan* (Code No. 05202), Public Information and Cultural Affairs Bureau, Ministry of Foreign Affairs, Tokyo, January 1981.

7   Sibatani, A., *Baiotekunorojii hihan* (Critique of biotechnology). Shakai hyōronsha, 1982, pp.134-144.

8   Sibatani, A., (Process of submission to governments on the safety of recombinant DNA). *Gijutsu to ningen* (Technology and Humans), no.5, 1983, pp.63-71.

9   Ada, G.L., 'Statement from RDMC Scientific Sub-committee: Addendum to Bartels (1983),' see note 21. *Search,* Sydney, vol.14, 1983, p.92.

10   Bartels, D., Naora, H. and Sibatani, A., 'Oncogenes, processed genes and safety of genetic manipulation', *Trends Biochem. Sci.* no.8, 1983, pp.78-80.

11 Bartels, D., 'Oncogenes: implications for the safety of recombinant DNA work', *Search, Sydney,* vol.14, 1983, pp.88-92.

12 Sibatani, A., *loc. cit.*

13 Sibatani, A., *loc. cit.,* pp.148-177.

14 Hiraoka, Y., (Why did the recombinant DNA controversy happen?). *Gendai no me,* May 1983, pp.158-167.

15 Sibatani, A., *loc. cit.,* pp.179-196.

16 Bartels, D., (Safety of recombinant DNA work). *Gijutsu to ningen.* June 1983, pp.58-70, (Sibatani, A., transl.).

17 Kiriyama, S., (Construction of the P4 laboratory in Tsukuba and opposition movements), in *Shimin ni yoru idenshi sosa hakusho* (White Paper on the Genetic Engineering: A Citizen's Submission). *Gijutsu to ningen.* Supplement 1983, pp.108-126.

18 Elliott, M., (ed.), *Ground for Concern: Australia's Uranium and Human Survival.* Penguin Books, Harmondsworth, 1977, pp.25-63. The aftermaths were reported in daily papers in Australia during 1978.

19 Anon., 'Scientists split on disease imports', *The Australian,* 25 August, 1982, p.3.

20 Sarma, V., 'Foot and mouth disease: Australian lab a white elephant?' *Nature,* no.303, 1983, p.190; 'Australian animal virology: politicians fear foot and mouth' *Nature,* no.303, 1983, p.463.

21 Tomura, I., *Shōsetsu: Sanrizuka* (Sanrizuka: a novel). Aki shobō, Tokyo, 1976. Tawara, S., *Genshiryoku sensō* (Nuclear power wars). Chikuma Shobō, Tokyo, 1976, in Japanese. These two volumes deal with the matter of Narita Airport Construction and Nuclear Power Stations, respectively, in the form of fiction. This was the only way to describe the truth because of the difficulty of mentioning the real names of those who were involved in the 'rackets'.

22 Nishio, B., *Genpatsu: Saigo no kake* (Nuclear power generation: the last gamble), Anvieru, Tokyo, 1981, pp.54-113.

23 Fukuda, M. and many others (Debate), *Hangenpatsu shinbun* (Anti-nuke Newspaper), Tokyo, no.60, 2-3; no.61, 2; no.62, 1 (1983). Anon., (Hearing for Shimane Nuke). *Asahi Shinbun.* 15 May, 1983, p.4.

24 Tawara, S., (Advocates of Japanese nuclear power: dialogues). 1. With Imai, R. *Genshiryoku kōgyō* (Nuclear Power Industry), vol.25, June 1979, pp.1-5.

25 Tawara, S., *ibid.,* no.2. With *Ōshima, K. Genshiryoku kōgyō* (Nuclear Power Industry), no.25, July 1979, pp.58-61; 5. With Mori, K., *ibid.,* 25, October 1979, pp.70-73.

26 Morimura, S., *Akuma no hōshoku* (Devil gluttony) (Kappa Novels). Kōbunsha, Tokyo, 1981. Takasugi, S., *731 butai saikinsen no ishi o oe* (Pursue medics of the Unit 731). Tokuma shoten, Tokyo, 1982. Takasugi. S., (Postwar corps for biological wars) *Gijutsu to ningen,* no.3, March 1982, pp.122-143.

27 Gomer, R., Powell, J.W. and Roeling, B.V.A.: 'Japan's biological weapons: 1930-1945', *Bull. Atomic Scientists,* no.37, October 1981, pp.43-53. Anon.; 'Japan's biological weapons: 1930-1945 — an update', *ibid.,* no.38, August 1982, p.62. McGill, P., 'US backed Japan's germ tests on mentally sick,' *The Observer,* 21 August 1983.

28 Anon., *Dai 21-kai Nippon igakukai sōkai gakujutsu kōen yōshi* (Abstracts of Scientific Papers Presented at the 21st General Assembly of All Japan Medical Societies), Osaka, 8-10 April 1983.

29 Shinohara, M. and Azechi, T., (Viewpoints in opposition to the 'revision' of the Eugenic Protection Law). *Gijutsu to ningen.* May 1983, pp.132-143.

30 Sibatani, A. (An open letter questioning the validity of biological arguments in the proposal to repeal the Eugenic Portection Law). *Asahi Journal,* 25 February 1985, pp.101-103; *Gijutsu to ningen.* March 1983, pp.71-75; In *Kanashimi o sabakemasu ka? Chʾuzetsu kinshi eno hammon* (Can you judge sorrow? A challenge to the Prohibition of abortion) (Family Planning Federation of Japan, eds), Ningen no kagakusha, Tokyo, 1983.

31 Shinohara, M. and Azechi, T., *loc. cit.,* no.29, p.12.

32 Sibatani, A., *Imanishi shinkaron hihan shiron* (An attempt of critique of the evolutionary theory of K. Imanishi). Asahi shuppansha, Tokyo, 1981, in Japanese.

33 Vogel, E.F., *Japan as Number One: Lessons for America.* Harvard University Press, Cambridge, Mass., 1979.

34 Hoshino. Y., Umeda, T. and Makino, K., (A debate: new science journalism in the boom of science and technology), *Gijutsu to ningen.* June 1983, pp.10-33.

35 Tawara, S., *Idenshi sangyō kakumei* (Industrial Revolution through Genes). Bungei shunjū, Tokyo, 1981. Tawara, S., *Sentan gijutsu jidai no sentaku* (Selection in the Frontier Technology Era). Sara Books, Futami shobō, Tokyo, 1982.

36 *Loc. cit.*

37 Sugimoto, Y. and Mouer, R., *Nihonjin wa 'Nihonteki' ka?* (Japanology reconsidered). Tōyō keizai shinpō sha, Tokyo, 1982. The English version of this book will appear under the title of *Images of Japan: A Study in the Social Construction of Reality,* Kegan Paul International, London, in press. An English-language monograph written jointly by these two authors and entitled *Japanese Society: Stereotypes and Realities* is available from Japanese Studies Centre, Melbourne (Wellington Road, Clayton, Victoria 3168).

38 Anon. (The relation between the right of collective self-defence and the Constitution: The unified view of the Government. 14 October 1972.) *Asahi Journal,* 27 May 1983, p.69.

39 Lummis, D., (Article 9 of the Constitution as a means to defend the nation). *Asahi Journal* 10 June 1983, p.114, (Kaji, E., trans.).

40 Seddon, G., 'Eurocentrism and Australian science: some examples,' *Search,* Sydney, no.12, 1980-81, pp.446-60. Ferguson, M., *The Aquarian Conspiracy.,* Routledge and Kegan Paul, London, 1981. Roszak, T., *Person/Planet.* Victor Gollancz, London, 1977. Schumacher, E. F., *A Guide for the Perplexed.* Jonathan Cape, London, 1977. Illich, I., *Jinrui no kibō* (People's Hope). Shinhyōron, Tokyo, 1981. Illich, I., *Vernacular Values.* Friends of the Earth/Chain Reaction Group, Tokyo, 1981.

41 Najita, T., 'Must we copy Japan?' *The New York Review of Books,* 21 February 1980, p.33. Keyworth, G.A., 'The role of science in a new era of competition,' *Science,* no.217, 1982, pp.606-609.

42 Shū, T. (Number one of the foreign faculty members in national universities), *Shizen.* June 1983, p.17.

43 Budiansky, S., 'Bio-Japan in Bethesda?' *Nature,* no.302, 1983, p.100.

44 Anon. (Editorial notes.) *Gendai no me,* May 1983, p.252. Revision of the Mercantile Law promulgated in October 1982 has now proved to be a step towards control of free speech. Among many periodicals which were forced to go out of business, both *Ryūdō* and *Gendai no me* have disappeared recently.

45 Kogawa, T., *Media no Rōgoku* (Prison of Media). Shōbunsha, Tokyo, 1982, pp.117-193. Japan IBM Co. has been publishing for some time *Mugendai* (Infinity). The recently started *Rekishi to Shakai* (History and Society) by Riburopōto (Libroport), Tokyo, is apparently sponsored by Seibu Department Store, Tokyo, a company which is mentioned by Kogawa in the above article. Both this company and Suntory Breweries Co. now run art galleries in Tokyo.

46 *Telos* (St Louis, Missouri, USA); *Social Alternatives* (Brisbane, Australia), *Radical Science Journal* (London, UK); and *Science for the People* (Boston, USA), all seem to be published by non-commercial groups of academics and intellectuals. In Japan, progressive or radical magazines are more frequently published by some large or small publishing companies on a commercial (rather than communal) basis.

47 Bahro, R., 'Rapallo — why not?' Reply to Gorz. *Telos,* no.51, 1982, pp.123-125

Index

Confederation of Labour (*Dōmei*), 116, 117, 133, 146
Confederation of Shipbuilding and Engineering Workers' Unions (*Zōsenjūki*), 116, 117
Constitution of Japan (1889), 10, 157, 228
Constitution of Japan *Kokken* (1947), 12, 45-46, 95, 98, 160, 163, 164, 184, 224; Article 9, 56-58, 121, 157, 241; Article 13, 225, 231; Article 38, 187; Article 96, 57-58; reforms, 174; sexual equality, 173, 182
Containment, 45
Control Society, 14, 16-17, 68-69, 235, 244-245
Convergence Theory, 65-66; Reverse (CT), 75
'corporate' unionism *see* enterprise unions
corruption, 49-50, 91, 230

Dahrendorf, R., 77, 89
Democratic Party, *see* Liberal Democratic Party
Democratic Socialist Party (DSP), 51, 116, 233-234
Deng Xiaoping, 47
Development Assistance Committee (DAC), 49
Diet, 57, 58, 71, 91, 96, 103, 112, 164, 178, 233; Ultranationalism and, 50
Divergence Theory, 65-66
Dore, Ronald, 16, 75

East Asian Anti-Japanese Armed Front, 191
Economic Advisory Council (1969), 77
Economic growth (Japan), 18, 24, 32, 36, 43; government and, 19, 171; problems with, 21, 27; technology and, 14, 26-27, 37, 55; rapid growth, 18, 27, 122, 149, 165, 232-233, 241-243; US and, 22, 122
Edo, 202
education, 14, 56, 59, 93-95, 97, 100, 104, 107, 111; discrimination in, 71, 100, 182; government control and, 13, 90-93, 109, 183, militarism and, 90, 100-101; reforms, 99, 102-103, 105; violence and, 70, 72, *see* also Imperial Rescript on Education
Ellsberg, Daniel, 63
Emperor system (*Tennōsei*), 50, 229
enterprise unionism, 13, 24, 30, 34, 119, 138-143 *passim*, 146, 149, 152, 165, *see* also General Council of Trade Unions, trade unions

Equal Opportunity Act, 175-178 *passim*, 185
Eugenic Protection Law (*Yūseihogohō*) (EP law), 178-179, 184-185, 222

fascism, 16-18, 46, 50, 58, 158, 232
Falwell, Jerry, 58
Family Registration System (*Koseki*), 69; womens' rights and, 175, 176
Federation of Auto Workers' Unions (*Jidōsha Sōren*), 117, 155
Federation of Economic Organisations (*Keidanren*), 116
Federation of Electrical Workers' Unions (*Denki Rōren*), 116, 117
Federation of Employers' Associations, Japan (*Nikkeiren*), 128, 141
Federation of Independent Unions (*Chūritsu Rōren*), 117
Federation of Iron and Steel Workers' Unions (*Tekkō Rōren*), 116
Fifteen Years War, 238; youth and, 240; Japan surrender, 241, *see* also World War II
foreign aid, 48-49, 60, 174, *see* also World Bank
France, 16, 23, 26, 31, 28, 38, 43, 46; Popular Front of, 21; economic stagnation, 24
Fujiwara Hirotatsu, 105
Fukuda Takeo, 58, 59, 167, 179
Fundamental Law of Education (1947), 93-95, 97, 102-103, 109-111

Galbraith, John Kenneth, 26, 43
General Council of Trade Unions (*Sōhyō*), 74, 115, 116-118 *passim*, 121-126 *passim*, 133, 141, 146, 147, 159, 177; Communist Party in, 119, 120, *see* also enterprise unionism, trade unions
Germany, 11, 21, 23, 29, 31, 46, 63; economic policy, 29; Fascism in, 21-22, 50, 178, 196; police in, 211; Socialist Democratic Party of, 116; US and, 22
Gorz, Andre, 88
Gotōda Masaharu, 59
Haken employment system, 84-85, 88, 135-136, 150, 177, 183; agencies of (*haken kaisha*), 85; women and, 136, 174

Hall, P., 175
Harvard University, 43
Hawke, Bob, 61, 238
Hayashi Yūjirō, 77
Hayden, Bill, 237, 238
Heath, E., 29, 36